The First Great Recession of the 21st Century

The First Great Recession of the 21st Century

Competing Explanations

Edited by

Óscar Dejuán

University of Castilla-La Mancha, Spain

Eladio Febrero

University of Castilla-La Mancha, Spain

Maria Cristina Marcuzzo

University of Rome La Sapienza, Italy

Edward Elgar

Cheltenham, UK • Northampton, MA, USA

Published by
Edward Elgar Publishing Limited
The Lypiatts
15 Lansdown Road
Cheltenham
Glos GL50 2JA
UK

Edward Elgar Publishing, Inc.
William Pratt House
9 Dewey Court
Northampton
Massachusetts 01060
USA

A catalogue record for this book
is available from the British Library

Library of Congress Control Number: 2010934051

MIX
Paper from
responsible sources
FSC® C018575
www.fsc.org

ISBN 978 1 84980 745 6

Typeset by Servis Filmsetting Ltd, Stockport, Cheshire
Printed and bound by MPG Books Group, UK

Contents

Figures

Tables

Contributors

Dirk J. Bezemer	Groningen University, the Netherlands
Ivars Brīvers	BA School of Business and Finance, Riga, Latvia
Óscar Dejuán	University of Castilla-La Mancha, Spain
Eladio Febrero	University of Castilla-La Mancha, Spain
Matthias Fiedler	Zeppelin University, Friedrichshafen, Germany
Davide Gualerzi	University of Padua, Italy
Jesús Huerta de Soto	King Juan Carlos University, Madrid, Spain
Steven Kates	RMIT University, Melbourne, Australia
Maria Cristina Marcuzzo	University of Rome La Sapienza, Italy
Jack Rasmus	Santa Clara University, California, USA
Gumersindo Ruiz	University of Malaga, Spain
Julio Segura	Complutense University of Madrid, Spain
Sunanda Sen	Jamia Millia University, New Delhi, India
Edith Skriner	Institute for Advanced Studies, Vienna, Austria
Ekaterina Svetlova	Zeppelin University, Friedrichshafen, Germany
Ramón Trías	AIS, Aplicaciones de Inteligencia Artificial, Barcelona, Spain
Adrian B. Winnett	University of Bath, UK
Catherine P. Winnett	University of Bath, UK

Introduction

Óscar Dejuán, Eladio Febrero and Maria Cristina Marcuzzo

The recession of 2008 (the First Great Recession of the 21st century) puzzled everybody. Economists were aware of the international trade imbalances and of the speculative bubbles in the real estate and stock exchange markets. However, few of them dared think that the recession was so close and that it was going to be so deep. Its severity is only comparable with the Great Depression of 1929.

The recession offers an opportunity to revise economic theories in order to identify their flaws. And also to compare different economic paradigms to find the one that provides a more plausible explanation and a more credible cure.

With this purpose, the University of Castilla-La Mancha (UCLM) and the European Society for the History of Economic Thought (ESHET) jointly organized an international symposium in January 2010 in Albacete, Spain, with the title 'The Recession of 2008. Do Economists Ever Agree on Analysis and Prescriptions?'[1] This book gathers together some of the papers presented, to which we have added a couple more in order to give a proper account of the broad array of the streams of thought in modern economics.

The book has been organized in three parts, following a train of thought that we hope will be made clear in this Introduction.

Part I – Economists on Trial – gathers together five papers that discuss which economists are to be praised and which are to be blamed in connection with the present crisis, and to which theories – Post-Keynesian or Neo-Austrian – we should turn to salvage this situation. What is wrong and what has been misinterpreted in economics is assessed from different theoretical perspectives, a task those authors undertake with equal concern for the present economic situation.

The first contribution, by Dirk J. Bezemer, scrutinizes the work of 12 economists who predicted the crisis. In seeking for some common features the author argues that in their analysis, unlike the forecasting models used by central banks (such as Dynamic Stochastic General Equilibrium models) these economists share the view that financial assets are prone to bubbles and that credit feeds the stock of debt. Most of these authors are Post-Keynesians or Institutionalists who have in common an approach that stresses uncertainty and non-optimizing behaviour; who favour empirical work rather than theoretical formalism and object to methodological individualism; and who recommend integrating flow-stock accounts from the financial and the real sides of the economy.

In the second contribution Jesús Huerta de Soto claims that the approach of the Austrian Business Cycle Theory of Ludwig von Mises and Friedrich Hayek is well equipped to explain recent events. According to the Austrian view there is no way in which the economy can escape the sacrifice of present consumption and bypass the discipline of accumulated saving: credit expansion and (fiduciary) inflation of the media of exchange offer no short cut to stable and sustained economic development. Money that does not originate from saving, but is generated only by credit expansion is bound to be channelled into 'bad' investments, which eventually result in a reduction of capacity and employment, produce inflation in good and asset markets, and give rise to speculative bubbles that are certain to burst sooner or later. Following the 'free market' prescriptions of the Austrian School, Huerta de Soto proposes privatizing and liberalizing financial markets, whose institutions are said to be unable to rule the business cycle, and are responsible for fostering rather than preventing disturbances in the markets.

In the third contribution, by Ekaterina Svetlova and Matthias Fiedler, the blame is laid on standard economic theory for failing to distinguish between uncertainty and risk, the former being identified with the latter by assigning probability values to all possible events. The current crisis has shown how models based on these assumptions have mispriced subprime mortgages, have facilitated unjustifiable risk-taking by lay and professional investors and have shut their eyes to the brewing crisis. Economists have to learn to cope with imperfect knowledge (not just 'imperfect information') and genuine uncertainty (not just 'risk'), taking inspiration from the work of Knight, Keynes and Shackle. Despite their theoretical differences, these three authors share a belief that the economy is pervaded by insufficient knowledge, true uncertainty, uniqueness of events and exposure to surprise, and that institutions are needed to monitor market confidence and stabilize markets.

Also, Gumersindo Ruiz and Ramón Trías – in the fourth contribution to this section – focus on the central role of risk management, as the 'raison d'être' of finance. Their account of the different methods of risk valuation introduced in the last quarter of the 20th century, is given as a historical background to current events. Risk theory was backward looking and statistically driven; it undervalued the dynamic characteristics of markets, boosted diversification and misused volatility as a proxy variable for risk measurement; it was clearly procyclical. What is required is a new approach to macroeconomics, which is forward looking. We need to devise measurement tools that can stabilize the valuation of assets all along the economic cycle, to have a better understanding of the relationship between risk and diversification and to provide new instruments to hedge those rare events known as fat-tail risk.

In the final contribution in this section, Julio Segura asks whether the 'efficient market hypothesis' (EMH) – on which modern finance relies – is at the root of the financial crash of 2007–08. The author believes the blame should be laid on the practitioners who use the models based on EMH, without being aware of the strict conditions to which they should be applied and academics who do not make these assumptions sufficiently explicit. Segura's point is that modern economics has recognized that financial markets suffer from insufficient transparency and asymmetric information; that agency problems and conflicts of interests in rating agencies are a source of market failures; that financial regulation becomes flawed when economic agents are able to 'capture' the regulator. It would therefore be equally wrong to invoke EMH to avoid any type of regulation or to accept as good whatever financial innovations markets may produce.

The economists on trial in this section are those, mainly heterodox, who are looked upon as sources of inspiration for the understanding of the crisis and those, mainly mainstream, who are seen as having inspired a type of behaviour that has fuelled the crisis. The well-known paragraph in the closing pages of *The General Theory* – 'Practical men, who believe themselves to be quite exempt from any intellectual influences, are usually the slaves of some defunct economist' (Keynes, 1936, p. 383) – comes to mind, but adapted to the present circumstances: it is in 'some living economists' that practitioners in financial markets have put too much faith. Perhaps it is now time to recognize that the road to travel is back to history.

The papers in Part II – What Does History Tell Us? – provide a historical background to the crisis, from the double perspective of economic history and history of economic thought. For more than a century some streams of thought have warned that capitalist market economies are crisis-prone, and those who continue in that tradition refer to the recession of 2008 as the key proof of the inherent instability of capitalism.

In the first contribution to the second section, Sunanda Sen compares the Great Depression of 1929 and the 1930s with the recession of 2008 from a Keynesian perspective. Similarities and parallels can be traced in the current account imbalances (although the main players have changed their roles; the USA used to be the biggest lender, now it is the biggest borrower); the increasing weight of international capital flows, more concerned with speculative gains than with production; exchange rate mismatches; deflationary policies in an attempt to gain international competitiveness (the control of inflation becomes the way); speculative bubbles in the stock exchange that compromise the solvency of the bank system in case of a sudden burst. Sen argues that to learn the lesson that history teaches us and to avoid the policy errors of the 1930s, we must follow Keynes's guidance, which points not only to fiscal expansion but also to financial regulation and international cooperation.

In the second contribution Catherine and Adrian Winnett draw attention to the rise in the 1930s of approaches that – unlike Keynes's exclusive concern with persistent unemployment *equilibrium* – focused on cycles and *dynamic disequilibrium*. The Stockholm School (Lundberg, Ohlin and Myrdal), the Austrian School (Hayek) and a thread in the Cambridge tradition (Roberston) all have in common explanations of the business cycle, which ultimately rested on the non-neutrality of money and the importance of real phenomena. In the same years, Schumpeter and Kalecki insisted on the key role of technical change, distribution and other determinants of growth and cycles. The lesson to be drawn from the 1930s' theories is that they are highly relevant to explain the recession of 2008, as triggered by financial problems, but reflecting weaknesses in the real side of the economy.

In the third contribution, Jack Rasmus coins the term 'Epic Recession' to denote major breakdowns in the economy. Outstanding examples are the US crisis of 1907–14, the international Great Depression of the 1930s and the current worldwide recession. The impact of an Epic Recession is broader and deeper than ordinary downturns and, as a consequence, the recovery will require more time (between seven and ten years). The common feature is that, unlike goods and wages, the supply of assets does not adjust, so that the price of assets will grow pari passu with speculative demand. The speculative bubble initially crowds out productive investment and later, when it bursts, as the most indebted firms and households default, it disrupts capacity and employment.

The next chapter in this part, by Edith Skriner, provides empirical support to the Austrian hypothesis that credit expansions (generally due to artificially low interest rates) cause assets bubbles and recessions. After scrutinizing an impressive amount of international economic data from 1974 to 2009 and building a broad array of economic variables, Skriner concludes that the current crisis responds to this pattern. Surprisingly enough, causality also operates the other way round, and with higher intensity. After a 1 per cent increase in asset prices, interest rates used to rise six basis points. In her opinion, central banks should include stock market prices in their monetary policy rules.

Finally, Steven Kates takes issue with the argument – used by governments worldwide fighting the current recession with Keynesian expansionary fiscal policies – that the Great Depression was defeated by Keynesian analysis and prescriptions. His view is that in the mid-1930s the only country in recession was the USA, despite the expansionary policies of the New Deal; the remaining economies had recovered applying classical remedies based on Say's Law. This brings into focus the role of the history of economic thought in understanding what Say and Keynes really meant and which conditions are required for a successful implementation of their prescriptions.

The records of facts and ideas from the past allow us to put current events in perspective, to find similarities and differences without which the analysis would be myopic. Knowledge of the history of discipline, makes room for the acceptance that there is more than one way to interpret phenomena in the real world, enriching the ability to understand and to prevent crisis. The stress on modelling and econometric exercises has misled economists into thinking that economics is closer to the physical world and the methods to employ are those of the natural sciences. It is interesting to be reminded of what a very successful market player, George Soros, has recently remarked:

> Financial markets should not be treated as a physics laboratory but as a form of history. The course of events is time-bound and one-directional. Predictions and explanations are not reversible. Some timelessly valid generalizations can serve to explain events but not to predict them. (Soros, 2010, p. 3)

Chapters in Part III – Country Cases in a Global Crisis – analyse the crisis from the angle of a specific country. By looking at the recession through the magnifying glass, small corners of the world come into focus as case studies. The knowledge that is gained by looking closer at individual countries allows us to get deeper into the consequences and who will bear the brunt of the costs of the crisis.

There is a common agreement that the origin of the current crisis is related to the expansion of subprime mortgages in the USA after 2002 and the diffusion of financial derivatives related to these mortgages all over the world. The 'Testimony' of Alan Greenspan before the Financial Crisis Inquiry Commission of the US Congress, on 7 April 2010, is probably the best way to approach it. At the beginning of this section we reproduce a part of his speech. The Chairman of the Federal Reserve from 1987 till 2006 admits that low interest rates played a role in the residential investment boom and subsequent bust. He considers, however, that what matters for residential investment is the long-term mortgage rate, not the overnight interest rate fixed by the Fed. According to him, mortgage rates were abnormally low because of the saving glut occasioned by the increasing trade surplus of China, India and other developing countries. Greenspan admits, however, that international imbalances should not conceal the responsibility of financial institutions in generating and spreading risks. A more demanding capitalization of financial institutions is required.

The core country is indeed the USA, from which many of the financial innovations and troubles originated. In the second chapter of this section Davide Gualerzi looks at the US economy from a long-term perspective that focuses on the real side, and at its structural low level of effective demand. In the golden age of capitalism (1950–70) the new markets for automobiles, industrial appliances and the like, justified a continuous flow of investment and were strong enough to overcome the ordinary fluctuations of demand. In the 1990s the new technologies of information took the relay as the new locomotive of the economy. So far, however, its creative impact on employment has been lower than the destructive one. The US economy recovered easily from the first stock market crash (the 'dot-com' bubble of 2001) because the housing market seemed promising. The recovery from the burst of the real estate bubble in 2007 and 2008, is taking longer than expected because US entrepreneurs do not see new markets that justify massive investments.

The next chapter examines the impact of the crisis on small, developing economies. Ivars Brīvers shows how at the turn of the century, when transition to a capitalist system was almost completed, Latvia experienced the highest rates of growth in its recorded history (around 10 per cent). However, the economic rally was more the mirage of speculative activities in the financial markets than the fruit of productive investment creating wealth and employment. As a matter of fact, at that time one-tenth of the Latvian population was forced to emigrate in search for a job. The locomotive of the economy was always outside the country and evolved in a three-step process: first came direct foreign investment to buy all the valuable assets stemming from the privatization of the former public enterprises. Later, foreign banks lent all the money necessary to allow Latvians to keep their standard of living in times of high inflation. The shrinking of liquidity that followed the international crisis put the entire economy on the verge of collapse.

The final chapter analyses a country, Spain, which at the time of writing (June 2010) is under the spotlight as one of the most fragile links in the eurozone. Óscar Dejuán and Eladio Febrero show that after joining the

European Monetary Union, Spain enjoyed the same nominal interest rates as Germany, but since inflation was one or two points above, long-term real interest rates became almost nil. In order to keep profitability up in an epoch of minimal interest rates, banks multiplied mortgage credits and lengthened monthly instalments. The result was the strongest expansion in output and employment among developed countries, but also the generation of three major disequilibria: (1) a current account deficit amounting to 10 per cent of GDP; (2) speculative bubbles in the real estate and the stock exchange; (3) an unbearable burden of debt whose deflationary effects will be felt for a long time. The Spanish crisis can be seen as the terminal station of an unsustainable pattern of growth propelled by a single sector (construction) and fed by cheap credit to households whose nominal wages grew at 3 per cent in a decade where house prices trebled.

The three countries under investigation have been severely hit by the crisis and in all the three cases we find a consistent pattern in which low interest rates, aggressive bank lending, inflated real estate prices set in motion a train of events that ultimately ended in high unemployment, repayment defaults and recession. The responsibility of financial institutions in generating and spreading the speculative bubble implies that a coordinated set of tighter regulations and binding capital requirements in all these countries might have prevented the disaster from occurring.

To the question posed to the participants of the Albacete Workshop: 'Do economists ever agree on analysis?', we feel that as far as the contributors to this volume are concerned, the answer is in the main affirmative. Here is a sample of the ideas that are recurrent in the chapters of the book:

- The roots of the recession of 2008 lie in the financial sector, which, in the last decades, has been growing in size and complexity. Financial innovation has decoupled the real and financial sectors, not always to the benefit of economic stability. Economists should give proper weight to financial variables and integrate them into their models.
- Genuine uncertainty (as opposed to statistical risk) is a key element in the generation of booms and busts. Economists have to integrate uncertainty into economic analysis. At the same time, financial economists should figure out how to make risks more transparent, how to price them and how to account for them.
- The integration of finance in economic variables starts by the recognition that rising flows of credit result in piling up stocks of debt. The repayment of this debt reduces disposable income and has a deflationary impact on aggregate demand. Over-indebtedness makes recessions deeper and longer, most of all, when the leverage ratio is above the normal levels.

- Speculative bubbles in the stock exchange markets and in real estate seem unavoidable and may have an impact on productive investment. Monetary policy should take asset inflation into consideration.
- Medium-term cycles are usually embedded in a long-term path of growth. The recovery will not be fully warranted unless there is a leading sector with an important potential market and with strong drawing effects on the rest of the economy.
- A 'proper' distribution of income is another condition to ensure a sustainable pattern of growth. The recession of 2008 evidences the unsustainability of a pattern of growth based on construction when the price of houses rose systematically above wages.
- Growth is not possible without savings. In a prodigal community that consumes the whole output, banks may grant increasing amounts of credit that will generate speculative bubbles in the asset markets, productive investment by no means leading to economic growth.
- The balance of payments constraint will continue to be operative even in a fully globalized economy with a common currency. A worldwide pattern of growth where some countries stand systematically as net borrowers, while others stand as net lenders, is unsustainable. The increasing pile of foreign debt will eventually result in prohibitive interest rates.

Are we also going to answer in the affirmative as far as the second question is concerned, that is, 'Do economists agree on prescriptions?' Which are the economic policies that need to be implemented and which are the institutional reforms to bring about so as to overcome the recession and to avoid it in the future? All the contributors to this volume strongly believe that the financial sector cannot be left unregulated as in the past, although this is more a question of quality than of quantity. We should figure out the right type of regulatory measures. Economic agents should enjoy the benefits of their successful decisions and suffer the losses of their wrong ones. The lack of accountability leads to agency problems, moral hazard situations, casino scenarios and the like. The key move advocated by most is to improve the transparency of financial products and to raise the capital requirements of agents engaged in risky operations.

Bearing in mind the errors of the Great Depression of 1929, governments, all over the world, hurried up to grant banks all the money necessary to prevent a financial collapse; central banks lowered the official rate of interest to historical minima in order to stimulate private investment; and fiscal authorities multiplied public expenditure to match the fall in private demand. Explicitly or implicitly, most of the authors in this volume admit the necessity of these Keynesian macroeconomic policies. But what should governments do if two years after the 'Great Recession' of 2008 the economy has not recovered as expected? And how can we interpret this policy failure?

Some authors in this volume point to the inefficiency of expansionary monetary and fiscal policies in over-indebted economies, most of all when the state of confidence of economic agents is at rock bottom. Others warn about the long-term undesirable consequences of 'permanent' expansionary policies. If banks know they will be rescued with public money in case of a failure, they won't pay enough attention to risk. If the interest rate falls in order to encourage private investment, we may soon reproduce another artificial boom, leading to an even worse recession. For sure, if public expenditure is unable to propel the private economy in a year or so, the pile of public debt will be added to the already existing private debt, making things worse for everybody. As a matter of fact, financial markets (which are a thermometer of the general estate of confidence) continue to be 'nervous'.

Will economics learn something from the 'Great Recession' of 2008 as usually happens after a major crisis? Certainly textbook economics, which has dominated the Washington Consensus and the curricula of prestigious universities, are unlikely to remain unscathed by the current crisis and the debates that have ensued. An interesting counterfactual exercise is to speculate that had Minsky and Keynes rather than Lucas or Fama been on the reading list of PhD courses in the 1980s, would we have had a generation of economists better equipped to foresee and even to prevent the 2008 meltdown? However, while there are signs that the profession is becoming more aware of the dangers of unregulated markets, we still have to see those radical changes that many of the contributors to this volume believe are necessary. We hope that the readers of this book, having scrutinized the logical coherence and explanatory power of the different approaches to the Great Recession of 2008 presented in this volume, will agree with our conclusion that diversity and pluralism of approaches in economics is the recipe for making economics a better and more useful science.

NOTE

1. The scientific committee was constituted by Óscar Dejuán, Eladio Febrero, Harald Hagemann, Maria Cristina Marcuzzo and Pedro Teixeira; and the local committee by Fabio Monsalve and María Ángeles Tobarra. We are grateful to all the participants for stimulating discussions and to ESHET and UCLM for their support.

REFERENCES

Keynes, J.M. (1936), *The General Theory of Employment, Interest and Money*, as reprinted (1964), New York: Harcourt, Brace and World.
Soros, G. (2010), 'Anatomy of crisis – the living history of the last 30 years: economic theory, politics and policy', paper presented at the INET Conference, Institute for New Economic Thinking, King's College, 8–11 April, available at: http://ineteconomics.org/sites/inet.civicactions.net/files/INET%20C%40K%20 Paper%20Session%201%20-%20Soros.pdf; accessed 2 September 2010.

PART I

Economists on trial

1. Who predicted the crisis and what can we learn from them?

Dirk J. Bezemer

1.1 INTRODUCTION

The recent credit crisis and recession are seen to have discredited the mainstream economic paradigm because so many economists 'got it so wrong' (Krugman, 2009). Friedman (2009) linked both when he wrote about 'the failure of the economy and the economists'. This paper takes this view as a starting point rather than a conclusion. It asks what, precisely, are the elements in the mainstream paradigm that caused many economists to misjudge the state of the economy so dramatically in the years leading up to the 2007 credit crisis and the 2008–09 recession? In order to address this question, this paper adopts an inductive approach. The research method involves scrutinizing the work of 12 economists who warned about the crisis, and to identify the common elements in their thinking. This is then contrasted with mainstream thinking. This is a new angle, as neither Krugman nor Friedman paid much attention to those economists who did *not* get it wrong (Galbraith, 2009). Moreover, it allows for the identification of critical elements of a more realistic economics based on the works of those economists themselves – rather than through the prism of those, like Krugman and Friedman, who did not warn beforehand that a financial crisis was brewing.

Previewing the results, we will find that those who 'saw it coming' in their analyses emphasized financial assets, debt, the flow of funds and the overarching accounting identities in the macroeconomy as the context and constraints to economic development – elements absent from most forecasting and scenario evaluation models in official use (such as Dynamic Stochastic General Equilibrium [DSGE] models). Their assumptions regarding economic behaviour included uncertainty and non-optimizing behaviour, also in contrast to mainstream theory. Methodologically, they favour empirical work rather than theoretical formalism, and they share an aversion to methodological individualism.

In the next section the common element of surprise among mainstream economists is described. Section 1.3 documents the views of those who did anticipate financial instability and section 1.4 draws out common elements in their thinking. Section 1.5 contrasts and compares this to the mainstream paradigm. Section 1.6 concludes with a summary and reflections.

1.2   THE CREDIT CRISIS SURPRISE

The view that '[n]o one foresaw the volume of the current avalanche', as Dutch Central Bank president Nout Wellink (2009) put it in a speech in April 2009, appears justified by the lack of discussion, in the academic and policy press, of the possibility that financial globalization harboured significant risks, or that the US real estate market and its derivative products were in murky waters. Wellink (2009) quoted a 2006 IMF report on the global real estate boom, asserting that there was 'little evidence . . . to suggest that the expected or likely market corrections in the period ahead would lead to crises of systemic proportions'. On the contrary, those developments now seen as culprits of the crisis were until recently lauded by policy-makers, academics and the business community. The following examples illustrate this.

In a speech on 27 September 2005 to the National Association for Business Economics, the then Federal Reserve Chairman Alan Greenspan spoke about the:

> development of financial products, such as asset-backed securities, collateral loan obligations, and credit default swaps, that facilitate the dispersion of risk. . . .. These increasingly complex financial instruments have contributed to the development of a far more flexible, efficient, and hence resilient financial system than the one that existed just a quarter-century ago. (Greenspan, 2005)

In line with these beliefs on increased 'resilience', Greenspan had, in February 2005, asserted to the US House Financial Services Committee that 'I don't expect that we will run into anything resembling a collapsing [housing] bubble, though it is conceivable that we will get some reduction in overall prices as we've had in the past, but that is not a particular problem'.

Similarly, the Canadian academic Philip Das in a 2006 survey article of financial globalization pointed out its benefits as:

> [f]inancial risks, particularly credit risks, are no longer borne by banks. They are increasingly moved off balance sheets. Assets are converted into tradable securities, which in turn eliminates credit risks. Derivative transactions like interest rate swaps also serve the same purpose [of *eliminating* credit risks].

Likewise, in August 2006, the IMF published 'Financial globalization: a reappraisal', which, despite its title, confirmed IMF conventional wisdom that 'there is little systematic evidence to support widely cited claims that financial globalization by itself leads to deeper and more costly crises' (Kose et al., 2006, p. 1). As for the business community, Landler (2007) reports that Klaus-Peter Müller, head of the New York branch of Kommerzbank for more than a decade, in a 2007 *New York Times* article asked 'Did I know in March of '04 that there was a U.S. subprime market that was going to face serious problems in the next few years? No, I didn't have the slightest idea. I was a happy man then'.

These assessments by the experts were carried over to the popular beliefs, enunciated in the mass media, that the recessionary impacts of the credit crisis came out of the blue. *USA Today* in December 2006 reported on the fall in house prices that had just started that summer. 'The good news is that far more economists are in the optimist camp than the pessimist camp. Although a handful, such as Baker, are predicting the economy will slide into a housing-led recession next year, the majority anticipate the economy will continue to grow' (Hagenbauch, 2006). Kaletsky (2008) wrote of 'those who failed to foresee the gravity of this crisis – a group that includes Mr. King, Mr. Brown, Alistair Darling, Alan Greenspan and almost every leading economist and financier in the world'.

The surprise at the seriousness of affairs was proportionate to previous optimism. Greenspan (2008a) in his October 2008 testimony before the Committee of Government Oversight and Reform professed to 'shocked disbelief' while watching his 'whole intellectual edifice collapse in the summer of [2007]'. Das (2008) conceded that contrary to his earlier view of financial globalization 'eliminating' credit risks, in fact '[p]artial blame for the fall 2008 meltdown of the global financial market does justly go to globalization'. The typical pattern was one of optimism shortly before and surprise shortly after the start of the crisis.

1.3   OTHER ASSESSMENTS

This mainstream view was not the only one, despite frequent assertions such as 'I do not know anyone who predicted this course of events', as Glenn Stevens, Governor of the Reserve Bank of Australia said on 9 December 2008 (RBA, 2008). Nor were the forebodings only vague, or the warnings made only by outsiders to the community of serious analysts. In this section I document analysis and public predictions of financial instability induced by falling real estate prices and leading to recession.

A major concern in collecting the data must be the 'stopped clock syndrome'. A stopped clock is put back on time twice a day, and the mere existence of predictions gives no useful information on the theoretical validity of such predictions since, in financial market parlance, 'every bear has his day'. Elementary statistical reasoning suggests that given a large number of commentators with varying views on any topic, it will be possible to find a prediction on that topic, at any point in time. With a large number of bloggers and pundits continuously making random guesses, erroneous predictions will be made and quickly assigned to oblivion, while correct guesses will be magnified and repeated after the fact. This in itself is no indication of their validity, but only of confirmation bias.

In distinguishing the lucky shots from insightful predictions, the randomness of guesses is a feature to be exploited. Random guesses are supported by all sorts of reasoning (if any at all), and will have little theory in common. Conversely, for a set of correct predictions to attain ex post credibility, it is additionally required that they are supported by a common theoretical framework. This study, then, aims to identify a set of predictions that are not only ex post correct but also rest on a common theoretical understanding. This will help identify the elements of a valid analytical approach to financial stability, and get the contrast into focus with conventional models.

In collecting these cases together in an analysis of the relevant literature, four selection criteria were applied. Only the analysts who provide some account of how they arrived at their conclusions were included. Second, the analysts included went beyond predicting a real estate or credit derivatives crisis, also making the link to real-sector recessionary implications, including an analytical account of those links. Third, the actual prediction must have been made by the analyst and have been available in the public domain, rather than being asserted by others. Finally, the prediction had to have some timing attached to it. Applying these criteria led to the exclusion of a number of (often high-profile) candidates so that the final selection is truly the result of critical scrutiny. At the same time, there is no pretension of completeness.

A summary overview of these analysts and their assessment is presented in Table 1.1. The 12 analysts described there – the number is entirely an outcome of the selection criteria – commented on the US, UK, Australian, Danish and global conditions in housing, finance and the broader economy. All except one are (or were) analysts and commentators of global fame. They are a mixed company of academics, government advisers, consultants, investors, stock market commentators and one graduate student, often combining these roles. Already between 2000 and 2006 they warned specifically about a housing-led recession within years, going against the general mood and official assessment, and well before

Table 1.1 Anticipations of the housing crisis and recession

Analyst	Capacity	Forecast
Dean Baker, USA	Co-director, Center for Economic and Policy Research	'plunging housing investment will likely push the economy into recession' (2006)
Wynne Godley, USA	Distinguished Scholar, Levy Economics Institute of Bard College	'The small slowdown in the rate at which US household debt levels are rising resulting from the house price decline, will immediately lead to a . . . sustained growth recession . . . before 2010' (Godley & Zezza, 2006). 'Unemployment [will] start to rise significantly and does not come down again' (Godley et al., 2007)
Fred Harrison, UK	Economic commentator	'The next property market tipping point is due at end of 2007 or early 2008. . . . The only way prices can be brought back to affordable levels is a slump or recession' (2005)
Michael Hudson, USA	Professor, University of Missouri	'Debt deflation will shrink the "real" economy, drive down real wages, and push our debt-ridden economy into Japan-style stagnation or worse' (2006b)
Eric Janszen, USA	Investor and *iTulip* commentator	'The US will enter a recession within years' (2006). 'US stock markets are likely to begin in 2008 to experience a "Debt Deflation Bear Market"' (2008)
Stephen Keen, Australia	Associate Professor, University of Western Sydney	'Long before we manage to reverse the current rise in debt, the economy will be in a recession. On current data, we may already be in one' (2006)
Jakob Brøchner Madsen & Jens Kjaer Sørensen, Denmark	Professor & graduate student, Copenhagen University	'We are seeing large bubbles and if they bust, there is no backup.. . . The outlook is very bad' (Madsen, in Agaard, 2008). 'The bursting of this housing bubble will have a severe impact on the world economy and may even result in a recession' (Sørensen, 2006)

Table 1.1   (continued)

Analyst	Capacity	Forecast
Kurt Richebächer, USA	Private consultant and investment newsletter writer	'The new housing bubble – together with the bond and stock bubbles – will invariably implode in the foreseeable future, plunging the US economy into a protracted, deep recession' (2001, in Bonner, 2007). 'A recession and bear market in asset prices are inevitable for the US economy. . .. All remaining questions pertain solely to speed, depth and duration of the economy's downturn' (2006b)
Nouriel Roubini, USA	Professor, New York University	'Real home prices are likely to fall at least 30% over the next 3 years'. 'By itself this house price slump is enough to trigger a US recession' (2005)
Peter Schiff, USA	Stock broker, investment adviser and commentator	'[T]he United States economy is like the Titanic. . .. I see a real financial crisis coming for the United States' (2006). 'There will be an economic collapse' (Schiff and Downes, 2007)
Robert Shiller, USA	Professor, Yale University	'[F]urther rises in the [stock and housing] markets could lead, eventually, to even more significant declines. . .. A long-run consequence could be a decline in consumer and business confidence, and another, possibly worldwide, recession' (in Karabell, 2009)

most observers turned critical from late 2007. Together they belie the notion that 'no one saw this coming', or that those who did were either professional doomsayers or lucky guessers.

   In the last part of this section we summarize the viewpoints of four of these analysts. This selection reflects diversity both in the countries they commented upon and in their methodological background. Fred Harrison commented on the UK situation, Jakob Brøchner Madsen and Jens Kjaer Sørensen on Denmark and the global housing bubble and Kurt Richebächer on the US credit markets. They are pluriform, as Harrison has published in the Georgist tradition, Richebächer wrote from an Austrian perspective, while Madsen does not clearly adhere to a specific methodological school and Sørensen's work is informed by Minsky's approach and hence perhaps best classified as Post-Keynesian. This diversity also holds for the entire set of analysts in Table 1.1, with the qualification that none is a mainstream economist. All are analysing the evolution of financial institutions and their impact on society over time, with attention to organizational and historical detail. They are, in this sense, operating in the Classical Institutionalist tradition. Importantly, although some are affiliated with mainstream institutions (Shiller is at Yale, Roubini at NYU, NBER and CEPR), all have distanced themselves in their writings from mainstream tenets such as rational individual optimization, the efficiency of financial markets or the irrelevance of financing methods (as in the Modigliani-Miller theorem). This common trait, in itself, is already a relevant finding, as it suggests that mainstream economics is unhelpful in anticipating financial instability and its implications. However, the aim of this paper is to go further and infer what, if anything, positively unites these contrarians.

The British economic commentator, Fred Harrison, in his first book, *The Power in the Land* (1983), forecast the recessions in the leading industrial economies in 1992. In 2005 he published *Boom Bust*, warning that the property market is subject to a sharp downturn at the end of a regular 18-year cycle, based on Harrison's study of UK property markets. At a time when the consensus among forecasters was that the boom in house prices would cool to an annual 2 per cent or 3 per cent rise over the following years, Harrison analysed that a 'winner's curse' phase of the cycle would see UK home prices rise by more than 10 per cent per annum – which they did during 2006 and 2007. An updated second edition of *Boom Bust* predicted that the next property market tipping point was due at the end of 2007 or early 2008. The reason for the instability, Harrison explained, was not the housing market itself but the land market. Economic expansion encourages speculation, with banks lending more against escalating asset values and reinforcing the upward spiral. The only way land prices can be brought back to affordable levels is a slump or recession, undermining the banking system and causing widespread unemployment and repossessions. The UK housing market started collapsing in November 2007, followed by the recession Harrison had forecast.

Jakob Brøchner Madsen, from Denmark, is a professor in economics at Monash University in Australia. From 2003, while he was professor in economics at the University of Copenhagen, he had questioned the sustainability of Denmark's growth. According to Madsen, Danes were living on borrowed time because of the mortgage debt, which 'had never been greater in our economic history'. The Danish business paper *Børsen* in its 4 December 2008 issue featured an overview of his forebodings (Agaard,

2008): In 2003 Madsen wrote 'I am very pessimistic. We are heading into something which is worse than what we experienced in 1982 [the last Danish recession]. It will be the worst recession since the Second World War'. In 2004: 'There is something completely wrong. We are seeing large bubbles and if they bust, there is no backup. House prices and shares are completely out of proportion. And it will go wrong.. . . The outlook is very bad for families in Denmark'. In 2005: 'I feel lost. Money growth is increasing, oil and commodity prices have doubled in the last 10 years. Therefore inflation and interest rates should increase, but nothing happens. All the models we use to predict inflation have broken down, it is chaos'.

One of his students, Jens Kjaer Sørensen, wrote an MA thesis in 2005–06 on 'The dynamics of house prices – international evidence', going back to the 1920s for a number of advanced economies (and to the 1840s for the Netherlands). In it, Sørensen demonstrated the existence of the first international synchronized housing boom in the UK, Norway, USA and the Netherlands. He showed that credit growth due to liberalization was the prime cause, and that it was a bubble, that is, prices would inevitably fall sharply to their long-run trends. The bursting of this bubble 'will have a severe impact on the world economy and may even result in a recession' (Sørensen, 2006, p. 97).

Jacob Brøchner Madsen moved to Monash University in 2006. His farewell talk at the University of Copenhagen on 1 July, 2006 was entitled 'Anatomy of the bubble–bust cycle in the Danish housing market'. In 2007, Madsen observed that 'houses are overvalued and it is only a matter of time before they will start falling' (Agaard, 2008). He predicted a decrease by up to 40 per cent. According to StatBank Denmark data, the growth in family homes prices in Denmark petered out in the third quarter of 2007, and economic growth halved from 3.3 per cent in 2006 to 1.6 per cent in 2007 and the economy contracted by 1 per cent in both 2008 and 2009 (source: StatBank Denmark).

Kurt Richebächer (1918–2007) wrote one of the longest-standing investment newsletters, *The Richebächer Letter*, which at various times also circulated as *Currencies and Credit Markets*. Richebächer was chief economist for Dresdner Bank from 1964 and moved into private consultancy in 1977. He warned against the bubble in technology stocks in the late 1990s. After its collapse, he warned against the bubble in housing, writing in September 2001: 'the new housing boom is another rapidly inflating asset bubble financed by the same loose money practices that fuelled the stock market bubble'. He went on to predict 'that the housing bubble – together with the bond and stock bubbles – will invariably implode in the foreseeable future, plunging the U.S. economy into a protracted, deep recession' (Bonner, 2007).

Writing in 2006, Richebächer held that 'the recovery of the U.S. economy since November 2001 has been dominated by an unprecedented consumer borrowing-and-spending-binge.. . . wealth creation through soaring asset prices has been driven by ultra-cheap and loose money and credit, and not by saving and investment' (Richebächer, 2006a, p. 4). Just before the turning of the US housing market in summer 2006, Richebächer in July 2006 commented that '[g]iven this precarious income situation on the one hand and the debt explosion on the other, it will be clear that in the foreseeable future there will be heavy selling of houses, with prices crashing for lack of buyers' (ibid., p. 11). As this prospect began to materialize in the next month, Richebächer wrote in his August 2006 newsletter that 'a recession and bear market in asset prices are inevitable for the U.S. economy.. . . This will not be a garden-variety recession, in which monetary easing unleashes pent-up demand, as it used to do in past business cycles'. He again emphasized its cause:

> the great trouble for the future is that the credit bubble has its other side in exponential debt growth. . .. The U.S. liquidity deluge of the last few years has had one single source: borrowing against rising assets backed by the Fed's monetary looseness . . . all hinging on further rises in asset prices. But they are going to plunge. (Richebächer, 2006b, pp. 1, 5, 9, 11–12)

And in September 2006 he wrote that 'housing bubbles, when bursting, generally do considerable damage to the economy. Today, they are bound to do far more damage' (Richebächer, 2006c, p. 4). The question was not if, but 'how fast the U.S. economy and its asset markets will turn down' (ibid., p. 9).

Paul Volker, former Chairman of the US Federal Reserve and a long-time friend of Richebächer, once remarked that the challenge for modern central bankers 'is to prove Kurt Richebächer wrong'. Richebächer regarded the expansion of credit under Greenspan as laying the foundation of the worst post-World War II economic contraction. He died on 24 August, 2007, two weeks after the events leading up to that contraction began (Bonner, 2007).

1.4 COMMON ELEMENTS OF THE ALTERNATIVE VIEWS

An analysis of these cases allows for the identification of a common underlying analytical framework, which apparently helps detect threats of instability. Surveying these assessments and forecasts, there indeed appears to be a set of interrelated elements central and common to the contrarians' thinking. This comprises a concern with financial assets as distinct from real-sector assets, with the credit flows that finance both forms of wealth, with the debt growth accompanying growth in financial wealth, and with the accounting relation between the financial and real economy. In the remainder of this section these issues will be discussed in turn.

A broadly shared element of analysis is the distinction between financial wealth and real assets. Several of the commentators (Schiff and Richebächer) adhere to the 'Austrian School' in economics, which means that they emphasize savings, production (not consumption) and real capital formation as the basis of sustainable economic growth. Richebächer (2006a, p. 4) warns against '"wealth creation" through soaring asset prices' and sharply distinguishes this from 'saving and investment' (where investment is in real-sector, not financial assets). Likewise Shiller (2003) warns that our infatuation with the stock market (financial wealth) is fuelling volatility and distracting us from more the durable economic prospect of building up real assets. Hudson (2006a) comments on the unsustainable 'growth of net worth through capital gains'.

A concern with debt as the counterpart of financial wealth follows naturally. 'The great trouble for the future is that the credit bubble has its other side in exponential debt growth' wrote Richebächer (2006b, p. 1). Madsen from 2003 worried that Danes were living on borrowed time because of the mortgage debt, which 'had never been greater in our economic history'. Godley and Zezza in 2006 published a paper titled 'Debt and lending: a *cri de coeur*' where they demonstrated the US economy's dependence on debt growth. They argued it would plunge the USA into a 'sustained growth recession . . . somewhere before 2010' (Godley and Zezza, 2006, p. 3). Schiff and Downes (2007) point to the low savings rate of the United States as its worst malady, citing the transformation from being the world's largest creditor nation in the 1970s to the largest debtor nation by the year 2000. Hudson (2006a) emphasized the same ambiguous potential of house price 'wealth' already in the title of his paper 'Saving, asset-price inflation, and debt-induced deflation', where he identified the 'large debt overhead – and the savings that form the balance-sheet counterpart to it' as the 'anomaly of today's [US] economy'. He warned that '[r]ising debt-service payments will further divert income from new consumer spending. Taken together, these factors will further shrink the "real" economy, drive down those already declining real wages, and push our debt-ridden economy into Japan-style stagnation or worse' (Hudson, 2006b, pp. 39–46.). Janszen (2009) notes how he had written in 2005 that:

> US households and businesses, and the government itself, had since 1980 built up too much debt. The rate of increase in debt was unsustainable. . .. Huge

imbalances in the US and global economy developed for over 30 years. Now they are rebalancing, as many non-mainstream economists have warned was certain to happen sooner or later.

Keen (2006) wrote that the debt-to-GDP ratio in Australia (then 147 per cent) 'will exceed 160 per cent of GDP by the end of 2007. We simply can't keep borrowing at that rate. We have to not merely stop the rise in debt, but reverse it. Unfortunately, long before we manage to do so, the economy will be in a recession'.

These quotes already reflect a further concern, that growth in financial wealth and the attendant growth in debt can become a determinant (instead of an outcome) of economic growth, undermining its sustainability and leading to a downturn. There is a recurrent emphasis (for example, Baker, 2002), that home equity-fuelled consumption has in recent years sustained stable growth (especially in the USA and UK) more than anything else, and that this was dangerous. Harrison (2007) juxtaposed his view to those who 'assume that the health of the property market depends upon the condition of the rest of the economy. In fact, . . . property is the key factor that shapes the business cycle, not the other way around'. Baker (2002) wrote that '[w]hile the short-term effects of a housing bubble appear very beneficial – just as was the case with the stock bubble and the dollar bubble – the long-term effects from its eventual deflation can be extremely harmful'. Godley and Wray (2000) argued that stable growth in the USA was unsustainable, as it was driven by households' debt growth, in turn fuelled by capital gains in the real estate sector. Their view was that as soon as debt growth slowed down – as it inevitably would within years – growth would falter and recession set in.

This recessionary impact of the bursting of asset bubbles is also a shared view. The bursting of the international housing bubble was seen to have 'a severe impact on the world economy and may even result in a recession' (Sørensen, 2006, p. 97). Richebächer (2006a, p. 4) in July 2006 commented that '[t]he one thing that still separates the U.S. economy from economic and financial disaster is rising house prices that apparently justify ever more credit and debt' and in August 2006 (Richebächer, 2006b) that 'a recession and bear market in asset prices are inevitable for the U.S. economy'. Again, '[t]here is no question that the U.S. housing bubble is finished. All remaining questions pertain solely to speed, depth and duration of the economy's downturn' (Richebächer, 2006c, p. 9). Roubini (2005) – only weeks after US house prices had started falling – already wrote that '[b]y itself this [house price] slump is enough to trigger a US recession'.

Finally, emphasis on the role of credit cycles in the business cycle leads to a long-term view on credit cycles. Sørensen (2006) criticizes most housing market analyses for not looking beyond the 1980s–2000s period. These were the years of a credit boom, and only by looking at longer periods can the dynamics and dangers of the housing market be detected, as he demonstrates. Also, others place the long credit boom that started in the mid-1980s as central to understanding economic performance, and assert that acceleration of growth in lending and debt has endangered stability since then. The assessment of the 2007–08 collapse is hence embedded in a longer-term view. 'This recovery has been fuelled by a housing bubble, just as the late 1990s cycle was fuelled by a stock bubble', commented Baker (2002). Accordingly, US economic growth since the 2000 dot-com crash, is viewed by several as a 'phony' growth in that it was (consciously or unwittingly) engineered by the monetary authorities via generous credit policies, rather than driven by real-sector performance.

1.5   COMPARING THE PARADIGMS

How did the analysts discussed above distinguish themselves from mainstream economics? A fundamental issue, from which more specific differences follow, is the organizing principle of market equilibrium induced by firms and households acting as rationally optimizing economic agents. In contrast to this feature of models used for official forecasts, the models used by the contrarians – whether formalized or not – have an emphasis on money, the flow of funds and accounting relations in the economy, on the role of uncertainty and on economic psychology and political economy as the key behavioural assumptions. Absence of the notion of equilibrium does not mean that their models are indeterminate. Some do have steady states (Godley, 1999) and the logical implications of flow-of-funds models such as those used by Godley et al. (2007) are determinant – in some respects more so than those of equilibrium models, as will be discussed below.

All of these analysts reject rational equilibrium on the basis of arguments related to economic psychology and to the Keynesian notion of 'radical uncertainty' (as opposed to calculable risks). Keen, in a 1995 article titled 'Finance and economic breakdown' (p. 612) explained that:

> Keynes argued that uncertainty cannot be reduced to 'the same calculable states as that of certainty itself' whereas the kind of uncertainty that matters in investment is that about which 'there is no scientific basis on which to form any calculable probability whatever. We simply do not know' (Keynes, 1937, pp. 213–224). Keynes argued that in the midst of this incalculable uncertainty, investors form fragile expectations about the future, which are crystallized

in the prices they place upon capital sets, and that these prices are therefore subject to sudden and violent change.

This view of human assessment and investment behaviour allows for a crisis of confidence in a way that equilibrium models – where investment is always guided by the marginal costs and benefits of underlying real capital assets – cannot. This possibility, in turn, allowed the above analysts to contemplate the plausibility that the general mood is not rational but mistaken, and that crisis looms amidst seemingly tranquil conditions.

Specifically, housing market participants in a credit boom are viewed as led to speculation by psychological mechanisms well-known in a bull market. Harrison (2005) observes that economic expansion encourages a speculation mentality, with banks lending more against escalating asset values and reinforcing the upward spiral. Shiller (2000, 2008) writes of the 'contagion effect' as the principal mechanism feeding bubbles. Beliefs about wealth creation through asset prices spread via a number of mechanisms such as 'new era' stories that justify the capital gains as being part of a 'new economy', where the novel aspect resides in, for instance, technology (in the 1990s) or globalization (in the 2000s). Shiller (for example, 2000) has articulated motivational models of human behaviour such as 'irrational exuberance', which allow for states of the economy such as euphoric booms, busts and recession – all of which are difficult to grasp in the conventional models. Other authors refer to related ideas as developed by Minsky (for example, 1978). Sørensen (2006) similarly explains the housing bubble by information cascades and herding behaviour, where investors observing gainful speculation are more likely to engage in speculation, regardless of the underlying fundamentals.

As for political economy, the boom was seen to be fuelled by monetary policies of generous credit flows and low interest rates and the untaxing of real estate gains via depreciation and interest payments tax rules. These policies are observed to have helped stave off (intentionally or otherwise) recession after the 1999 dot-com collapse, even though in fostering a wealth-cum-debt bubble they stored up the present trouble. Janszen (2001) 'expected that after the technology bubble crash the Federal Reserve and government was certain via tax cuts, rate cuts, and stealth dollar devaluation to induce a reflation boom like the 1934–1937 reflation created after the 1929 stock market bubble bust'. Richebächer (2006a, p. 9) writes of 'ultra-cheap and loose money and credit', and that '[t]he U.S. liquidity deluge of the last few years has had one single source: borrowing against rising assets backed by the Fed's monetary looseness' (Richebächer, 2006b, p. 9).

This underlying difference with the neoclassical equilibrium assumption finds expression in the way models are structured. Models of the macro-economy (of either type) consist of equations of two sorts: identities describing per-definition relations between variables, and behavioural equations capturing researchers' assumptions about decisions by eco-nomics agents on saving, investment, borrowing, lending, employment and transactions. In equilibrium models, the action is in the behavioural assumptions, which drive model responses to shocks and determine per-formance forecasts. The typical behavioural assumption is individual optimization by economic agents of their objective function (consumption for households; profit for firms) to some equilibrium level.

Unlike equilibrium models, the equations in flow-of-funds models such as those used by Godley represent a transactions (flow) matrix and a balance sheet (stock) matrix. Thus, the flow of funds is at the very heart of these models, unlike the mere unit-of-account function of money in equilibrium models. Explicit flow-of-funds models, such as those developed not only by Godley (1999) but also Graziani (2003), Keen (2006), Hudson (2006b) and Godley and Lavoie (2007a) are grounded in the 'endogenous money' view of the economy, where banks' credit creation is viewed as central and indis-pensable for transacting and thus for economic activity at large. Levels of wealth and debt are recognized to affect banks', firms' and the public's balance sheets, and thus economic activity. The contrast is with neoclass-ical economics on which equilibrium models are based, where wealth plays no (or only a small) role and money is incidental to the economic process, which is seen as driven by real-sector fundamentals. This emphasis on financial balance sheets and the monetary nature of the economy is what distinguishes flow-of-funds models also from input-output models, which describe flows of goods and services perhaps denominated in money terms, but without finance and the flow of funds it generates playing a role in the model dynamics. For instance, '[f]lows of interest are not often discussed in the literature, although a model of the whole system cannot be solved unless they are explicitly included' (Godley, 1999, p. 397).

As to behavioural equations, equating of marginal cost and revenue would be inconsistent with the radical uncertainty theorized by Keynes. This implies that firms are in a state of uncertainty over future sales and revenues and do not even know their precise objective function, let alone have the computing power to continually solve it, as in neoclassical theory. Hence firms cannot respond to future prices while planning future pro-duction. Rather, firms may be assumed to respond to sold quantities, via changes in their inventories.

The introduction of uncertainty, and the absence of maximizing to a single optimum, likewise shapes the behavioural assumptions on house-holds and the government. For instance, in Godley's approach households are assumed to hold wealth in a number of assets, allocating over assets according to their expected returns. Consumption, in turn, depends on these wealth-holding preferences as well as income. As expectations can be volatile, 'when unexpected things happen, these assets move in correspondingly unexpected ways' (ibid.), and so does consumption, demand and the wider economy. They depend, not on some equilibrium condition, but on how flows of funds and goods adjust to changes in stocks. Changes in this theoretical system therefore can be much more abrupt and economy-wide crisis, resulting from perceptions and wealth changes, is possible.

As to underlying model philosophy, 'a model, of necessity, is an abstraction from the full detail of the real world', as Greenspan (2008b) reminded his readers and himself after the crash. In contrast, flow-of-funds models (whether formalized or not) differ from equilibrium models in what they abstract from. Equilibrium models abstract from the flow of funds and the stocks of credit and debt, and the systemic risks implied in them; they focus on the individual optimization problems facing individuals. It is assumed that any impact of the flow of funds and the stocks of credit and debt are fully reflected in returns and risks at the individual level, so that this is what analysis needs to focus on. Flow-of-funds models abstract from optimization problems and focus on the flow of funds and the stocks of credit and debt. The assumption is that individual decisions will always be reflected in the aggregate flow of funds and the stocks of credit and debt, and that this is where an economy's rate of return and systemic risks are formed; and so that this is what a model needs to chart.

But when Greenspan (2008b, p.9) wrote that 'we will never have a perfect model of risk', he meant individual-level, not systemic risk. His (and the mainstream) view is that systemic analysis is not valid scientifically without an individual-level underpinning ('micro-fundamentals'), and is redundant with it. 'He espoused the idea that mathematical econometric models of individual behaviour are the only tools we will ever have' (Shiller, 2008, p.42). This contrasts to the analyses discussed in section 1.3, which are all pinned on the level of the economic system, not the individual one.

Similarly, an important difference between equilibrium models and the flow-of-fund models used explicitly by Godley and Keen and implicitly by Hudson, is that identity equations in a flow-of-funds model aim to reflect the flow of funds in the economy in a complete (though obviously stylized) manner. It is specified where each flow of funds comes from and where it goes. Each transaction is by some sector with some other sector (both well specified) and leads to two equal changes in balance sheets. In contrast, equilibrium models do not aim at such completeness. For instance, an increase in the money supply in a flow-of-funds model is reflected in changes in the accounts of banks and lenders, whereas an increase in the money supply in the typical macroeconomic model is simply an increase in the value of the money stock (M2 or M3) ex nihilo; the actual money creation process, and the accompanying flow of funds (principal and interest payments) is not specified. Thus, conventional equilibrium models tend to be detailed on hours worked, productivity and the like but completely miss the tendency of variables such as debt build up.

Finally, in equilibrium models, solving the optimization problems is what determines the model's outcome. In flow-of-funds models, its completeness drives the outcome. For instance, in flow-of-funds models including a private sector (firms and households), a government sector and a foreign sector, Godley and Lavoie (2007b, p. xxxvi) note the 'strategic importance' of the 'accounting identity which says that, measured in current prices, the government's budget deficit less the current account deficit is equal, by definition, to private saving minus investment'. This identity allowed Godley and Wray (2000) to conclude that 'Goldilocks was doomed': with a government surplus and current account deficit, US economic growth had to be financed by private debt growth. Equilibrium models do not permit for such conclusions.

1.6   SUMMARY, REFLECTIONS AND CONCLUSIONS

This paper has sought to contribute to the debate on what economics can learn from the credit crisis and recession. It asks what are the elements in the mainstream paradigm that caused many economists to misjudge the state of the economy so dramatically in the years leading up to the 2007 credit crisis and the 2008–09 recession? It has applied a factual, inductive approach by scrutinizing the work of 12 economists who warned about the crisis, and by identifying the common elements in their thinking. These are then contrasted with mainstream thinking.

Those who 'saw it coming' in their analyses emphasized financial assets, debt and the flow of funds. These are elements that are absent from most forecasting and scenario evaluation models in official use (for example, DSGE models). Regarding behavioural assumptions, these include uncertainty, bounded rationality and non-optimizing behaviour, also in contrast to mainstream theory. Methodologically, these analysts favour empirical work rather than theoretical formalism, and they share an aversion to methodological individualism. To sum up, neoclassical economists should stop neglecting money, wealth and debt, and turn away from an individualistic and towards a systemic view of the economy.

These are not shockingly novel findings: they have been extensively discussed in the heterodox literature. This paper's contribution is a corroboration of those concerns based not on theoretical considerations, but on a factual investigation of what 'works' in terms of crisis anticipation. The straightforward conclusion is that mainstream theory should start paying attention to these elements if it is to be more successful in anticipating financial instability when 'it' happens again (Minsky, 1963). The problem will be that most of these elements are incompatible with core tenets of the neoclassical paradigm. In personal communications and at seminar presentations of this paper, officials from central banks and forecasting agencies often asserted that a monetary module is being added to their standard model, addressing the concerns raised here. This may be true for some issues such as ignoring or tracing the size (if not the impact) of debt. But when it comes to fundamental choices such as equilibrium solutions or accounting identities and taking a systemic or individualistic perspective, the question is not how they can best match. They are incompatible. Therefore, following Kuhn's (1962) view on scientific revolutions, it is more likely that the credit crisis and recession will result in increased efforts towards the construction of theoretical 'protective belts' rather than modification of economics' theoretical core. The continuing challenge for heterodox economists will be to develop and publicize a more realistic kind of economics. In addressing this task for the field of monetary economics and macro financial stability, there are solid foundations to be built on, as this paper has sought to demonstrate.

REFERENCES

Agaard, J. (2008), 'Fact: this is what the housing crisis prophet said', *Børsen*, 4 December (translation by Jens Sørensen).

Baker, D. (2002), 'The run-up in home prices: is it real or is it another bubble?', Washington, DC: Center for Economic and Policy Research, August, available at: http://www.cepr.net/documents/publications/housing_2002_08.pdf; accessed 3 September 2010.

Baker, D. (2006), 'Recession looms for the U.S. economy in 2007', available at http://ideas.repec.org/p/epo/papers/2006-29.html; accessed 17 September 2010.

Bonner, B. (2007), 'Requiem for an economist. (Kurt Richebächer: *in memoriam*)', *The Daily Reckoning*, 24 August, available at http://www.sane.org.za/docs/views/showviews.asp?ID=243; accessed 3 September 2010.

Das, D. (2006), 'Globalization in the world of finance: an analytical history', *Global Economy Journal*, **6** (1), article 2.

Das, D. (2008), 'Contemporary phase of globalization: does it have a serious downside?', *Global Economic Review*, **37** (4), 507–526.

Friedman, B.M. (2009), 'The failure of the economy and the economists', *New York Review of Books*, **56** (9), 42–45, 28 May.

Galbraith, J. (2009), 'Who are these economists, anyway?', *Thought and Action*, Fall, 85–97.

Godley, W. (1999), 'Money and credit in a Keynesian model of income determination', *Cambridge Journal of Economics*, **23** (4), 393–411.

Godley, W. and M. Lavoie (2007a), 'Fiscal policy in a Stock-Flow Consistent (SFC) model', *Journal of Post Keynesian Economics*, **30** (1), 79–100.

Godley, W. and M. Lavoie (2007b), *Monetary Economics: An Integrated Approach to Credit, Money, Income, Production and Wealth*, London: Palgrave/Macmillan.

Godley, W. and L.W. Wray (2000), 'Is Goldilocks doomed?', *Journal of Economic Issues*, **34** (1), 201–207.

Godley, W. and G. Zezza (2006), 'Debt and lending: a *cri de coeur*', The Levy Economics Institute of Bard College Policy Note No. 06-4, available at: http://www.levyinstitute.org/pubs/pn_4_06.pdf; accessed 3 September 2010.

Godley, W., D. Papadimitriou, G. Hannsgen and G. Zezza (2007), 'The U.S. economy: is there a way out of the woods?', The Levy Economics Institute of Bard College Strategic Analysis, November, available at: http://www.levy institute.org/pubs/sa_nov_07.pdf; accessed 3 September 2010.

Graziani, A. (2003), *The Monetary Theory of Production*, Federico Caffè Lectures, Cambridge, New York and Melbourne: Cambridge University Press.

Greenspan, A. (2005), '*Economic flexibility*', Remarks by Chairman Alan Greenspan to the National Association for Business Economics Annual Meeting Chicago, IL, 27 September, available at http://www.federalreserve.gov/board docs/speeches/2005/20050927/default.htm; accessed 2 September 2010.

Greenspan, A. (2008a), 'Testimony' of Dr. Alan Greenspan before the Committee of Government Oversight and Reform, 23 October, available at: http://clipsand comment.com/wp-content/uploads/2008/10/greenspan-testimony-20081023. pdf; accessed 2 September 2010.

Greenspan, A. (2008b), 'We will never have a perfect model of risk', *Financial Times*, 17 March, p. 9.

Hagenbauch, B. (2006), 'Growth or recession in 2007?', *USA Today*, 12 December.

Harrison, F. (1983) *The Power in the Land*, New York: Universe Books.

Harrison, F. (2005) *Boom Bust: House Prices, Banking and the Depression of 2010*, London: Shephear-walwyn.

Harrison, F. (2007), 'House prices: expect the worst', *MoneyWeek*, 7 November.

Hudson, M. (2006a), 'Saving, asset-price inflation, and debt-induced deflation', in L.R. Wray and M. Forstater (eds), *Money, Financial Instability and Stabilization Policy*, Cheltenham, UK and Northampton, MA, USA: Edward Elgar, pp. 104–124 (graphs also reproduced at http://www.itulip.com/forums/Showthread.php/891-Saving-Asset-Price-Inflation-and-Debt-Induced-Deflation; accessed 3 September 2010.

Hudson, M. (2006b), 'The new road to serfdom: an illustrated guide to the coming real estate collapse', *Harper's Magazine*, April.

Janszen, E. (2001), 'Questioning fashionable investment advice', www.itulip.com, August, available at: http://www.itulip.com/gold.htm; accessed 3 September 2010.

Janszen, E. (2006), iTulip's Eric Janszen interviews noted economist James Galbraith, 28 November 2006, available at: http://www.itulip.com/forums/Showthread.php/654-Dr.-James-K.-Galbraith-Interview-Janszen; accessed 17 September 2010.

Janszen, E. (2008), 'Debt deflation bear market. Update Part I; 2009 Windup', available at: http://news.goldseek.com/foldseek/1227251100.php; accessed 17 September 2010.

Janszen, E. (2009), 'Debt deflation bear market windup update. Part I: 2009', www.itulip.com, available at: http://www.itulip.com/forums/showthread. php?p=61898#post61898; accessed 3 September 2010.

Kaletsky, A. (2008), 'It's an emergency. Long-term cures must wait', *The Times*, 13 November.

Keen, S. (1995), 'Finance and economic breakdown: modelling Minsky's Financial Instability Hypothesis', *Journal of Post Keynesian Economics*, **17** (4), 607–635.

Keen, S. (2006), 'The lily and the pond', interview reported by the Evatts Foundations, available at http://evatt.org.au/news/445.html; accessed 3 September 2010.

Kose M.A., E. Prasad, K. Rogoff and S.-J. Wei (2006), 'Financial globalization: a reappraisal', IMF Working Papers No. 06/189, August.

Krugman, P. (2009), 'How did economists get it so wrong?', *New York Times*, 6 September.

Kuhn, T. (1962), *The Structure of Scientific Revolutions*, Chicago: University of Chicago Press.

Landler, M (2007), 'A banker in Germany says trouble is not over', *New York Times*, 27 November, available at: http://www.nytimes.com/2007/11/27/business/ worldbusiness/27subprime.html?scp=1&sq=Klaus-Peter+M%FCller&st=nyt; accessed 2 September 2010.

Minsky, H. (1963), 'Can "it" happen again?', as reprinted in D. Carson (ed.), *Banking and Monetary Studies*, Homewood, IL, R.D. Irwin, pp. 101–111.

Minsky, H. (1978), 'The financial instability hypothesis: a restatement', *Thames Papers in Political Economy*, London: Thames Polytechnic.

Reserve Bank of Australia – RBA (2008), 'Interesting times', speech by Glenn Stevens, Governor of the Reserve Bank of Australia, to the Australian Business Economists Annual Dinner, Sydney, 9 December, available at: http://www.rba. gov.au/Speeches/2008/sp-gov-091208.html; accessed 2 September 2010.

Richebächer, K. (2006a), *The Richebächer Letter. Monthly Analysis of Currencies and Credit Markets*, July.

Richebächer, K. (2006b), *The Richebächer Letter. Monthly Analysis of Currencies and Credit Markets*, August.

Richebächer, K. (2006c), *The Richebächer Letter. Monthly Analysis of Currencies and Credit Markets*, September.

Roubini, N. (2005), 'The biggest slump in US housing in the last 40 years . . . or 53 years', available at: http://www.roubini.com/roubini:-monitor/142759/the_ biggest_slump_in_US_housing_in_the_last_40_years_or_53_years; accessed 17 September 2010.

Schiff, P. (2006), CBNC *Interview*, August.

Schiff P. with J. Downes (2007), *Crash Proof: How to Profit From the Coming Economic Collapse*, Hoboken, NJ: John Wiley & Sons.

Shiller, R. (2000), *Irrational Exuberance*, Princeton, NJ: Princeton University Press.

Shiller, R. (2003), *The New Financial Order: Risk in the 21st Century*, Princeton, NJ: Princeton University Press.

Shiller, R. (2008), *The Subprime Solution. How Today's Global Financial Crisis Happened, and What to Do about It*, Princeton, NJ: Princeton University Press.

Sørensen, J. (2006), 'The dynamics of house prices – international evidence', Social Science Research Network Paper, available at: http://papers.ssrn.com/sol3/papers.cfm?abstract_id=1273183; accessed 3 September 2010.

Wellink, N. (2009), *Ruijs de Beerenbroucklezing*, 9 April, available at: http://www.dnb.nl/ (author's translation); accessed 2 September 2010.

2. A brief note on economic recessions, banking reform and the future of capitalism

Jesús Huerta de Soto

The financial crisis of 2008–09 and the current worldwide economic recession is one of the most important problems we have to cope with now. The Austrian Business Cycle Theory can help us to understand its causes and the best approach to economic recovery (Huerta de Soto, 2009a).

Having witnessed the intellectual and practical defeat of socialism especially during the last decades of the 20th century (Huerta de Soto, 2010), one of the main challenges that still remains for the future of capitalism is the urgent need to privatize money by dismantling the organ of central monetary planning: the Central Bank. In other words, real socialism, represented by state money, central banks and financial administrative regulations, is still in force in the monetary and credit sectors of the so-called free market economies. As a result, we regularly experience, in the area of money and credit, all the negative consequences established by the Theorem of the Economic Impossibility of Socialism discovered by those distinguished members of the Austrian School of Economics, Ludwig von Mises and Friedrich Hayek (Mises, 1981; Hayek, 1997).

Specifically, the central planners of state money cannot know, follow and control the changes in both the demand and supply of money. Furthermore, the whole financial system is based on the legal privilege given by the state to private bankers to act with a fractional reserve ratio in relation with the demand deposits they receive from their clients. As a result of this privilege, private bankers are not true financial intermediaries, but are mainly creators of deposits that materialize in credit expansions. These credit expansions are artificial and do not correspond to any previous increases in the voluntary savings of citizens. In this way, the current fractional reserve banking system tends to worsen and amplify the systemic inter-temporal distortions and investment misallocations that the macroeconomic planners working for central banks induce in the production structure of the whole real economy. These distortions manifest themselves in the stages of financial bubbles, economic boom, overall poor investment and afterwards in the stages of financial crisis, deep economic recession and unemployment.

The expansionary cycle that has now come to a close was set in motion when the US economy emerged from its last recession in 2001 and the Federal Reserve embarked, again, on a major artificial expansion of credit and investment, an expansion that was not backed by a parallel increase in voluntary household saving. For several years the money supply, in the form of banknotes and deposits, grew at an average rate of over 10 per cent per year (which meant that every seven years the total volume of money circulating in the world doubled). The media of exchange originating from this severe fiduciary inflation had been placed on the market by the banking system as newly created loans granted at extremely low (and even negative in real terms) interest rates. This fuelled a speculative bubble in the shape of a substantial rise in the prices of capital goods, real estate assets, and the securities that represent them and are exchanged on the stock market, where indexes soared (Bismans and Mougeot, 2009).

Curiously, as in the 'roaring' years prior to the Great Depression of 1929 and 1930s (Rothbard, 2000), this monetary growth shock has not significantly influenced the prices of the subset of consumer goods and services (approximately only one-third of the total number of goods). The last decade, like the 1920s, has seen a remarkable increase in productivity as a result of the introduction, on a massive scale, of new technologies and significant entrepreneurial innovations that, were it not for the 'money and credit injection', would have given rise to a healthy and sustained reduction in the unit price of the goods and services all citizens consume. Moreover, the full incorporation of the economies of China and India into the globalized market has gradually raised the real productivity of consumer goods and services even further. The absence of a healthy 'deflation' in the prices of consumer goods in a stage of such considerable growth in productivity, as that of recent years, provides the main evidence that the monetary shock has seriously disturbed the whole economic process.

Economic theory teaches us that, unfortunately, artificial credit expansion and the (fiduciary) inflation of the media of exchange offer no short cut to stable and sustained economic development, nor a way of avoiding the necessary sacrifice and discipline behind high rates of voluntary saving. In fact, particularly in the United States, voluntary saving until recently has not only failed to increase, but in the past years has even fallen to a negative rate. Indeed, the artificial expansion of credit and money is never more than a short-term solution even at best. In fact, today there is no doubt about the recessionary quality the monetary shock always has in the long run: newly created loans (of money without the backup of citizens' savings) immediately provide entrepreneurs with purchasing power they use in overly ambitious investment projects (especially in the building sector and real estate development in recent years). In other words, entrepreneurs acted as if citizens had increased their saving, when they had not actually done so.

Widespread lack of coordination in the economic system results in the financial bubble ('irrational exuberance') exerting a harmful effect on the real economy, and sooner or later the process reversing itself in the form of a financial crisis, which marks the beginning of the painful and necessary readjustment (economic recession). This readjustment invariably requires the reconversion of the entire real productive structure, which inflation has distorted (Garrison, 2001). The specific triggers of the end of the euphoric monetary 'binge' and the beginning of the recessionary 'hangover' are many, and they can vary from one cycle to another. In this crisis, the most obvious triggers have been the rise in the price of raw materials, particularly oil, the subprime mortgage crisis in the United States, and finally, the failure of important banking institutions when it became clear in the market that the value of their debts exceeded that of their assets (mortgage loans granted).

At present, numerous self-interested voices are demanding further reductions in interest rates and new injections of money that would permit those who so desire to complete their investment projects without suffering losses. Nevertheless, this escape forward would only temporarily postpone problems at the cost of making them far more serious later. The crisis has hit because the profits of capital-goods companies (especially in the building sector and in real estate development) have disappeared due to the entrepreneurial errors provoked by cheap credit, and because the prices of consumer goods have begun to perform relatively less poorly than those of capital goods. At this point, an inevitable, painful readjustment begins, characterized by a drop in production and an increase in unemployment.

The most rigorous economic analysis and the coolest, most balanced interpretation of recent economic and financial events lead inexorably to the conclusion that central banks (which are true financial central-planning agencies) cannot possibly succeed in finding the most advantageous monetary policy at every moment in time. This is exactly what became clear in the case of the unsuccessful attempts to organize the former Soviet economy from above. To put it another way, the Theorem of the Economic Impossibility of Socialism, which the Austrian economists Ludwig von Mises and Friedrich A. Hayek discovered, is fully applicable to central banks in general, and to the Federal Reserve and (formerly) to Alan Greenspan and (currently) to Ben Bernanke in particular. According to this theorem, it is impossible to organize society, in terms of economics, based on coercive commands issued by a planning agency, since such a body can never obtain the information it needs to infuse its commands with a coordinating nature (Hayek, 1988). Indeed, nothing is more dangerous than to indulge in the 'fatal conceit' – to use Hayek's useful expression – of believing oneself omniscient or at least wise and powerful enough to be able to keep the most suitable monetary policy fine tuned at all times. Hence, rather than soften the most violent ups and downs of the economic cycle, the Federal Reserve and, to a lesser extent, the European Central Bank, have most likely been the main architects and the culprits in their own downturn.

Therefore, the dilemma facing Ben Bernanke and his Federal Reserve Board, as well as the other central banks (beginning with the European Central Bank), is not a comfortable one. For years they have shirked their monetary responsibility, and now they find themselves in a blind alley. They can either allow the recessionary process to follow its path, and with it the healthy and painful readjustment, or they can escape forward toward a 'renewed inflationist' cure. With the latter, the chances of even more severe recession (even inflationary recession) in the not too distant future exponentially increase. This was, precisely, the error committed following the 1987 stock market crash, an error that led to inflation at the end of the 1980s and concluded with the sharp recession of 1990–92. Furthermore, the reintroduction of a cheap-credit policy at this stage will only hinder the necessary liquidation of unprofitable investments and company reconversion further. It could even end up prolonging the recession indefinitely, as in the Japanese economy, which, after all possible interventions were tried, ceased to respond to any stimulus involving monetarist credit expansion or Keynesian methods.

It is in this context of 'financial schizophrenia' that we must interpret the 'shots in the dark' fired in the last two years by the monetary authorities (who have two totally contradictory responsibilities: both to control inflation and to inject all the liquidity necessary into the financial system to prevent its collapse). Thus, one day the Fed rescues Bear Stearns (and later AIG, Fannie Mae, Freddie Mac or City Group) and the next it allows Lehman Brothers to fail, under the amply justified pretext of 'teaching a lesson' and refusing to fuel moral hazard. Finally, in light of the way events were unfolding, the US and European governments launched multi-billion-dollar plans to purchase illiquid (i.e., worthless) assets from the banking system and even to buy bank shares, nationalizing totally or partially the private banking system. If those plans are financed by taxes (and not more inflation), it will mean a heavy tax burden on households, precisely when they are least able to bear it.

In comparison, the economies of the European Union are in a somewhat better state (if we forget about the relatively greater European rigidities, particularly in the labour market, which tend to make recessions in Europe longer and more painful). The expansionary policy of the European Central Bank, though not free of grave errors, has been somewhat less irresponsible than that of the Federal Reserve. Furthermore, fulfilment of the convergence criteria involved, at the time, a healthy and significant overhaul of the chief European economies. Only some countries on the periphery, like Ireland and especially Spain, were immersed in considerable credit expansion from the time they initiated their processes of convergence. The case of Spain is paradigmatic. The Spanish economy underwent an economic boom that, in part, was due to real causes (like the liberalizing structural reforms that originated with José María Aznar's administration). Nevertheless, the boom was also largely fuelled by an artificial expansion of money and credit, that in Spain grew at a rate nearly three times more than the corresponding rates in France and Germany. Spanish economic agents essentially interpreted the decrease in interest rates that resulted from the convergence process in the easy-money terms traditional in Spain as a greater availability of easy money and mass requests for loans from Spanish banks (mainly to finance real estate speculation), loans that these banks granted by creating the money ex nihilo while European central bankers looked on unperturbed. When faced with the rise in prices, the European Central Bank tried to remain faithful to its mandate and at least for some months decided to maintain interest rates despite the difficulties of those members of the Monetary Union, which, like Spain, were already discovering that much of their investment in real estate had been erroneous and that they were now heading for a lengthy and painful reorganization of their real economy.

Under the current circumstances, the most appropriate policy would be to liberalize the economy at all levels (especially in the labour market) to permit the rapid reallocation of productive factors (particularly labour) to profitable sectors. Likewise, it is essential to reduce public spending and taxes, in order to increase the available income of heavily indebted economic agents who need to repay their loans as soon as possible. Economic agents, in general, and companies, in particular, can only overhaul their finances by cutting costs (especially labour costs) and paying off loans. Essential to this aim is a very flexible labour market and a much more austere public sector. These factors are fundamental if the market is to reveal as quickly as possible the real value of the erroneously produced investment goods and thus lay the foundation for a healthy, sustained economic recovery in a not too distant future.

Now, let us make some comments on the influence of the new accounting rules on the current economic and financial crisis. Very often we hear and read in the media that the financial crisis and the stock market crash are the result of the lack of confidence produced by accountancy and management scandals. But the so-called 'creative accounting' of the bubble years and the subsequent scandals are not the cause of our current problems, but just the opposite. They are one of the most typical by-products of the feverish market pressures on business during a long period of 'irrational exuberance'. Accounting is the language of business and its traditional century-old foundations based on the principle of very prudent valuation of assets (namely the lower of cost or market) cannot be substituted by new principles based on the very volatile so-called 'fair market value' and the artificial inflation of balance sheets in bubble markets without destroying the whole capitalist system. We must not forget that a central feature of the recent period of artificial expansion was a gradual corruption, on the North American continent as well as in Europe, of the traditional principles of accounting as practised globally for centuries. To be specific, acceptance of the International Accounting Standards (IAS) and their incorporation as law in most countries has meant the abandonment of the traditional principle of prudence and its replacement by the principle of fair value in the assessment of the value of balance sheet assets, particularly financial assets.

In this abandonment of the traditional principle of prudence, a highly influential role has been played by brokerages, investment banks and, in general, all the parties interested in 'inflating' book values in order to bring them closer to supposedly more 'objective' stock market values, which in the past rose continually in an economic process of financial euphoria. In fact, during the years of the 'speculative bubble', this process was characterized by a feedback loop: rising stock market values were immediately entered into the books, and then these accounting entries were used as a justification for further artificial increases in the prices of financial assets listed on the stock market.

We see that new accounting rules act in a procyclic manner (Huerta de Soto, 2009b) by heightening volatility and erroneously biasing business management. In times of prosperity, they create a false 'wealth effect', which prompts people to take disproportionate risks. When, from one day to the next, the errors committed come to light, the loss in the value of assets immediately decapitalizes companies, which are obliged to sell assets and attempts to recapitalize at the worse possible moment, when assets are worth the least and financial markets are drying up. Clearly, accounting principles that have proven so disturbing must be abandoned as soon as possible, and all of the recently enacted accounting reforms must be reversed. This is not only so because these reforms mean a dead end in a period of financial crisis and recession, but especially because it is vital that in periods of prosperity we stick to the principle of prudence in valuation, a principle that has shaped accounting systems from the time of Luca Pacioli at the beginning of the 15th century to the adoption of the false idol of International Accounting Standards.

In short, the greatest error of the accounting reform, recently introduced worldwide, is that it scraps centuries of accounting experience and business management when it replaces the prudence principle, as the highest ranking among all traditional accounting principles, with the 'fair value' principle, which is simply the introduction of the volatile market value for an entire set of assets, particularly financial assets. This Copernican turn is extremely harmful and threatens the very foundations of the market economy for several reasons.

First, to violate the traditional principle of prudence and require that accounting entries reflect market values is to provoke, depending upon the conditions of the economic cycle, an inflation of book values with surpluses that have not materialized and that, in many cases, may never materialize. The artificial 'wealth effect' this can produce, especially during the boom phase of each economic cycle, leads to the allocation of paper (or merely temporary) profits, the acceptance of disproportionate risks, and, in short, the commission of systematic entrepreneurial errors and the consumption of the nation's capital, to the detriment of its healthy productive structure and its capacity for long-term growth.

Second, I must emphasize that the purpose of accounting is not to reflect supposed 'real' values (which in any case are subjective and which are determined and vary daily in the corresponding markets) under the pretext of attaining a (poorly understood) 'accounting transparency'. Instead, the purpose of accounting is to permit the prudent management of each company and to prevent capital consumption (Hayek, 1935). This requires the application of strict standards of accounting conservatism (based on the prudence principle and the recording of either the historical cost or the market value, whichever is less), standards that ensure at all times that distributable profits come from a safe surplus that can be distributed without, in any way, endangering the future viability and capitalization of each company.

Third, we must bear in mind that in the market there are no equilibrium prices a third party can objectively determine. Quite the opposite is true; market values arise from subjective assessments and fluctuate sharply, and hence their use in accounting eliminates much of the clarity, certainty and information that balance sheets contained in the past. Today, balance sheets have become largely unintelligible and useless to economic agents. Furthermore, the volatility inherent in market values, particularly over the economic cycle, robs accounting based on the 'new principles' of much of its potential as a guide for action for company managers and leads them to systematically commit major errors in management, errors that have been on the verge of provoking the severest financial crisis to ravage the world since 1929.

To create a truly free and stable financial and monetary system in this new 21st century, it will be necessary to take three steps: (1) the re-establishment of a 100-per cent reserve requirement on all bank demand deposits and equivalents; (2) the elimination of central banks as lenders in the last resort (which would be unnecessary if the preceding principle were applied, and harmful if they continued to act as financial central-planning agencies); and (3) the privatization of the current, monopolistic and fiduciary state-issued money and its replacement with a classic gold standard. This radical, definitive reform would essentially mark the culmination of the 1989 fall of the Berlin Wall and real socialism, since the reform would mean the application of the same principles of liberalization and private property to the only sphere, that of finance and banking, which has until now remained bogged down in central planning (by 'central' banks), extreme interventionism (for instance, the fixing of interest rates, the tangled web of government regulations) and state monopoly (through legal tender laws that require the acceptance of the current, state-issued fiduciary money) (Huerta de Soto, 2009a, chap. 9).

All these considerations are crucially important in light of the critical state of the international financial system. Nevertheless, while it is tragic that we have arrived at the current situation, what is even more tragic, if that were possible, is the widespread lack of understanding regarding the causes of the phenomena that plague us, and especially the atmosphere of confusion and uncertainty prevalent among experts, analysts and most economic theorists. In this area at least, we can hope that the revival of the Austrian School approach to economic theory and business cycles may contribute to the theoretical training of readers, to the intellectual rearmament of new generations, and eventually, to the much needed institutional overhaul of the entire monetary and financial system of current market economies.

REFERENCES

Bismans, F. and C. Mougeot (2009), 'Austrian Business Cycle Theory: empirical evidence', *The Review of Austrian Economics*, **22** (2), 241–257.

Garrison, R.W. (2001), *Time and Money: The Macroeconomics of Capital Structure*, London and New York: Routledge.

Hayek, F.A. (1935), 'The maintenance of capital', *Economica*, **2** (7), 241–276;

reprinted in (1979), *Profits, Interest and Investment and Other Essays on the Theory of Industrial Fluctuations*, New Jersey: Augustus M. Kelley.

Hayek, F.A. (1988), *The Fatal Conceit: The Errors of Socialism*, Chicago: The University of Chicago Press.

Hayek, F.A. (1997), *Socialism and War: Essays, Documents and Reviews*, as reprinted in B. Caldwell, *Collected Works of F.A. Hayek*, vol. X, Chicago: The University of Chicago Press.

Huerta de Soto, J. (2009a), *Money, Bank Credit, and Economic Cycles*, Auburn, Alabama: Ludwig von Mises Institute.

Huerta de Soto, J. (2009b), 'The fatal error of Solvency II', *Economic Affairs*, **29** (2), 74–77.

Huerta de Soto, J. (2010), *Socialism, Economic Calculation and Entrepreneurship*, Cheltenham, UK and Northampton, MA, USA: Edward Elgar.

Mises, L. von (1981), *Socialism: An Economic and Sociological Analysis*, Indianapolis: Liberty Fund.

Rothbard, M.N. (2000), *America's Great Depression*, Auburn, Alabama: Ludwig von Mises Institute.

3. Understanding crisis: on the meaning of uncertainty and probability

Ekaterina Svetlova and Matthias Fiedler

3.1 INTRODUCTION

The financial crisis of 2007–09 caused significant discontent about the current state of economic theory. In the manifesto 'The financial crisis and the systemic failure of academic economics', Colander et al. (2009, p.2) wrote of 'a systemic failure of the economic profession'. They argued that:

> [T]he current academic agenda has largely crowded out research on the inherent causes of financial crises. There has also been little exploration of early indicators of system crisis and potential ways to prevent this malady from developing. In fact, if one browses through the academic macroeconomics and finance literature, 'systemic crisis' appears like an otherworldly event that is absent from economic models. Most models, by design, offer no immediate handle on how to think about or deal with this recurring phenomenon. (Ibid., p.2)

In this paper, we draw on the ideas of a neglected line of economic research to discuss the causes and consequences of the recent crisis. Against the background of the failure of traditional economic tools to analyse the financial turmoil of the last years, we explore the concepts of Frank Knight, John Maynard Keynes and George L.S. Shackle to search for an alternative explanation.

These three economists belonged to one thematic school of economic thought. This school differs from the economic mainstream by its focus on knowledge about the future related to the understanding of risk and uncertainty. Those issues were considered to have been resolved by economists of both earlier and later schools. For example, Friedman (1976, p.282) considered Knight's suggestion of distinguishing between risk and uncertainty as useless because, in his view, subjective probabilities can always be assigned; hence an economist can treat every situation with uncertain outcomes as a situation of risk. While the neoclassical tradition was focused on risk measurement based on probability calculus, Knight, Keynes and Shackle argued that uncertainty, rather than mathematical probability, governs the economic world. They did not consider knowledge and expectation formation as unproblematic, but rather as issues at the very heart of economic theory. Due to this common ground, we consider this non-mainstream line of economic thought as a separate thematic school that deserves greater attention.

The rest of our paper is structured as follows. In the second section, we will discuss the views of Knight, Keynes and Shackle on probabilities and uncertainty in detail. The concepts outlined will then be applied analytically to the recent crisis in the third section. Consequently, the third section contains a discussion of the challenges that economic theory should master. In the fourth section, our conclusions can be found.

3.2 KNOWLEDGE AND UNCERTAINTY AS UNDERSTOOD BY KNIGHT, KEYNES AND SHACKLE

This section outlines the main arguments of Knight, Keynes and Shackle. We are aware that these three economists did not form a historical school of economic thought: Knight was a part of the Chicago School, Keynes established his own influential line of thought and Shackle's approach has never been classified. But we believe that these three scholars formed one thematic line of thought of which they were not the only representatives. There were also other thinkers in the first half and middle of the 20th century who seriously analysed knowledge and uncertainty, for example, Friedrich von Hayek and Joseph Schumpeter. However, we will concentrate on the relevant ideas of Knight, Keynes and Shackle and will emphasize the many commonalities in their arguments. We will present their thinking as a single line of thought that is pertinent to an analysis of today's financial crisis.

3.2.1 Incompleteness of our Knowledge about the Future

The only thing of which we can have certain knowledge is the past. Thus, the only way to anticipate the future is to evaluate and to interpret our knowledge of the past. The easiest way to do this is to assume the uniformity of the past and the future. Though this assumption is often made, it poses a philosophical problem: when it comes to inferring from past particulars to future generalizations there is an absence of deductive certainty. This is the famous problem of induction formulated by Hume

(1938). What we know at present is linked to the future through 'constant conjunction' (ibid., p. 11), which refers to similar causes creating similar effects. Hume argues that this sense of causation rests upon experience and that it would be circular reasoning to argue that the future will be like the past because the past futures have been like past pasts (ibid., p. 14).

In Hume's view, inductive methods are not necessarily false, but he showed that their validity cannot be proved (Keynes, 1921, p. 272). In Hume's own words: 'suppose the future conformable to the past . . . however easy this step may seem, reason would never, to all eternity, be able to make it' (cited in Meeks, 1991, p. 138). The fact that we regard the past to be like the future is our unjustified habit or custom (Hume, 1938, p. 16). Such a custom is reflected by the common assumption that regards current market prices as a correct guide to future prospects, for example.

The absence of deductive certainty about the future was the point of departure for the thinking of Knight, Keynes and Shackle. There is evidence that Hume's work significantly influenced Keynes (Meeks, 1991, p. 137f). In *Risk, Uncertainty and Profit*, Knight (1921), though he doesn't cite Hume, criticizes 'the assumption of practical omniscience on the part of every member of the competitive system'. He further emphasizes that many 'economic phenomena . . . are connected with the imperfection of knowledge' (ibid., p. 197), primarily with the imperfection of knowledge about the future.

It was crucial for those economists to understand the imperfect nature of knowledge. For them, as for Hume, this was not identical to the problem of imperfect or asymmetrical information. Hume's scepticism was not affected by the amount of information available. Hume, as one of the first modern philosophers, was sceptical about inductive reasoning itself, independent of the level of information (Hacking, 2001, p. 248). Knight, Keynes and Shackle were fascinated with the problem of uncertainty because they believed that there is something like 'inherent unknowability in the factors, not merely the fact of ignorance' (Knight, 1921, p. 219). Ignorance is based on incomplete information and can, theoretically, be abolished. It is the foundation of epistemological uncertainty. But Knight, Keynes and Shackle considered the possibility of ontological indeterminacy as a legitimate fact of economic life (for example, Knight, 1921, p. 197ff, esp. 219ff; Skidelsky, 2009, p. 88). A detailed discussion of these issues follows in the next sections.

3.2.2   Probability Concepts as Measures of Ignorance

If valid inductive inference is impossible, how can this problem be avoided? There are several approaches to the question of knowledge under conditions of uncertainty. The description of non-valid arguments or uncertain consequences in terms of probability is a possible approach, and it falls roughly into three categories: theoretical probability, experimental probability and probability as a degree of belief. The first can be predicted using counting principles (by rolling dice for example), the second describes the frequency of an outcome given a repeated trial and the last expresses a judgment of the likelihood of an event. The degree of belief type probabilities can be distinguished further. There is a subjective and a logical probability. Subjective probability, also called personal probability, refers to a statement such as 'I am very confident that inflation pressure is going to increase'. It is subjective, but obeys the basic rules of probability such as normality, certainty and additivity. Normality holds that every probability is a fraction between zero and one. Certainty states that a certain hypothesis has a probability of one, and additivity requires that the probabilities of mutually exclusive hypotheses add up to unity (for example, Ramsey, 1926; de Finetti, 1980). In contrast to subjective probability, logical probability is always related to evidence. An advocate of logical probability would make the following argument: 'Given the evidence, it is reasonable to have a high degree of belief in mounting inflation'.

Probability concepts of different types were developed to avoid the induction problem, that is, the impossibility of inferring from the known (the past) to unknown (the future). They imply that probability is capable of reducing uncertainty about the future to a number or a fraction, that is, that uncertainty can be expressed and analysed in terms of probability.

This notion was contested by Knight, Keynes and Shackle. Knight and Keynes concentrated on criticizing the first two types of probabilities; Shackle doubted that probabilities in general can be useful to an analysis of economic reality. These three thinkers argued that probabilities do not always help to bridge the knowledge gap between the past and the future and searched for alternatives. Though they followed quite different lines of argument, some commonalities between them can be highlighted. This will be done in the following sub-sections.

3.2.3   Critiques of Probabilities and Alternative Concepts

Though the discussion about uncertainty is often reduced to the problem of the measurability of probabilities, the common starting point for Knight, Keynes and Shackle was to ask if probability calculus as such is sufficient to account for individual actions under uncertainty.

3.2.3.1   Knight: a distinction between risk and uncertainty
Knight's critique refers to the first two types of probabilities (theoretical and experimental), which he calls a priori and statistical probabilities

(Knight, 1921, p. 216). He considers the determination of probabilities to be based on a classification of the possible outcomes. For him, a priori and statistical probabilities differ from each other in the accuracy of such classifications. However, Knight suggests that those two categories do not exhaust all the possibilities for defining a probability situation. Knight (1921, p. 223) adds 'estimates': 'The distinction here is that there is no valid basis of any kind for classifying instances. This form of probability is involved in the greatest logical difficulties of all' (ibid., p. 225). Knight refers to this last situation as a situation of uncertainty, while he defines the first two situations as 'risk' (ibid., p. 233).

Knight argues that the classification of outcomes is sometimes impossible because circumstances are unique:

> The practical difference between the two categories, risk and uncertainty, is that in the former, the distribution of the outcome in a group of instances is known (either through calculation *a priori* or from statistics of past experience), while in the case of uncertainty this is not true, the reason being in general that it is impossible to form a group of instances, because the situation dealt with is in a high degree unique. (Ibid.)

Here, Knight's argument coincides with Shackle's line of reasoning, which will be discussed later.

Furthermore, Knight argues that the uncertainty situation is typical in business. He describes a manufacturer who considers increasing the capacity of his enterprise: 'He "figures" more or less on the proposition, taking account as well as possible of the various factors more or less susceptible of measurement, but the final result is an "estimate" of the probable outcome of any proposed course of action' (ibid., p. 226). Due to insufficient knowledge, the manufacturer cannot classify possible events, but he can make 'a judgment of probability' (ibid.), or 'an estimate of an estimate' (ibid., p. 227):

> The business man himself not merely forms the best estimate he can of the outcome of his action, but he is likely also to estimate the probability that his estimate is correct. The 'degree' of certainty or of confidence felt in the conclusion after it is reached cannot be ignored, for it is of the greatest practical significance. (Ibid., p. 226f)

Here we can see some intersections with Keynes's idea of 'the state of confidence', discussed later.

Knight's 'estimate of an estimate' is associated with subjective probability (ibid., p. 233). Subjective probabilities can always be formed under conditions of uncertainty; however, objective probabilities (mathematical and statistical) cannot be calculated under such conditions. Here lies the crucial distinction between risk and uncertainty: risk is the situation where probabilities are measurable; under uncertainty they are not, though they take the form of 'a ratio, expressed by a proper fraction' (ibid., p. 231). Thus:

> a measurable uncertainty, or 'risk' proper . . ., is so far different from an immeasurable one that it is not in effect an uncertainty at all. We shall accordingly restrict the term 'uncertainty' to cases of non-quantitative type. It is . . . 'true' uncertainty, and not risk. (Ibid., p. 20)

To sum up, Knight pleads for a sharp distinction between risk and uncertainty. He argues that people in business situations that are unique face 'true' uncertainty. Thus, they lack any valid basis to calculate probabilities and have to rely on subjective judgment, or 'an estimate of an estimate'.

3.2.3.2   Keynes: an immeasurable relationship

Now we will discuss how Keynes's notion of probability allows for a definition of uncertainty. Following Lawson (1985), Keynes's uncertainty is defined as the absence of a probability relation. This assertion will be discussed in more detail.

Keynes begins his analysis in his book *Treatise on Probability* (1921) with considerations about the nature of knowledge. He distinguishes between direct and indirect knowledge. These are obtained directly or by argument, respectively. Keynes associates the latter with the realm of probability and regards probability as a non-subjective logical relationship between a premise and a conclusion. The premise consists of a proposition h and the conclusion of a proposition a. If knowledge of h allows a rational belief in a, there is a probability relation of degree α (ibid., p. 4). Keynes defines the cases where such a probability relation exists as 'secondary propositions' (ibid., p. 10).

Besides the logical relation, another concept supplements the probability description. It is called the 'weight of the argument'. It refers to the size of the evidence supporting the probability relation and it increases with evidence available, but could decrease the probability of an argument (ibid., p. 71). Probability refers to a relation between a and h, whereas weight is concerned with the 'magnitude' of the evidence of h. Weight is positively correlated with evidence, that is, low weight implies less relevant information and an increase in h entails an increase in weight, but not necessarily probability. O'Donnell (1990, p. 256) understands weight as an indicator of 'confidence'. An increase in evidence of h implies a broader base for the argument.

To sum up, both measures are used to make an inference. Probability establishes the degree of rational belief in the conclusion and the weight expresses confidence about the probability. According to Lawson (1985) and Runde (1990), those two main dimensions of Keynes's probability concept define Keynes's notion of uncertainty. It is related to the absence of a secondary proposition. The absence of a secondary proposition does not allow for calculating a numerical value for the probability relation between premise and conclusion (Keynes, 1921, p. 34f; Lawson, 1985, p. 913). This notion is crucial to Keynes's thought. Lawson concludes that the absence of a secondary proposition, or the lack of a probability relationship, constitutes uncertainty. The evidence for the proposition is not measurable numerically and not comparable. In Keynes's words: 'It is not possible to say of every pair of conclusions, about which we have some knowledge, that the degree of our rational belief in one bears any numerical relation to our degree of rational belief in the other' (1921, p. 37). He goes on to argue that it is not 'always possible to say that the degree of our rational belief in one conclusion is either equal to, greater than, or less than the degree of our belief in another' (ibid.).

Lawson (1985, p. 914) summarizes: 'Thus uncertainty is not merely a situation in which the probability relation is known and the primary proposition, *a* say, relative to the evidence, gives rise to a numerical probability that is less than unity'. Rather, it refers to an immeasurable relationship between premise and conclusion in the absence of a secondary proposition.

In the absence of a secondary proposition, no comparison between magnitudes of probabilities of different contingent outcomes is possible, and uncertainty prevails. In this case, Keynes argues in unison with Knight that we lack a valid basis to form probabilities. Keynes suggests that such uncertainty exists, for example, in the case of predicting the price of copper or the interest rate 20 years hence: 'About these matters there is no scientific basis on which to form any calculable probability whatever. We simply do not know' (Keynes, 1937, p. 113). Lack of knowledge is related to the insufficient scientific basis, or as Keynes terms it, the insufficient rational basis. There are cases, he writes (1921, p. 30), 'in which no rational basis has been discovered for numerical comparison. It is not the case here that the method of calculation, prescribed by theory, is beyond our powers or too laborious for actual application. No method of calculation, however impracticable, has been suggested'. This situation implies more than epistemological uncertainty, which we can remove by becoming more skilful in calculation or by collecting more information. It refers to ontological uncertainty which we cannot cope with by means of probability.

Nevertheless, as Keynes suggested, 'the necessity to action and for decision compels us as practical men to do our best to overlook this awkward fact and to behave exactly as we should if we had behind us a good Benthamite calculation' (1937, p. 114), that is, to assign probabilities. Those probabilities lack any scientific basis, however, which is the same point that was raised by Knight. The assignment of probabilities and the building of expectations on this ground has become one of the many conventions that people use to cope with uncertainty in business situations: we are 'calculating where we can, but often falling back for our motive on whim or sentiment or chance' (Keynes, 1936, p. 163), or 'animal spirits' (ibid., p. 162), that is, the non-calculative motivation to act. Those conventions are the basis of the expectations that guide action.

Keynes's discussion of long-term investment expectations in Chapter 12 of *The General Theory of Employment, Interest, and Money* (1936) seems to be especially relevant to understanding the recent crisis. Keynes describes two components of expectations, namely the most probable forecast and the state of confidence. Referring to Keynes's concepts of probability and weight of the argument, Gerrard (1994, p. 331ff) explains: 'The most probable forecast is the agent's best estimate of the likely future outcome. The state of confidence reflects the likelihood of the most probable forecast turning out to be wrong'. This similarity to Knight's 'estimate' and 'estimate of the estimate' is striking.

Long-term expectations are formed in a situation of uncertainty. The knowledge base is insufficient to be certain of the future. As mentioned above, according to Keynes, the most probable forecast is based on a convention:

> The essence of this convention . . . lies in assuming that the existing state of affairs will continue indefinitely, except in so far as we have specific reasons to expect a change. This does not mean that we really believe that the existing state of affairs will continue indefinitely. . ... Nevertheless the above conventional method of calculation will be compatible with a considerable measure of continuity and stability in our affairs, *so long as we can rely on the maintenance of the convention*. (Keynes, 1936, p. 152, original emphasis)

This statement is related to Hume's concept of 'custom', which he showed to be groundless. People make estimations about the future, but as they know that those estimations are imprecise, they make subjective judgments of these estimations. The formation of this judgment is crucial for understanding behaviour under uncertainty; however, this topic is notoriously under-researched in economics. One of the reasons is that:

> [b]y its very nature the state of confidence is not amenable to formal technical analysis. But, given its crucial importance in determining actual behavior,

Keynes argues that the state of confidence needs to be the subject of careful analysis by economists. Any model of investment which excludes the state of confidence is likely to be seriously misspecified. (Gerrard, 1994, p. 332)

To sum up, Keynes contested the idea of a calculable future and developed the concept of probability as a logical relation. He showed that this relation is undetermined in situations of uncertainty, so that probabilities are not calculable or comparable. In this situation, people form expectations based on probabilities without any scientific basic. They fall back on conventions, or 'animal spirits'. As in Knight's understanding, the estimate of the most probable forecast ('the state of the confidence') plays a crucial role.

Keynes's work was a significant departure from previous traditional approaches to probability and expectations. G.L.S. Shackle shared most of Keynes's objections to probability, though he doubted that Keynes's concept of probability was the solution. Shackle's two main arguments are outlined in the next sub-section.

3.2.3.3   Shackle: a non-probabilistic alternative

In his early writings, Shackle (for example, 1949) objected primarily to frequency probability. Frequency probability refers to the relative outcome of an event in a large number of trials under equal conditions. Shackle's first line of argument stems from the distinction between different courses of action, rendering frequency probability meaningless. Shackle's second line of argument extends from the critique of frequency probability and questions the usefulness of all probability concepts, including subjective probability.

Shackle begins by classifying decision situations, or experiments. The throw of a die can be repeated indefinitely and its results can be added up. The latter constitutes a divisible experiment because it consists of a series of trials (Shackle, 1955, p. 23). The underlying reasoning is similar to Knight's grouping of cases with respect to rolling a die, or a priori probability (Knight, 1921, p. 224). According to Shackle, most economic decisions cannot be repeated indefinitely and do not rest upon various single trials that can be grouped together. A non-divisible experiment consists of just one trial. However, certain individual non-divisible experiments can be turned into divisible experiments in the aggregate. Such experiments are called 'seriable' (Shackle, 1955, p. 24). Fire insurance is an example of a seriable experiment. Although there is no probability that an individual house will burn down, if there are enough pooled results, a (statistical) probability will emerge.

Furthermore, Shackle (1949, p. 6) argues that most economic decisions are unique (this is in line with Knight's argument). A unique experiment is non-divisible and non-seriable. For example, an investment decision is made just once or a career is chosen only once in a lifetime. Shackle goes on to argue that frequency ratios are irrelevant in such cases and that frequency probability is only admissible if it provides some certain knowledge of the relevant outcome. In Shackle's words (1955, p. 28f):

> Suppose, for example, that a probability of 1/6 is assigned ex ante to some hypothesis concerning the outcome of a non-divisible non-seriable experiment. Then if the hypothesis proves false, the decision-maker was plainly wrong not to assign it a probability of zero instead of 1/6 while if it proves true, he was plainly wrong not to assign it a probability of unity.

In other words, frequency ratios are irrelevant in unique cases. In such cases, it is impossible to set up a Bernoulli trial in order to attain long-term objective stability. There are also cases when frequency ratios are not just irrelevant, but also cannot be determined; these are called crucial experiments. The crucial experiment inevitably alters the conditions under which it was performed. A chess move reflects such a crucial experiment because it will subsequently be impossible to perform a similar experiment again (ibid., p. 25). Economic decisions are crucial because they destroy the very conditions under which they were performed. This makes a repeated trial impossible. Frequency probability cannot account for crucial experiments because they preclude a repeated trial, which is necessary to establish objective stability. However, crucial experiments do not exclude subjective interpretations of probability, as they do not rely on repeated trials. Now, we will outline Shackle's second objection to the use of numerical probability.

This objection refers to the absence of an exhaustive list of possible consequences. Traditional probability calculus assumes that the list of consequences over which it is distributed is an exhaustive list of hypotheses. However, if there is a residual hypothesis, that is, the list of possible consequences is incomplete, the numerical probability model runs into trouble. By adding a hypothesis to the list of possible hypotheses, each corresponding probability of the previously known hypotheses has to be revised downwards (ibid., p. 27). If five possible hypotheses are considered and a sixth hypothesis is added and additivity and normality are assumed, the probability of each of the initial five hypotheses is subsequently lower. This objection applies to both approaches, namely frequency probability and belief-type probability, because neither can incorporate a residual hypothesis.

How, then, can an economic agent make an inconclusive argument conclusive if the probabilities approach is not applicable? Shackle, like Keynes, asserted that an individual is guided by expectations. Although the concept of expectations formulated by Keynes (1921, 1936) and Shackle's idea of expectations are not the same, both concepts arguably have a common starting point, that is, the aforementioned insufficiency of probability calculus to account for uncertainty. Shackle (1979) differs substantially from Keynes as he emphasizes the rational degree of belief less than imagination or 'originative audacity' (p. 75), whereas in the absence of knowledge Keynes refers to conventional expectations rather than a creative act.

Shackle's (1949, p. 1) definition of expectations makes this difference obvious:

> By expectation I mean the act of creating imaginary situations, of associating them with named future dates and of assigning to each of the hypotheses thus formed a place on a scale measuring the degree of our belief that a specified course of action on our own part will make this hypothesis come true. Such a hypothesis I call an expectation.

The crucial prerequisite to understanding Shackle's non-probabilistic approach is to distinguish between the certainty of a hypothesis being true and the absence of disbelief of that hypothesis (Shackle, 1955, p. 30). The latter refers to a state of mind that makes an individual decision-maker unsurprised to see a particular hypothesis come true.

Shackle (ibid., p. 31) introduces the concept of disbelief to meet some of the shortfalls implied by numerical probability because expressing perfect confidence in one mutually exclusive hypothesis would imply a belief in the falsity of all its rivals.

The absence of disbelief is not certainty. If an individual learns that a hypothesis is true that she had assigned an absence of disbelief to, the individual will not be surprised or experience any kind of shock. Shackle (ibid.) refers to disbelief as 'potential surprise'. The absence of disbelief can accordingly be regarded as zero potential surprise.

Potential surprise resolves the previously outlined dilemma by expressing a perfect possibility without implying perfect certainty by assigning zero potential surprise to a hypothesis. Furthermore, the potential surprise assigned is independent of the number of other hypotheses considered and the list of non-excludable hypotheses can be extended without affecting the second independent variable of a rival hypothesis. In addition, potential surprise is a measure that does not contain a faulty judgment, unlike the frequency ratio, which is proven wrong unless it is zero or one. If a hypothesis that had a potential surprise larger than zero is proved to be true, the degree of misjudgment is reflected by the degree of potential surprise. Finally, potential surprise allows for considering a hypothesis and its contradiction to be equally plausible.

Shackle argues that uncertainty is necessarily linked with surprise. It is reflected by 'potential surprise', which, unlike probability, does not focus on the truth of a hypothesis, but rather whether it would surprise the decision-maker. Therefore, a true hypothesis does not imply zero potential surprise. An exhaustive list of rival hypotheses is the precondition for additivity. Such an exhaustive list does preclude any surprise.

The existence of a residual hypothesis among its set of rival hypotheses allows an individual to expect to be surprised. Anything not capable of surprising him would have occurred to him (Shackle, 1955, p. 60).

To sum up, Shackle proposed an independent measure for uncertainty that does not rely on numerical probability. Furthermore, he took into account that the list of possible hypotheses is not exhaustive, that is, that a decision-maker never knows all the possible outcomes. By introducing a non-additive measure such as potential surprise, he allowed for the addition of hypotheses without affecting each single hypothesis. In addition, potential surprise allows for the existence of a residual hypothesis. Shackle was very much aware that this proposal is far from orthodox decision theory. He states that 'those accustomed to think in terms of the actuarial calculation of the result will find this hard to appreciate' (ibid., p. 42f). However, the proposal does address some of the aforementioned objections.

3.3   UNDERSTANDING FINANCIAL CRISIS

Now let us consider what implications the uncertainty concepts of Knight, Keynes and Shackle have for understanding the recent financial and economic turmoil.

Risk seems to be the key concept in mainstream economic theory's understanding of the recent crisis. The German Ifo Institute states in its *Report on the European Economy* in 2009 that excessive risk-taking by financial institutions was one of the main features of the crash (EEAG, 2009, p. 59). In the words of Alan Greenspan, 'the underpricing of risk worldwide' played a major role in the origins of the crisis (as cited in Skidelsky, 2009, p. 3).

In this context, uncontrollable risk-taking refers to new financial instruments like ABS (asset-backed securities), CDO (collateral debt obligations) and CDS (credit default swaps). Those products were the result of the mortgage securitization, which developed rapidly as US house prices rose 124 per cent between 1997 and 2006 (ibid., p. 5). Mortgage volume, including subprime mortgages, increased significantly in this time period. As those loans became securitized, uncontrollable risk-taking commenced.

The underlying securitization scheme works as follows:

> By issuing a mortgage loan to a household or a firm, a bank or financial inter-
> mediary is the originator of an asset that generates a cash flow paid regularly
> over time (the monthly installments). Securitization occurs when the origina-
> tor sells this cash flow to a special purpose vehicle SPV . . ., administered by
> a financial institution called the administrator or the sponsor of the program.
> Because mortgage holders may default on their loans, however, the (nominal)
> face value of the cash flow is not sure. To deal with default risk, the SPV . . .
> purchases a well-diversified portfolio of mortgages, pooling together the cash
> flows from many borrowers. . . .. The trick consists of slicing the cash flow from
> a well-diversified pool of mortgages into tranches of increasing risk/return
> profiles. (EEAG, 2009, p. 63f)

There are low-risk (senior) tranches, medium- and high-risk tranches.
Those risk levels are related to the possibility of future default. Though the
future is uncertain, financial institutions, as well as rating agencies, treated
this issue as 'risk' in the sense used by Knight and Keynes. Existing risk
models are based on the assumption that risk can be calculated as future
events and that their effects are known and can be assigned probabilities.
However, in the recent crisis, such models notoriously underestimated
risk. How could this have happened?

Generally, to assess risks related to new products, banks and rating
agencies had to assess the corresponding default risks. The Moody's/
KMV credit risk company defines this kind of risk as follows:

> Default risk is the uncertainty surrounding a firm's ability to service its debts
> and obligations. Prior to default, there is no way to discriminate unambigu-
> ously between firms that will default and those that won't. At best we can only
> make probabilistic assessments of the likelihood of default. (Crosbie and Bohn,
> 2003, p. 5)

In this definition, the confusion of risk with uncertainty is quite clear;
like most market participants, rating agencies were not concerned with
the crucial distinction made by Knight and Keynes. The terms 'risk' and
'uncertainty' are used interchangeably. However, the confession that 'there
is no way to discriminate unambiguously between firms that will default
and that won't' does call to mind the Keynesian statement that 'we simply
do not know'. Unlike Keynes, however, who suggested that probabilities
cannot be calculated under such conditions, the credit risk company states
that probability assignment is the only way to deal with the situation.
Hence, we should ask if the situation faced by economic participants in
2007–09 was a situation of risk or uncertainty and if probability calculus
was applicable. Perhaps this distinction will allow for a more profound
understanding of the causes of the crisis.

Because financial institutions and economic agencies used models of risk that are based on the calculation of default probability, they saw themselves operating under conditions of risk as Knight and Keynes understood the term. For example, Moody's approach to rating CDOs was based on the evaluation of expected loss. In the first stage, the probability distribution for each level of loss of the underlying assets was determined; then the correlation between tranches was taken into account; and eventually the total expected loss of the CDO note was calculated using a complicated correlated binomial method (Witt and Xie, 2005). Standard and Poor's and Fitch Ratings based their assessments of credit risk entirely on default probabilities.

All of these default calculations were grounded in an assessment of the future development of the security issuer based on historical data, that is, statistics about the company and industry. This means that risk models relied on statistical probabilities.

The other model used to assess the risk of loss, Value at Risk, should also be mentioned. Value at Risk is:

> defined as the worst loss possible under *normal market conditions* for a given time horizon. For example, an investment position that loses a maximum of $100 million for the next year, no more than 1 percent of the time, will be viewed by some managers as having a value at risk of $100 million for the next year. (Hillier et al., 2008, p. 794, original emphasis)

Thus, Value at Risk is also based on a known probability distribution, given normal market conditions. The probability distribution is usually assumed to be normal, or to follow the Gaussian bell curve.

Why did rating agencies' models and Value at Risk models underestimate risk during the crisis? First, many of their calculations were simply wrong. Many reasons for this have been discussed in the academia and in the press. Adverse incentives were created as agencies were paid by product issuers. This induced agencies to produce the ratings required by clients, that is, to assign high ratings to papers that were in fact high risk. Agencies were able to easily manipulate ratings because their models were non-linear and very sensitive to input. They often used unreliable, that is, unaudited, information to estimate risks. But do the problems not lie deeper?

We believe that it is wrong to define the situation of the credit crisis as a situation of risk. Economic participants faced a situation of uncertainty that could not be reduced to risk. Thus, it was misleading to assume that the future is calculable and to analyse the situation in terms of probabilities.

The economic conditions that have prevailed since 2007 have been entirely unique, though they resembled other crashes. This is exactly Shackle's point, the argument that business situations are crucial, non-seriable and non-divisible experiments. Ongoing risk assessments changed the very conditions under which they were initially performed. The under-estimation of risk led to increased demand for risky assets; subsequently, more risky assets were issued and bought. The volume of structured finan-cial instruments that were traded around the globe increased dramatically, creating a unique situation.

According to the theories of Knight, Keynes and Shackle, in such a situation, frequency probabilities cannot be used, but this is exactly what banks and rating agencies did. Their risk models were based on historical data that did not apply to the new unique situation. The actual problem was that the financial instruments that were assessed by the risk models didn't have a price history (Croft, 2009, p. 21). There was no scientific basis on which to estimate and to model their parameters. For example, one such uncertain parameter was the correlation between assets included in CDOs. Calculations of those correlations rested upon the assump-tion that such correlations are stable and, thus, 'made no allowance for unpredictability' (Salmon, 2009).

The other example refers to the Value at Risk formula. As structured products had a short and unique history, their liquidity became an uncertain parameter. According to Jane Croft (2009, p. 21):

> VAR [Value at Risk] was not designed for illiquid products as it assumed the sale of products within 24 hours and the 10-day holding period is a neces-sary extra buffer. . .. Putting really illiquid products into VAR, where you are looking at short-term moves in prices, is not appropriate because you will be locked in for a longer period and potentially suffer larger price moves. VAR will understate risk.

In other words, the underpricing of risk occurred because there was no way to estimate liquidity except to assume it to be high and stable, as it was in the past.

In general, a lack of knowledge prevailed in the system, implying that economic agents acted under conditions of uncertainty. Oliver Blanchard, the chief economist at the International Monetary Fund, described the situation in his Munich lecture. He stated that banks did not just hold mortgages on their books, but:

> these mortgages were basically securitized and re-securitized and re-securitized which made some sense from the point of view of risk allocation. It allowed to provide securities that are more tailored to the people who wanted a lot of risk or little risk but that made the assets extremely opaque in the sense of

understanding the value of the assets became nearly impossible because the asset was claim on a claim on a claim and basically nobody, even in the business, really understood what these assets were worth with the implication that as soon as there were uncertainties about the ultimate value of the assets at the beginning (subprime mortgage or prime mortgage), then basically there was enormous uncertainty as to exposure you had by holding these derived assets, securitized assets. (Blanchard, 2008)

According to Knight, Keynes and Shackle, it was inappropriate to use probabilities to assess such a situation because there is no valid scientific basis to do so. In addition, no exhaustive list of possible future events was available. Economic agents simply didn't know what they and their counterparts had on their books. They faced uncertainty but continued to treat the situation as one of risk. Their decisions were based on the assumption of a high degree of predictability. Exactly as Keynes described, economic agents behaved as if they were able to make 'a good Benthamite calculation' based on the assignment of probabilities, but few realized at the time that this calculation was empty. Importantly, as Shackle demonstrated, this argument applies to probabilities of any kind when facing a crucial experiment. Thus, the point of Friedman and Savage that the assignment of subjective probabilities would be a solution is not valid. We think that an understanding of this fact could add a lot to our understanding of the crisis.

Knight, Keynes and Shackle further argued that if measurable probabilities cannot be assigned, market participants use judgments or build expectations to bridge the gap of uncertainty between the past and future. Now, let us analyse how the ideas of Knight, Keynes and Shackle could help us to understand expectations and their contribution to the recent financial turmoil in more detail.

We will continue to tell the story of the crisis from the point where we left off: economic agents faced enormous uncertainty concerning the value of assets on their books and the books of their counterparts. This uncertainty prevailed in the summer and autumn of 2007, when first banks like Northern Rock and IKB suffered from the liquidity squeeze and from deteriorating asset quality. This happened because financial institutions started to doubt whether the securities on their books were as risk-free as their ratings suggested.

In terms of Keynes's theory, investors' most likely forecast that high ratings corresponded to high security quality was based on the convention of believing in the judgments of rating agencies. In general, it can be easily demonstrated that during the crisis investors relied heavily on the assumption of the uniformity of the past and the future, which, according to Hume, cannot be proved valid. However, people fell back on this 'custom' and built their estimations upon it. Blanchard described the real events as follows:

> And the question is why is it that we were basically fooled as a system, as a collection of individuals and institutions, into producing of these assets and thinking that they were riskless. And I think here is basically the inability, with support in human nature really, the inability to think about risk when you haven't seen it for a while. In the US, housing prices have gone up every year since World War II; even in the recession of 2001 we hadn't seen them come down. So when you were told 'Look, basically you can buy risk because housing prices were not to go down', you looked at history, you looked at the last recession and you could convince yourself fairly easily that this would continue. (Blanchard, 2008)

However, as Keynes argued, this could not continue forever, but only until investors saw 'specific reasons to expect a change' (Keynes, 1936, p. 152). As the discrepancy between the past and the future became clear, market participants changed their 'state of confidence' or the Knightian 'estimate of an estimate'. They knew that the quality of structural products backed by mortgages was generally estimated to be high, but their estimate of this estimate reflected the expectation that the quality of such products might not, in fact, be sound. This change led to a situation whereby financial institutions stopped extending credit to each other and liquidity dried up. The 'confidence' factor became crucial.

Similarly, when, at the beginning of 2008, the discussion evolved round whether a 'hard' or 'soft' landing was the most likely scenario, the factor of 'confidence' also played a significant role for further developments. Markets believed in the likelihood of a soft landing because they were confident that the problems that had already occurred in the money markets were manageable. There was a conviction that 'central banks would make up for the lack of liquidity in the interbank markets' and that they 'would intervene on a case-by-case basis to support banks under threat of failure' (EEAG, 2009, p. 82). However, 'the state of confidence' changed dramatically during the summer of 2008, when markets were surprised by the Lehman Brothers bankruptcy. Expectations based on the convention that the US Central Bank had always functioned as a lender of last resort in the past, and therefore would continue to do so, no longer held. Capturing this change properly would have been a far more accurate predictor of the hard landing than risk probability models.

Shackle's related concepts of disbelief and non-numerical expectations could help to provide a more detailed understanding of the situation in 2008. As we see ex post facto, there were not just two hypotheses (that is, 'soft' and 'hard' landing). There was also a residual hypothesis of 'very hard landing'. The list of possible scenarios was not complete (which is an additional argument for why probability calculus could not work under such circumstances). However, market participants discussed only two scenarios, both of which appeared to be possible. They discussed arguments for and against soft landing that expressed their degree of disbelief. They assigned zero potential surprise to both scenarios. At the beginning of the crisis, a hard landing was a counter-expected event with a high degree of disbelief. The occurrence 'very hard landing' was an entirely unexpected event. It was not imagined at all by the majority. This is the answer to Queen Elizabeth's question at the London School of Economics briefing in 2008, 'Why did nobody see it coming?'

One might ask what we gain if we structure the decision situation this way. We think that it allows for a more precise description of the set of alternatives under conditions of uncertainty. In the absence of reliable knowledge people do not exclude any hypothesis completely, but consider all hypotheses as possible, assigning different degrees of disbelief to each of them. The use of imagination, a concept emphasized by Shackle, seems to have been low, with financial players limiting their hypotheses to those shaped by historical experience. For example, as people saw central banks helping financial institutions in trouble in 2007 and in the first half of 2008, they didn't imagine and didn't discuss the possibility that central banks might cease to function as lenders of last resort and would let a big bank go bankrupt. People do not imagine beforehand the unexpected events that surprise them, even though such unexpected events continue to occur.

This leads us to the last issue, namely expectation and surprise, which should be briefly discussed in light of Knight's, Keynes's and Shackle's ideas. We learn from them that expectations and surprises are inseparable. This fact has been widely neglected by standard economic theory. Surprises are not only events to which nobody can assign a probability, but they are events that no one can imagine. Surprises are unexpected events that play a crucial role in economic life because they destroy conventions and force people to change their expectations. Their role should be recognized and explored further. This is one of the important theoretical lessons we learn from the representatives of the line of economic thought that focuses on knowledge and uncertainty.

3.4   OUTLOOK

To conclude, we can draw some important lessons from the discussion above. Above all, we are concerned with lessons for economic theory, which was heavily criticized as the crisis evolved. Criticisms varied from the argument that standard theory was unable to analyse and predict the crisis to the allegation that theory itself caused the turmoil. To provide an example of the last accusation, we turn to Akerlof and Shiller's (2009, p. 1) statement:

> What had people been thinking? Why did they not notice until real events – the collapse of banks, the loss of jobs, mortgage foreclosures – were already upon us? There is a simple answer. The public, the government, and most economists had been reassured by an economic theory that said that we were safe. It was all OK. Nothing dangerous could happen. But that theory was deficient.

Against the backdrop of such criticisms, the ideas of Knight, Keynes and Shackle experience a true revival. In their book *Animal Spirits: How Human Psychology Drives the Economy, and Why It Matters for Global Capitalism*, the two star economists Akerlof and Shiller seized on Keynes's concept of confidence and non-rational motivation for action, suggesting that economics should open itself to psychology. They envision behavioural economics as the root of future developments in economic theory.

Though a detailed analysis of people's motives and beliefs is important, we would prefer not to relegate the ideas of Knight, Keynes and Shackle solely to the realm of psychology. The most important lesson from the above discussion should be that economics has to seriously confront the problem of imperfect knowledge (not imperfect information) and uncertainty. The financial crisis demonstrated clearly that standard economic theory could not meet high scientific standards in such a difficult situation because it neglected those important issues. Standard economic theory treats every economic situation as a situation of risk, and this has dire consequences, such as the facilitation of unjustifiable risk-taking and the failure to predict the crisis.

The line of economic thought represented by Knight, Keynes and Shackle draws attention to the genuine nature of every economic situation. Its major features – insufficient knowledge, true uncertainty, uniqueness and exposure to surprise – have to become the focus of mainstream economic theory. This line of thought provides us with new perspectives on the crucial topic of risk. Are the situations faced by markets daily truly 'risk'? If these situations are not risk, as Knight and Keynes suggest, then models that are based on numerical probabilities do not make sense. The obsession of modern science with risk measurement should be called into question and the role of financial models should be revised.

Undoubtedly, there is a tendency to pay more attention to these issues in light of the recent crisis. There is an evolving discussion about those issues; however, it obviously still takes place on the periphery, not in the heart of economic science. There is still no consistent research programme that addresses these issues. From this perspective, the history of economic thought could be an important source of ideas on how to address the crucial questions that have still not been resolved by economic science.

REFERENCES

Akerlof, G.A. and R.J. Shiller (2009), *Animal Spirits. How Human Psychology Drives the Economy, and Why It Matters for Global Capitalism*, Princeton, NJ: Princeton University Press.

Blanchard, O. (2008), 'The financial crisis: initial conditions, basic mechanisms, and appropriate policies', Munich Lecture, 18 November, available at: http://www.cesifo-group.de/portal/page/portal/ifoHome/a-winfo/d7teachmat/10videolect/_VIDEOLECT?item_link=lect-blanchard2008.htm; accessed 4 September 2010.

Colander, D., H. Föllmer, A. Haas, M.D. Goldberg, K. Juselius, A. Kiirman, T. Lux and B. Sloth (2009), 'The financial crisis and the systemic failure of academic economics', University of Copenhagen, Dept. of Economics, Discussion Paper No. 09-03, 9 March, available at: http://ssrn.com/abstract=1355882; accessed 3 September 2010.

Croft, J. (2009), 'Modeling adapts as catastrophic clouds clear', *Financial Times*, 21, 5 October.

Crosbie, P. and J. Bohn (2003), *Modeling Default Risk*, San Francisco: KMV.

EEAG – European Economic Advisory Group at CESifo (2009), *The EEAG Report on the European Economy 2009*, Munich, Germany: Ifo Institute for Economic Research, 25 February, available at: http://www.cesifo-group.de/portal/page/portal/ifoHome/B-politik/70eeagreport/20PUBLEEAG2009; accessed 4 September 2010.

Finetti, B. de (1980), 'Foresight: its logical laws, its subjective sources', in H.E. Kyburg (ed.), *Studies in Subjective Probability*, Huntington, NY: Krieger, pp. 97–158.

Friedman, M. (1976), *Price Theory: A Provisional Text*, Chicago: Aldine.

Gerrard, B. (1994), 'Beyond rational expectations: a constructive interpretation of Keynes's analysis of behaviour under uncertainty', *Economic Journal*, **104** (423), 327–337.

Hacking, I. (2001), *An Introduction to Probability and Inductive Logic*, Cambridge: Cambridge University Press.

Hillier, D., M. Grinblatt and S. Titman (2008), *Financial Markets and Corporate Strategy*, New York: McGraw-Hill.

Hume, D. (1938), *An Abstract of a Treatise of Human Nature*, edited by J.M. Keynes and P. Sraffa, Cambridge: Cambridge University Press.

Keynes, J.M. (1921), *A Treatise on Probability*, New York: MacMillan.

Keynes J.M. (1936), *The General Theory of Employment, Interest and Money*, as reprinted in (1973), *Collected Writings of John Maynard Keynes*, vol. VII, London: Macmillan.

Keynes, J.M. (1937), *General Theory and After. Part II Defence and Development*, as reprinted in (1973), *Collected Writings of John Maynard Keynes*, vol. XIV, London: Macmillan.

Knight, F.H. (1921), *Risk, Uncertainty and Profit*, Mineola, NY: Dover Publ.

Lawson, T. (1985), 'Uncertainty and economic analysis', *The Economic Journal*, **95** (380), 909–927.

Meeks, J.G.T. (1991), 'Keynes on the rationality of decision procedures under uncertainty: the investment decision', in J.G.T. Meeks (ed.), *Thoughtful Economic Man: Essays on Rationality, Moral Rules and Benevolence*, Cambridge: Cambridge University Press, pp. 126–160.

O'Donnell, R. (1990), 'An overview of probability, expectations, uncertainty and rationality in Keynes's conceptual framework', *Review of Political Economy*, **2** (3), 253–266.

Ramsey, F.P. (1926), 'Truth and probability', in R.B. Braithwaite (ed.), *The Foundations of Mathematics and Other Logical Essays*, London: Kegan, pp. 156–198.

Runde, J. (1990), 'Keynesian uncertainty and the weight of arguments', *Economics and Philosophy*, **6** (2), 275–292.

Salmon, F. (2009), 'Recipe for disaster: the formula that killed Wall Street', *Wired*, 24 September, available at: http://www.wired.com/techbiz/it/magazine/17-03/wp_quant?currentPage=all; accessed 4 September 2010.

Shackle, G.L.S (1949), *Expectations in Economics*, Cambridge: Cambridge University Press.

Shackle, G.L.S. (1955), *Uncertainty in Economics and Other Reflections*, Cambridge: Cambridge University Press.

Shackle, G.L.S. (1979), *Imagination and the Nature of Choice*, Edinburgh: Edinburgh University Press.

Skidelsky, R. (2009), *Keynes: The Return of the Master*, London: Penguin.

Witt, G. and M. Xie (2005), 'Moody's modeling approach to rating structured finance: cash flow CDO transactions', Moody's Investor Service, 26 September.

4. Financial crisis and risk measurement: the historical perspective and a new methodology

Gumersindo Ruiz and Ramón Trías

> The revolutionary idea that defines the boundary between modern times and the past is the mastery of risk: the notion that the future is more than a whim of the gods and that men and women are not passive before nature. Until human beings discovered a way across that boundary, the future was a mirror of the past or the murky domain of oracles and soothsayers who held a monopoly over knowledge of anticipated events.
> Peter L. Bernstein (1996, p. 1)

> Slowly it began to dawn on me that what we faced was not so much risk as uncertainty.
> Emanuel Derman (2004, p. 259)

4.1 RISK CONTROL IN FINANCE: A RECENT HISTORY

In his book: *Against the Gods: A Remarkable Story of Risk*, Peter L. Bernstein (1996) makes a thorough historical analysis of the concept of risk. He starts from the development of the laws of probability and the pretension of having statistical rules that permit the decision-making process, and arrives at the 20th century to make a distinction between risk and uncertainty, the former being valuable and measurable while the latter is not.

In economics, the concept of risk management as a practical technique, together with the use of statistical methods under certain theoretical assumptions, was introduced by Kenneth Arrow (1951, 1971) who was aware of the impossibility of predicting the future and its associated contingencies. Therefore, he developed a whole theory of diversification and insurance. The relevance of his thoughts lies in the fact that he considers the differences between the quantifiable and the non-quantifiable. That is why we regard him as a reference for global risk management both as a theory and as a practical application to assure diversification and control.

In an economic system, given long-term equilibrium conditions, time being the main variable, the probabilities of unexpected events are compensated. This could be like the stock exchange case in which bull and bear periods produce, on average, positive results, providing that we can maintain our investments in the long run. But uncertainty means that these regularities do not exist, and past data are by no means useful to predict the future. For that reason Keynes, after analysing uncertainty, designed an economic policy model, with targets and instruments, trying to control the future and avoid risks.

The next step in the history of risk is to take into account economic behaviour, as developed in Wärneryd (2001). Game theory shows us that uncertainty depends on the behaviour of the other players. Strategies, formal and informal contracts, deals and herd behaviour are parts of the theory. In finance, diversification is a game theory strategy that seeks to maximize the probabilities of survival if there are failures in risk calculations. These developments are loaded with quantitative techniques: the theory of probabilities, sample techniques, spreads around an average, the trade off between risk and profitability and the expected utility for investors. In Ruiz et al. (2000) we analyse market, credit, operational, technological, liquidity, and legal risks. In theory, any aspect of risk could be considered, such as identifying risk to measuring and managing it, and to valuing the managers according to their long-run performance, but in practice some risks are not taken into account, or are approached only through probabilistic methods.

As a theoretical and practical subject, risk management deals with risk valuation as well as with uncertainty, that is, situations that may be completely unknown. The following are three characteristics of uncertainty. Economic agents do not have enough information and understanding for decision-making, and their economic models do not catch the complexity of economic reality. The historical view does not provide tools for proper risk management, that is, sound analytical methods with predictive power. Correlations between financial markets (bonds, commodities, equities, private equity, emerging countries, rates of exchange) that have been studied and established can change from positive to negative and vice versa, with devastating consequences for a portfolio aiming at diversification.

George A. Akerlof and Robert J. Shiller (2009) returned to a human behaviour analysis of risk-taking. This methodology has deep roots in the history of financial risk thought, but lacks the tools for implementing their main ideas and principles. As we know, there are not predictive models for herd behaviour, considered as a non-efficient market hypothesis, neither for extreme risk aversion nor for risk appetite. Nevertheless, their hindsight is worth taking into account for financial risk analysis.

In the 1980s, Banker Trust tried to calculate a profit–capital ratio in terms of risk. The cost of the capital related to specific business and its profits was the implicit cost of risk taken to obtain these profits. The method was called 'Risk Adjusted Return on Capital' (RAROC). For example, sales of options on equities can deliver high premium profits, but the risk of strong losses was also very high. For that reason the need for capital to match these losses is bigger in the options business than in others such as simple trading, with no risk retained. Both are bank activities but their profitability should be weighted by the risk that they carry and by the theoretical capital that each one requires. This policy was extended to every kind of business in the bank, such as the wages and bonuses policy for high-level employees, considering the amount of capital that everyone 'used'.

Risk analysis requires an operational data basis. The easiest risk to monitor is the most frequent one, and it is very difficult to extend risk management to unforeseen risk events that are unlikely to happen. But we can not remove the basic idea that some factors of risk could be hidden within some good performances. This is especially true for the huge benefits of leverage in the years before the 2008 crisis that had an implicit risk of illiquidity.

In the late 1980s, banking institution J.P. Morgan (1997) developed a methodology for risk management. RiskMetrics is a variance model to calculate 'Value at Risk' (VaR), a matrix of volatility correlations. Historical data of correlations and volatilities provide the maximum expected loss for a portfolio, for a period of time (say a day, a week, a month). The VaR calculation failed in the recent crisis due to the strong deviations in correlations and volatilities. New methods to measure risks are required and in this paper we introduce Risk Dynamics into the Future (RDF) as an alternative methodology to VaR (AIS, 2009).

During the late 1990s, Coopers & Lybrand, an audit and consulting firm that merged with Pricewaterhouse, developed a system called: 'Generally Accepted Risk Principles' (GARP), which tried to deal with almost every situation of risk, encouraging the creation of independent departments for risk control and risk management, and setting out clear definitions of responsibilities for firms. These departments were not only compliance and procedures reviewers, but real risk control departments aiming at establishing limits to every line of products and business.

Also in the late 1990s, Goldman Sachs along with the Swiss Bank Corporations developed the concept of 'stress testing' as a practical methodology for risk management. This idea was not new, but at that time hardware and software facilities could work with statistical methods, picturing different scenarios for risk. Nevertheless the 'worst case scenario' is a concept that belongs to the realm of uncertainty as shown by the Long-Term Capital Management fund (LTCM – a huge investment fund that needed to be rescued by a group of investment banks). New methods combining macroeconomics and scenarios for specific asset portfolios were needed.

The following are new facts and issues in the recent history of financial risk. They could also be considered as a shortlist of sources of problems in the present crisis.

Securitization was a technique favoured as a way to spread risk out and obtain liquidity. However, there was a lack of responsibility in both its origin and structuring: that is, on the left side of the balance sheet of the securitization vehicles, because of the poor quality of the assets, and on the right side due to an excess of leverage. Moreover, there were imperfections in credit rating, and illiquidity problems for high-rated assets were not considered.

Capital requirements boost and shrink the balances of financial institutions in the high and low phases of the economic cycle. This fact accentuates GDP growth and employment deviations from potential growth and the natural rate of employment. Regulators allowed big banks to have lower capital requirements if they had sophisticated risk models, but these models had produced ambiguous measures of risk. Large international banks as well as local financial institutions push in the same direction, developing better financial technology and models rather than basic credit and risk assessment.

We have learned from the crisis that risk changes depending on who holds it. Increasing capital acts as a buffer in financial institutions, making them countercyclical, focusing on loans as basic measures of risk. These are important issues but are insufficient to avoid liquidity troubles in the future. One main idea surging from the crisis is that liquidity risk is best held by institutions that do not require liquidity like pension funds, life insurance or private equity firms. On the other hand, credit risk is best held by institutions that have plenty of credit risk with which to diversify such as retail banks and hedge funds.

These ideas are intended for the long run and as a way to deal with risk behaviour and management. They are a kind of consensus in today's financial thought about uncertainty, but we need to go from consensus to action. We propose a methodology to test stress scenarios: 'Risk Dynamics into the Future' (RDF). RDF allows us to assess the risk in different situations and should be considered as an accepted method in modern financial thought.

4.2 RISK MANAGEMENT AFTER THE CRISIS

Some of the main issues in post-crisis risk management for financial institutions were: the need for stronger regulatory core capital; to take into account that high-rated assets could be illiquid; to gain more transparency in transactions; improvements in risk control, governance and compliance. Unsuitable policies related to the appointment of directors, bonus and payment systems have been identified as causes of poor risk management. Off-balance-sheet operations deserve more attention as they constitute a new form of risk. Profits and dividends should be approached in a long-run context.

At the beginning of the crisis there was a movement against financial complexity, but new financial instruments such as securitization remain the only way to provide liquidity for the real economy. Today securitization, previously blamed for the current financial problems is a solution for private, financial and non-financial, and public problems. But more transparency is needed on both sides of the securitization structures balance sheet.

Today risk management is a more complex subject than in the past and an agreement should be reached on the following principles:

- The increase of core capital should be related to trading operations rather than to stable positions; and it is essential to avoid the full business cycle impact on the needs of capital. Bank reserves against credit default must be anti-cyclical, that is, more and less relative reserves in both the lower and higher phases of the cycle.
- The effects of asset valuation on balance sheets need to be diminished, looking for more stable long-run valuations. Mark-to-market valuations provide very good information, but the specific role of each kind of asset in a business must be taken into account to determine its valuations.
- An upper limit to leverage will avoid the excess of credit that comes with optimistic expectations about the economy. Liquidity deserves new regulation and supervision rules. The more long-term investment is matched with short-term liquidity positions, the greater the systemic risk for the financial system.
- Supervision needs to be extended to credit rating agencies. A discussion should be started regarding rating agencies' criteria for valuation.
- Regulatory codes for directors' payments and bonuses must be implemented. What is essential is to know how a payment system can introduce a bias in the management of the firm. Changes

are necessary in regulation and supervision to analyse business plans and risk-taking strategies. More international coordination in regulation and supervision is needed.

Shiller (2008) went back to the ideas of Kenneth Arrow to insure against an unexpected increase (or decrease) in the price of assets. Insurance was the field Arrow explored as a way to deal with uncertainty. Schiller suggested that in the case of mortgages, an index could be used to adjust the payment of mortgages to the cycle, while the risk of undesirable volatility in houses and mortgages could be covered by derivatives. Some of these ideas are theoretical and there is not a real market where they could be implemented. Furthermore, insurance in finance lacks the stability common to life, house, or car insurance; the volatility of credit default swaps (CDS), or derivatives on commodities are good examples of this. Only a good system for monitoring credit and loans can establish a sound basis for risk management.

One lesson that has been learned from this crisis is the need to emphasize risk control in anything that can make us more vulnerable, like basic risks in loans, mortgages and liquidity. Risk should be analysed and valued in-house with the specific knowledge held by each financial institution. External valuations by rating agencies are an input for risk management but not a substitute for internal valuations because they lack business experience and relevant local information. Size and risk concentration are important issues. Business strategies in a boom market can be very profitable in the short run but a big source of risk for the future. And last but not least, macroeconomic scenarios deserve more attention than they have received in the past.

How have we arrived at the present situation? There is a tradition in financial risk thought of determining how to identify, measure and manage risk. In Ruiz (2008) we present the case of a financial entity with a sound financial risk management that was unable to avoid liquidity and credit problems in this crisis. From a theoretical point of view every issue with risk involved was taken into account, market illiquidity included. It managed to discover the extremely narrow spreads in debt credit and the abnormal prices in the real estate market. It also conducted the stress tests for liquidity. Loans and risky assets were continuously monitored and valued mark-to-market. However, complex structures were not; rating agencies provided the value for collaterals and it accepted them. From a risk management point of view, complex structures were in a no man's land between loans and tradable assets.

But the main source of troubles came from the sales departments, because incentives to sell created a dangerous bias in the whole organization in favour of sales and against risk control. Test control departments were strongly regulated and internal control and compliance were well implemented. But in practice, and from the point of view of the whole organization, these departments were considered just a necessary inconvenience for day-to-day business. Financial deals were carefully prepared in the back office and sales departments, and risk control departments did not have the time to study these complex operations in depth. Almost every deal was finalized in a rush in a world full of opportunities and hopeful about the future. In this situation it was very difficult to discuss each operation properly. A sound methodology was needed to halt this movement in sales and leverage from the outset.

Our main point in this paper is that a model of scenarios can provide a wide consensus that would help to implement a long-run culture for the long run and for a steady rise in business. Maybe the comment that best explains what happened is found in the interview Chuck Prince, CEO of Citigroup gave to the *Financial Times* in the summer of 2008: 'So long as the music is playing, you have got to get up and dance. We are still dancing'. This statement reflects not only herd behaviour but the inability of a CEO to control his or her complex organization, focusing on a risk dynamic into the future approach.

Considering risk scenarios involves an important change in financial behaviour. Historical analysis is relevant but just a part of a more complex type of analysis. Risk spread and insurance cannot cover every kind of risk because there is no true market to cover them. After the crisis, diversification is no longer the solution. When different markets move in the same direction, as happened in this crisis, we have illiquid markets for assets that historically were never synchronized. VaR methodology and historical data are useful as inputs for the analysis to avoid risk concentration, but we should be able to design and build complex scenarios where different risks could materialize. We propose a methodology for risk management that takes into account the historical perspective for predictions putting together the macroeconomic historical approach, a model for plausible scenarios and the specific circumstances of a portfolio, business or firm.

4.3   METHODS TO MEASURE RISK AND THE RECESSION OF 2008

Today, risk management in financial institutions requires a better measurement of their performance as intermediaries between savings and investment. Risk and uncertainty control are appraised by financial institutions applying two basic concepts – selection and diversification.

Information, frequently very asymmetrical, is highly relevant, in the selection for the expected loss estimation, and in diversification for the decrease of variability and difficulties in controlling extreme portfolio losses. The early applications of these analyses were carried out by investment banks taking advantage of an almost continuous flow of information about bonds portfolios. However, when these concepts had to be calculated for the portfolio of a retail bank and the new financial instruments and assets in the balance sheet of investment banks, it was necessary to redesign the way they were calculated.

Over the last few years, risk measurement methods and their use in crisis situations have been found to have important drawbacks that underestimated risk. This statement has now become the main argument against the use of models in finance, in a process that recalls Ned Ludd's early 19th-century followers. Craftsmen destroyed machines thinking they were the cause of the poor working conditions they suffered, just like today when many in the economic profession oppose models as a tool of valuation and support in decision-making and risk calculation.

Analytical tools and techniques used in financial markets are focused on risk measurement and do not take into account uncertainty. It is impossible to be against this idea because economic conditions in the period 2003 to 2007 were unique. In this situation frequency probabilities and correlations techniques are not enough to deal with the markets.

Risk measurement and financial models are just a part of risk management, and they indeed make sense when considering either risk or uncertainty. In the stock exchange we have stocks that are more volatile or risky depending on certain characteristics that we can identify and measure by probability methods. Loss function for a loan or mortgage portfolio depends on variables that maintain some stability throughout the economic cycle.

In everyday life we continuously assign probabilities to many difficult hypotheses, integrating information and experience. Pre-established ideas, theoretical concepts and practical information give reality to things. The need for a change is not for financial instruments and methods, but for risk behaviour and management. This is not an easy task because the way we approach information and knowledge determines the outcome, and risk perception differs according to the risk bearer. But the fact is that managers are paid for making decisions and they need some sort of guide to do that. They live in a peculiar world in which they need conventional probability methods for risk management and, at the same time, to gain knowledge about uncertainty, to do their everyday work.

Sound research programmes revising mainstream financial models are not a new thing. Over the course of more than 40 years Benoit Mandelbrot

(Mandelbrot and Hudson, 2004) has established that modern financial theory is founded on a few shaky myths that lead us to underestimate real risk in financial markets. Specifically he has been influential in critical approaches to VaR measures. His three basic ideas are the following:

- The most important failing of conventional models is that they grossly underestimate market turbulence and the frequency of extreme events.
- A second problem with orthodox financial models is that they ignore timing. Unlike the random walk, markets have their own sense of time. And volatility clusters together in a burst of turbulence.
- Irregularity in markets is not a minor departure from an idealized theory, but a fundamental characteristic of markets.

Instead of making a general critical assessment of the financial models, we will focus on the underlying model of risk appraisal in Basel II directives. The Vasicek model and other frequently used models such as the Gaussian Copula models and the CreditMetrics/RiskMetrics by J.P. Morgan have similar weaknesses.

The probabilistic event base for the Vasicek model is the concept of bankruptcy as formalized by US economist Robert Merton: bankruptcy occurs when total liabilities exceed total assets, which is a stochastic variable. The value of the assets is supposed to be formed by two components: a common factor to all the elements and another for each investment, the first known as 'systemic risk' or 'state of the economy' and the second as 'specific risk' or 'idiosyncratic', which is dismissed because it is considered irrelevant due to diversification. It is convenient to see that this criterion will provide us with two levels of analysis: the conditioned loss to a certain level of the 'state of economy' and the probability function of losses, obtained by integrating the former function with the probability of occurrence of each possible 'state of the economy'.

Vasicek's development is very elegant, at the expense of assuming some quite restrictive hypotheses, with risk estimates sometimes overstated and, unfortunately much more frequently and intensely, undervalued.

The single risk factor   In investment, when only one risk factor or kind of risk is considered, this risk is neglected in a diversified portfolio. Nevertheless, diversification underestimates the intrinsic risk of a portfolio, providing that the single risk factor hypotheses do not come true. Besides, the explanation of systemic risk cannot be exhausted by a single variable or a common arbitrary combination to form a single artificial variable.

Granularity   Some of the hypotheses issued to justify its validity should not be taken into account. Infinite granularity is the one that introduces more bias, assuming that the portfolio is composed of an (almost) infinite number of loans, each of them of an (almost) infinitesimal amount. The existence of singular investments of a great volume sharing risks with portfolios composed of small or medium loans invalidates this hypothesis.

Diversification   In the credit paradox, the quality of risk usually moves in the opposite way to diversification. If a bank becomes a specialist in a particular class of credit (sector, product) it usually results in a better expected risk for the portfolio of this particular class of credit. But, under this assumption, the same specialized position will cause the bank to be in a weaker position if a crisis beats the sector where it has accumulated a high concentration of risk.

This becomes more serious if we want to apply stress testing to credit portfolios to evaluate the worst case scenario in crisis situations. The current models of risk measurement calculate the correlations between economic sectors as the average along the whole economic cycle. The risk could be undervalued by this procedure. For example, the furniture and construction industries are considered as poorly correlated sectors, but in the present crisis the real correlation between these two sectors becomes extremely high. In the retail sector this fact becomes even more apparent: mortgages on residential dwellings in remote places probably had scanty correlation in times of prosperity, but in a general recession their correlated probability of non-payment increases significantly.

We can conclude by saying that these average methods of the cycle undervalued the correlations between variables and therefore unexpected risk. The diversification effect wished for in the financial institutions credit portfolio is overvalued by these types of methods. To accommodate the reality of the complexities and dynamics of markets and fat-tailed events into a probability distribution requires the concept of portfolio diversification to be broadened beyond current approaches.

Expected value vs. worst case scenario   Implementing stress testing on credit portfolios gives the expected loss from adverse macroeconomic scenarios. That is the case in 'The Supervisory Capital Assessment Program' from the Federal Reserve System for US banks. This procedure avoids the effect of variables not included in the scenario and microeconomic models estimation errors. Clearly we do not obtain the worst case scenario, but the expected value from this specific adverse scenario. In order not to underestimate the potential loss, the conditioned loss function to the adverse scenario should be estimated to obtain its Value at Risk conditioned to the aforementioned scenario.

Scenarios Though there is no standard classification of stress scenarios, the specialist literature distinguishes at least three classes:

- Historical scenarios, backward looking and statistically driven. The basis for this type of analysis is the supposition that the past can repeat itself. Its limitation is that the future can be different.
- Hypothetical scenarios based on external opinions or internal expert opinions of the financial institution. This type of definition of scenarios can be very simple or fairly complex. For example, if we gather in a wide-ranging survey the opinions of the branch managers of the financial institution to define a scenario.
- Systematic scenarios evaluating risk impact through a selection of scenarios with different variations in risk factors. Scenarios based on multivariate statistical models (VARMA, GARCH).

Current statistical risk models are based on past information, exploiting the regularity of the situations. These models allow for future predictions but they are unable to gather scenarios that have not yet happened. This drawback can be solved by choosing hypothetical or systematic scenarios that allow reach where statistical models do not.[1]

4.4 MARKET CORRELATIONS, RISK AND THE RECESSION OF 2008

In this section we present a study of index correlations, picturing the global economy. Risk diversification is one of the main features of VaR measurement, and strong changes in correlations among financial assets challenge VaR as an instrument for risk valuation.

Markowitz's portfolio theory works on the mean-return and variance-risk criteria. Calculating the portfolio mean-return is not very difficult, we take the expected return for each stock and multiply it by its weighting in that portfolio. On the other hand, the risk of the portfolio is measured by its variance. Nevertheless, return and risk do not add up so simply, and it is not just a weighted average since it depends on how stocks correlate. Two stocks that tend to crash at the same time are going to make for a riskier portfolio than two stocks with the same individual variance but moving in opposite directions. So, higher asset correlation in a portfolio means higher variance and risk. The mean-return and variance-risk are calculated by historical data using the bell curve math or normal distribution.

Table 4.1 shows correlation among 21 indexes covering (top to bottom or left to right) United States and Europe, Emergent Countries, Japan, China, France, Germany stock exchanges, rate of interest, corporate bonds, high yields, emergent bonds, public debt for different durations, commodities, energy, commodities ex-energy, gold, and global hedge fund index.

Correlations are calculated for 21 months from October 2006 to June 2008, excluding commodities volatility in summer 2008. Correlations go from 0 signifying no relationship to 1 total correlation. Negative correlations are rare, indicating assets that move in the opposite direction.

Strong correlations can be spotted in five main groups of assets: correlation among US stock exchanges; Emergent Countries, Japan and China; correlations among European stock exchanges; investment grade corporate bonds and public debt; high yields and emergent countries bonds; and commodities and energy.

Table 4.2 displays correlations among the same 21 indexes, calculated for 21 months from July 2008 to March 2010. After the 2008 recession the financial assets relationship changes dramatically. The no-correlation surface (white and light shade) is reduced, showing strong correlation among US and European stock exchange indexes. Commodities, considered historically as an independent asset class, uncorrelated to other securities, are now correlated to stock exchange and emerging countries; and correlations between China and Europe, strength. Hedge funds diminished correlations because they were able to implement quick changes in their portfolios, adapting them to the new circumstances. Only public debt continues uncorrelated except to corporate debt. As a special example, the price of petrol and the S&P 500 index had a clear negative correlation prior to 2008, which was positive afterwards.

These changes in correlations are striking, with serious consequences on implementing VaR in portfolios. An examination of these topics by Fox (2009, pp. 238–239) illustrated that the response of the markets was not as simple as adjusting the portfolios to the new correlations. Portfolio managers, following Markowitz's theory, calculated maximum expected losses for a period, taking into account individual risks and risk assets correlations. Because the strong changes in historical correlations increased portfolios value at risk, if a portfolio manager was trying to keep the VaR below a certain level, he or she might then have to sell off securities to push the VaR back down. This was the VaR's power to exacerbate a downturn, and the role of correlations, as a basic part of mainstream theory on risk economics, in the recession of 2008.

Table 4.1   Securities correlations prior to July 2008

	RUSSELL 3000 VALUE IDX	RUSSELL 3000 GROWTH IDX	S&P 500 INDEX	ESTX 50 € Pr	MSCI EM	NIKKEI 225
RUSSELL 3000 VALUE IDX	1.00	0.95	0.99	0.44	0.29	0.07
RUSSELL 3000 GROWTH IDX	0.95	1.00	0.98	0.48	0.35	0.11
S&P 500 INDEX	0.99	0.98	1.00	0.47	0.31	0.08
ESTX 50 € Pr	0.44	0.48	0.47	1.00	0.60	0.30
MSCI EM	0.29	0.35	0.31	0.60	1.00	0.66
NIKKEI 225	0.07	0.11	0.08	0.30	0.66	1.00
HANG SENG INDEX	0.05	0.08	0.06	0.24	0.77	0.66
CAC 40 INDEX	0.46	0.49	0.48	0.98	0.62	0.31
DAX INDEX	0.42	0.46	0.45	0.97	0.61	0.32
Eonia Capitalization Index Cap	0.00	0.00	0.01	−0.01	−0.03	−0.06
ISHARES IBOXX INV GR CORP BD	−0.30	−0.31	−0.31	−0.15	−0.02	0.02
PIMCO-GLB H/Y BD-INST ACC	0.17	0.17	0.16	0.38	0.61	0.36
BAIF OS OEF EM MKT DEBT	0.13	0.17	0.15	0.34	0.56	0.25
ISHARES BARCLAYS 1–3 YEAR TR	−0.54	−0.55	−0.55	−0.27	−0.17	−0.08
ISHARES BARCLAYS 7–10 YEAR	−0.53	−0.53	−0.54	−0.27	−0.18	−0.09
ISHARES BARCLAYS 20+ YEAR TR	−0.41	−0.42	−0.42	−0.26	−0.16	−0.08
ETFS ALL COMMOD DJ-UBSCISM	0.00	0.04	0.01	0.17	0.30	0.14
ETFS ENERGY DJ-UBSCISM	−0.10	−0.07	−0.09	0.02	0.14	0.05
ETFS EX-ENERGY DJ-UBSCISM	0.05	0.09	0.06	0.24	0.40	0.22
GOLD SPOT $/OZ	0.05	0.07	0.06	0.10	0.23	0.02
HFRX Global Hedge Fund Index	0.60	0.68	0.63	0.59	0.72	0.35

Table 4.1 (continued)

	HFRX Global Hedge Fund Index	GOLD SPOT $/OZ	ETFS EX-ENERGY DJ-UBSCISM	ETFS ENERGY DJ-UBSCISM	ETFS ALL COMMOD DJ-UBSCISM	ISHARES BARCLAYS 20+ YEAR TR	ISHARES BARCLAYS 7–10 YEAR	ISHARES BARCLAYS 1–3 YEAR TR	BAIF OS OEF EM MKT DEBT	PIMCO-GLB H/Y BD-INST ACC	ISHARES IBOXX INV GR CORP BD	Eonia Capitalization Index Cap	DAX INDEX	CAC 40 INDEX	HANG SENG INDEX	NIKKEI 225	MSCI EM	ESTX 50 € Pr	S&P 500 INDEX	RUSSELL 3000 GROWTH IDX	RUSSELL 3000 VALUE IDX
HANG SENG INDEX	0.41	0.06	0.24	0.06	0.15	0.01	-0.02	-0.04	0.33	0.39	0.10	-0.01	0.26	0.26	1.00	0.66	0.77	0.24	0.06	0.08	0.05
CAC 40 INDEX	0.61	0.10	0.24	0.04	0.18	-0.26	-0.27	-0.26	0.36	0.40	-0.15	0.00	0.94	1.00	0.26	0.31	0.62	0.98	0.48	0.49	0.46
DAX INDEX	0.60	0.11	0.24	0.03	0.19	-0.26	-0.26	-0.27	0.34	0.39	-0.14	0.00	1.00	0.94	0.26	0.32	0.61	0.97	0.45	0.46	0.42
Eonia Capitalization Index Cap	-0.01	-0.01	-0.04	-0.09	-0.01	0.08	0.03	0.00	0.00	0.05	0.09	1.00	0.00	0.00	-0.01	-0.06	-0.03	-0.01	0.01	0.00	0.00
ISHARES IBOXX INV GR CORP BD	-0.02	-0.16	-0.05	-0.06	-0.07	0.72	0.74	0.60	0.12	0.30	1.00	0.09	-0.14	-0.15	0.10	0.02	-0.02	-0.15	-0.31	-0.31	-0.30

PIMCO-GLB H/Y BD-INST ACC	0.17	0.17	0.16	0.38	0.51	0.36	0.39	0.40	0.39	0.05	0.30	1.00	0.45	0.12	0.13	0.12	0.09	-0.02	0.17	0.10	0.46
BAIF OS OEF EM MKT DEBT	0.13	0.17	0.15	0.34	0.56	0.25	0.33	0.36	0.34	0.00	0.12	0.45	1.00	0.04	0.04	0.06	0.32	0.16	0.39	0.46	0.50
ISHARES BARCLAYS 1–3 YEAR TR	-0.54	-0.55	-0.27	-0.17	-0.08	-0.04	-0.26	-0.27	-0.27	0.00	0.60	0.12	0.04	1.00	0.85	0.70	-0.05	-0.01	0.00	0.04	-0.35
ISHARES BARCLAYS 7–10 YEAR	-0.53	-0.53	-0.54	-0.27	-0.18	-0.09	-0.02	-0.27	-0.26	0.03	0.74	0.13	0.04	0.85	1.00	0.92	-0.06	-0.02	-0.05	0.01	-0.36
ISHARES BARCLAYS 20+ YEAR TR	-0.41	-0.42	-0.26	-0.16	-0.08	0.01	-0.26	-0.26	-0.26	0.08	0.72	0.12	0.06	0.70	0.92	1.00	-0.04	-0.02	-0.05	0.01	-0.30
ETFS ALL COMMOD DJ-UBSCISM	0.00	0.04	0.01	0.17	0.30	0.14	0.15	0.18	0.19	-0.01	-0.07	0.09	0.32	-0.05	-0.06	-0.04	1.00	0.62	0.69	0.41	0.31
ETFS ENERGY DJ-UBSCISM	-0.10	-0.07	-0.09	0.02	0.14	0.05	0.06	0.04	0.03	-0.09	-0.06	-0.02	0.16	-0.01	-0.02	-0.02	0.62	1.00	0.41	0.27	0.14
ETFS EX-ENERGY DJ-UBSCISM	0.05	0.09	0.06	0.24	0.40	0.22	0.24	0.24	0.24	-0.04	-0.05	0.17	0.39	0.00	-0.05	-0.05	0.69	0.41	1.00	0.52	0.41

Table 4.1 (continued)

	GOLD SPOT $/OZ	HFRX Global Hedge Fund Index
HFRX Global Hedge Fund Index	0.36	1.00
GOLD SPOT $/OZ	1.00	0.36
ETFS EX-ENERGY DJ-UBSCISM	0.52	0.41
ETFS ENERGY DJ-UBSCISM	0.27	0.14
ETFS ALL COMMOD DJ-UBSCISM	0.41	0.31
ISHARES BARCLAYS 20+ YEAR TR	0.01	−0.30
ISHARES BARCLAYS 7–10 YEAR	0.01	−0.36
ISHARES BARCLAYS 1–3 YEAR TR	0.04	−0.35
BAIF OS OEF EM MKT DEBT	0.46	0.50
PIMCO-GLB H/Y BD-INST ACC	0.10	0.46
ISHARES IBOXX INV GR CORP BD	−0.02	−0.16
Eonia Capitalization Index Cap	−0.01	−0.02
DAX INDEX	0.11	0.60
CAC 40 INDEX	0.10	0.61
HANG SENG INDEX	0.06	0.41
NIKKEI 225	0.02	0.35
MSCI EM	0.23	0.72
ESTX 50 € Pr	0.10	0.59
S&P 500 INDEX	0.06	0.63
RUSSELL 3000 GROWTH IDX	0.07	0.68
RUSSELL 3000 VALUE IDX	0.05	0.60

Source: Bloomberg.com.

Table 4.2 Securities correlations after July 2008

	RUSSELL 3000 VALUE IDX	RUSSELL 3000 GROWTH IDX	S&P 500 INDEX	ESTX 50 € Pr	MSCI EM	NIKKEI 225
HFRX Global Hedge Fund Index	0.50	0.55	0.52	0.56	0.63	0.33
GOLD SPOT $/OZ	0.06	0.09	0.07	0.11	0.16	0.10
ETFS EX-ENERGY DJ-UBSCISM	0.32	0.36	0.34	0.54	0.51	0.21
ETFS ENERGY DJ-UBSCISM	0.23	0.25	0.24	0.48	0.46	0.25
ETFS ALL COMMOD DJ-UBSCISM	0.27	0.30	0.29	0.53	0.50	0.24
ISHARES BARCLAYS 20+ YEAR TR	−0.41	−0.42	−0.41	−0.32	−0.29	−0.03
ISHARES BARCLAYS 7–10 YEAR	−0.39	−0.40	−0.40	−0.30	−0.30	−0.03
ISHARES BARCLAYS 1–3 YEAR TR	−0.45	−0.45	−0.46	−0.36	−0.27	0.02
BAIF OS OEF EM MKT DEBT	0.26	0.28	0.27	0.48	0.61	0.51
PIMCO-GLB H/Y BD-INST ACC	0.21	0.21	0.21	0.42	0.51	0.56
ISHARES IBOXX INV GR CORP BD	0.26	0.28	0.28	0.26	0.26	0.11
Eonia Capitalization Index Cap	−0.11	−0.12	−0.11	−0.04	−0.09	−0.02
DAX INDEX	0.67	0.67	0.68	0.96	0.72	0.35
CAC 40 INDEX	0.60	0.61	0.61	0.98	0.74	0.39
HANG SENG INDEX	0.32	0.35	0.34	0.47	0.82	0.65
NIKKEI 225	0.11	0.12	0.12	0.38	0.65	1.00
MSCI EM	0.53	0.55	0.54	0.74	1.00	0.65
ESTX 50 € Pr	0.63	0.63	0.64	1.00	0.74	0.38
S&P 500 INDEX	0.99	0.99	1.00	0.64	0.54	0.12
RUSSELL 3000 GROWTH IDX	0.96	1.00	0.99	0.63	0.55	0.12
RUSSELL 3000 VALUE IDX	1.00	0.96	0.99	0.63	0.53	0.11

Table 4.2 (continued)

	HFRX Global Hedge Fund Index	GOLD SPOT $/OZ	ETFS EX-ENERGY DJ-UBSCISM	ETFS ENERGY DJ-UBSCISM	ETFS ALL COMMOD DJ-UBSCISM	ISHARES BARCLAYS 20+ YEAR TR	ISHARES BARCLAYS 7–10 YEAR	ISHARES BARCLAYS 1–3 YEAR TR	BAIF OS OEF EM MKT DEBT	PIMCO-GLB H/Y BD-INST ACC	ISHARES IBOXX INV GR CORP BD	Eonia Capitalization Index Cap	DAX INDEX	CAC 40 INDEX	HANG SENG INDEX	NIKKEI 225	MSCI EM	ESTX 50 € Pr	S&P 500 INDEX	RUSSELL 3000 GROWTH IDX	RUSSELL 3000 VALUE IDX
HANG SENG INDEX	0.44	0.08	0.27	0.27	0.24	0.14	−0.17	−0.13	0.44	0.40	0.25	0.00	0.47	0.47	1.00	0.65	0.82	0.47	0.34	0.35	0.32
CAC 40 INDEX	0.58	0.10	0.55	0.48	0.51	−0.32	−0.36	−0.29	0.47	0.41	0.29	−0.04	0.91	1.00	0.47	0.39	0.74	0.98	0.61	0.61	0.60
DAX INDEX	0.52	0.11	0.51	0.45	0.52	−0.32	−0.34	−0.31	0.46	0.38	0.21	−0.02	1.00	0.91	0.47	0.35	0.72	0.96	0.68	0.67	0.67
Eonia Capitalization Index Cap	−0.29	−0.03	−0.11	−0.08	−0.04	0.10	0.09	0.12	−0.14	−0.14	−0.03	1.00	−0.02	−0.04	0.00	−0.02	−0.09	−0.04	−0.11	−0.12	−0.11
ISHARES IBOXX INV GR CORP BD	0.43	−0.07	0.13	0.03	0.11	0.11	0.14	−0.08	0.12	0.30	1.00	−0.03	0.21	0.29	0.25	0.11	0.26	0.26	0.28	0.28	0.26

	C1	C2	C3	C4	C5	C6	C7	C8	C9	C10	C11	C12	C13	C14	C15	C16	C17	C18	C19	C20	C21
PIMCO-GLB H/Y BD-INST ACC	0.21	0.21	0.42	0.51	0.56	0.40	0.41	0.38	−0.14	0.30		1.00	0.56	−0.01	0.07	0.00	0.30	0.28	0.22	0.07	0.52
BAIF OS OEF EM MKT DEBT	0.26	0.28	0.27	0.48	0.61	0.51	0.44	0.47	0.46	−0.14	0.12	0.56	1.00	−0.08	−0.05	−0.06	0.45	0.43	0.43	0.27	0.52
ISHARES BARCLAYS 1-3 YEAR TR	−0.45	−0.45	−0.46	−0.36	−0.27	0.02	−0.13	−0.36	−0.34	0.12	−0.08	−0.01	−0.08	1.00	0.74	0.61	−0.28	−0.18	−0.25	0.09	−0.34
ISHARES BARCLAYS 7-10 YEAR TR	−0.39	−0.40	−0.40	−0.30	−0.30	−0.03	−0.17	−0.29	−0.31	0.09	0.14	0.07	−0.05	0.74	1.00	0.91	−0.22	−0.20	−0.27	0.07	−0.22
ISHARES BARCLAYS 20+ YEAR TR	−0.41	−0.42	−0.41	−0.32	−0.29	−0.03	−0.14	−0.32	−0.32	0.10	0.11	0.00	−0.06	0.61	0.91	1.00	−0.24	−0.22	−0.29	0.02	−0.25
ETFS ALL COMMOD DJ-UBSCISM	0.27	0.30	0.29	0.53	0.50	0.24	0.24	0.51	0.52	−0.04	0.11	0.30	0.45	−0.28	−0.22	−0.24	1.00	0.80	0.77	0.27	0.43
ETFS ENERGY DJ-UBSCISM	0.23	0.25	0.24	0.48	0.46	0.25	0.27	0.48	0.45	−0.08	0.03	0.28	0.43	−0.18	−0.20	−0.22	0.80	1.00	0.66	0.20	0.39
ETFS EX-ENERGY DJ-UBSCISM	0.32	0.36	0.34	0.54	0.51	0.21	0.27	0.55	0.51	−0.11	0.13	0.22	0.43	−0.25	−0.27	−0.29	0.77	0.66	1.00	0.37	0.46

Table 4.2 (continued)

	GOLD SPOT $/OZ	HFRX Global Hedge Fund Index
HFRX Global Hedge Fund Index	0.16	1.00
GOLD SPOT $/OZ	1.00	0.16
ETFS EX-ENERGY DJ-UBSCISM	0.37	0.46
ETFS ENERGY DJ-UBSCISM	0.20	0.39
ETFS ALL COMMOD DJ-UBSCISM	0.27	0.43
ISHARES BARCLAYS 20+ YEAR TR	-0.02	-0.25
ISHARES BARCLAYS 7–10 YEAR	0.07	-0.22
ISHARES BARCLAYS 1–3 YEAR TR	0.09	-0.34
BAIF OS OEF EM MKT DEBT	0.27	0.52
PIMCO-GLB H/Y BD-INST ACC	0.07	0.52
ISHARES IBOXX INV GR CORP BD	-0.07	0.43
Eonia Capitalization Index Cap	-0.03	-0.29
DAX INDEX	0.11	0.52
CAC 40 INDEX	0.10	0.58
HANG SENG INDEX	0.08	0.44
NIKKEI 225	0.10	0.33
MSCI EM	0.16	0.63
ESTX 50 € Pr	0.11	0.56
S&P 500 INDEX	0.07	0.52
RUSSELL 3000 GROWTH IDX	0.09	0.55
RUSSELL 3000 VALUE IDX	0.06	0.50

Source: Bloomberg.com.

4.4.1 RDF (Risk Dynamics into the Future) Method

In an informal comment by Donald R. van Deventer in Geneva, December 2002, Robert Merton was asked what advice he could give to financial institutions using the Merton model to manage their risk. After a long pause, Professor Merton said: 'Well, the first thing you have to remember is that the model is twenty-eight years old'.

It is very important to check the hypotheses under which the models correctly explain what the reality is. We are able to lighten up many of the simplifications that Merton or Vasicek methods incorporate for reasons of calculation feasibility. The speed of calculation has increased since the end of the 1980s up to today approximately 100000 times, which means that what took two-and-half months can now be done in a minute. In addition to this, vast quantities of information can be store and organized.

Following the analysis of risk in Ruiz et al. (2000), we will show how measurable risk can be integrated with uncertainty (not measurable) using a method that combines econometric models and expert economic scenarios. This method, initially designed to forecast capital needs under stress situations, has become a useful tool for decision-making either strategic or operational. It has already been tested on the real arena as a risk management tool for several financial institutions.

Measurable risk is controlled by means of macroeconomic models that not only allow the forecast of the significant variables in their expected values, but can also estimate the joint probability distribution function of these outcomes. Afterwards, uncertainty is integrated by means of the instantiation of some of the variables defining a macroeconomic scenario. As a result, we will have a reduced space of that probability distribution function, with the marginal probability distribution function with equivalent statistical properties.

We propose a new scope beyond current risk concepts –'Conditioned Value at Risk' (CVaR), 'Conditioned Unexpected Risk' (CUR), 'Conditioned Shortfall' – extending them to a 'Risk Conditioned to an Economic Scenario', improving the 'What-if' method, traditionally limited to the 'expected value if a certain condition is met'.

RDF combines a set of models allowing, by way of sophisticated econometric models, the simulation of unfavourable economic scenarios, and the calculation of the distribution of losses in these scenarios, providing support for strategic planning and business development. Our method includes an innovative analytical solution for the integration of the loss function, which complements the more traditional Monte Carlo solution.

The main criteria used in the construction of RDF are:

- The sources of variability that produce the risk arise essentially (but not only) from the macroeconomic situation. An econometric or macro model allows this domain to be controlled.
- Depending on the severity of a possible crisis, the companies and retail exposures of the portfolio will either be able or not to cope with it. Modelling their response capacity requires combining the macroeconomic variables and the characteristics of the instrument and each sub-portfolio, in the so-called micro models. The model could be developed at an aggregated level, although the treatment of sub-portfolios seems the most suitable.
- The micro models that relate the macroeconomic situation to the losses in each sub-portfolio have their own residual variables. These random variables will be categorized as risk drivers, linking a single multivariate distribution (in this case as independent variables) integrated into the macroeconomic model.
- The macroeconomic model (macro model) enriched with the residual variables of the models, optionally multi-period, is integrated in a single dimension multivariate distribution (number of periods multiplied by the number of macro and micro variables). The indirect effect and the interactions are thus controlled.
- The risk measurements incorporate the distribution of the losses from the micro and macro models through the indicated multivariable distribution. CVaR ('Conditioned Value at Risk'), CShortfall ('Conditioned Shortfall') or CUR ('Conditioned Unexpected Risk') can be calculated in a conditioned scenario.
- We understand scenarios as the instantiation of some variables in some periods (hypothetical or expert scenarios). The system must be capable of calculating the probability of the occurrence of this instantiation and of generating the resulting marginal distribution.
- The diversification effect is computed at its correct level of residual risk, considering the risk concentrations for singular investments, extraordinary, granular and common effects of extreme circumstances on different sub-portfolios.

One lesson we have learned from the recession of 2008 is that mainstream theory on risk measurement and valuation was flawed. Risk theory was backward focused and statistically driven. It undervalued the dynamic characteristics of the markets, emphasizing diversification, and using volatility as a proxy variable to risk measurement. This approach strongly influenced risk management in different fields like capital needs calculations, probability of losses in loan portfolios, or asset allocations as shown in our example. An unexpected consequence was that implementing these principles made things worse in the downturn. Future developments require a forward-looking macroeconomic approach, measurement tools for stabilized valuation along the economic cycle, a better understanding of the relationship between risk and diversification, and looking for a way to hedge those rare events known as fat-tail risks.

NOTE

1. References on these subjects are the following: Vasicek (1987); Caouette et al. (1998); Arvanitis and Gregory (2001); Ávila et al. (2002); Bessis (1998); Cossin and Pirotte (2000); Credit Suisse FP (1997); Gordy (2002a, 2002b); Gundlach and Lehrbass (2004); Márquez and Lopez (2006); Ong (1999); Reiss (2003); Saunders (1999); Shimko (1991) and Wilson (1997).

REFERENCES

AIS, Aplicaciones de Inteligencia Artificial (2009), *Risk Dynamics into the Future (RDF)*, GNU Free Documentation Licenses.

Akerlof, G.A. and R.J. Shiller (2009), *Animal Spirits. How Human Psychology Drives the Economy, and Why It Matters for Global Capitalism*, Princeton, NJ: Princeton University Press.

Arrow, K.J. (1951), 'Approaches to the theory of choice in risk-taking', in Arrow, J. (1971), *Essays in the Theory of Risk-bearing*, Chicago: Markham Publishing Company, pp. 1–21.

Arrow, K.J. (1971), *Essays in the Theory of Risk-bearing*, Chicago: Markham Publishing Company.

Arvanitis, A. and J. Gregory (2001), *Credit. The Complete Guide to Pricing, Hedging and Risk Management*, London: Risk Books.

Ávila, F., J. Márquez and A. Romero. (2002), *Implantación del Modelo CyRCE*, México: Banco de México.

Bernstein, P.L. (1996), *Against the Gods. The Remarkable Story of Risk*, New York: John Wiley & Sons.

Bessis, J. (1998), *Risk Management in Banking*, New York: John Wiley.

Caouette, J.B., E.I. Altman and P. Narayanan (1998), *Managing Credit Risk: The Next Great Financial Challenge*, New York: John Wiley.

Cossin, D. and H. Pirotte (2000), *Advanced Credit Risk Analysis. Financial Approaches and Mathematical Models to Assess, Price and Manage Credit Risk*, London and New York: John Wiley & Sons.

Credit Suisse Financial Products (1997), 'CreditRisk+: A credit risk management framework', London, available at: www.csfb.com/creditrisk; accessed 4 September 2010.

Derman, E. (2004), *My Life as a Quant*, New York: John Wiley & Sons.

Fox, J. (2009), *The Myth of the Rational Market*, New York: Harper.

Gordy, M.B. (2002a), 'A risk-factor model foundation for ratings-based bank capital rules', Board of Governors of the Federal Reserve System.

Gordy, M.B. (2002b), 'Saddlepoint approximation of CreditRisk⁺', *Journal of Banking and Finance*, **26** (7), 1335–1353.

Gundlach, M. and F. Lehrbass (2004), *CreditRisk⁺ in the Banking Industry*, Berlin: Springer.

J.P. Morgan (1997), 'CreditMetrics technical documentation', London: available at www.creditmetrics.com; accessed 4 September 2010.

Mandelbrot, B.B. and R.L. Hudson (2004), *The (Mis)behaviour of Markets. A Fractal View of Risk, Ruin, and Reward*, New York: Basic Books.

Márquez, J. and F. Lopez (2006), 'Un modelo de análisis del riesgo de crédito y su aplicación para realizar una prueba de estrés del sistema financiero mexicano', *Estabilidad financiera*, **10**, 25–54.

Ong, M.K. (1999), *Internal Credit Risk Models. Capital Allocation and Performance Measurement*, London: Risk Books.

Reiss, O. (2003), 'Fourier inversion algorithms for Generalized CreditRisk+', WIAS- Preprint No. 817.

Ruiz, G. (2008), *Un mundo en crisis. Auge y caída de la liquidez y el crédito*, Málaga: Cámara de Comercio.

Ruiz, G., J.L. Jiménez and J.J. Torres (2000), *La gestión del riesgo financiero*, Madrid: Pirámide.

Saunders, A. (1999), *Credit Risk Measurement. New Approaches to Value at Risk and Other Paradigms*, New York: John Wiley & Sons.

Shiller, R.J. (2008), *The Subprime Solution. How Today's Global Financial Crisis Happened, and What to Do about It*, Princeton, NJ: Princeton University Press.

Shimko, D. (1991), *Credit Risk-Models and Management*, London: Risk Books.

Vasicek, O. (1987), 'Probability of loss on loan portfolio', KMV Corporation Working Paper.

Wärneryd, K.E. (2001), *Stock-market Psychology. How People Value and Trade Stocks*, Cheltenham, UK and Northampton, MA, USA: Edward Elgar.

Wilson, T.C. (1997), 'Portfolio Credit Risk', I and II, *Risk Magazine*, September, 111–117 and October, 56–61.

5. Did economic analysis fail in the current financial crisis?[1]

Julio Segura

5.1 INTRODUCTION

Crises are the proper moment to reflect on the inadequacies of analytical and policy instruments that should help us to detect problems and defects in the legal framework in advance, in order to face and avoid crisis in advance. The debate about the errors of the regulatory and policy measures implemented to tackle the crisis, which started in the fall of 2007, has been, and still is, very intense. However, the academic debate on possible errors in the approach and the type of economic analysis prevailing in the decades prior to the crisis has been slower. The aim of this paper is to try to answer two questions. First, what went wrong with the economic analysis that prevailed in the decades prior to the crisis? Second, how have we, the economists, failed?

I will start by pointing out that some widespread and vulgar criticisms do not disturb me. I will give a couple of examples. The first one puts the blame on economists for not being able to foresee the crisis. As we shall see later, this is not true, but in the end, due to the crucial role that expectations play in the financial world, if a model existed that could foresee a crisis with a high degree of accuracy, the effect would be to bring the crisis about at an earlier date. The second example is the criticism of economic analysis because it uses simplified models that do not take into account all of the idiosyncratic and institutional characteristics of the real world. As Joan Robinson pointed out (1962, p. 33) with a sharpness not devoid of irony, and everybody knows, the only useful maps are those with a 1:1 scale.

I am old enough to have lived through various waves of naive criticism of economic analysis, such as the ones I have just described, by those who neither understand it nor work on it. These people make use of economic analysis in a biased way – I will comment on this point a bit later – and they benefit from crisis situations to try to improve their academic curricula to gain the attention of the media. This does not surprise me at all.

My main worry is focused on trying to discern whether the prevailing approach in economic analysis and in financial markets in the last decades has been kept alive by erroneous hypotheses. There are two fundamental hypotheses: in the area of macroeconomics, the hypothesis of rational expectations and in financial analysis, the efficient market hypothesis (EMH).

Since my area of expertise is microeconomics in economic analysis and I am working as a market supervisor at the moment, I shall focus my analysis exclusively on the analysis of EMH. First of all, I shall present a somewhat technical description that I shall translate, straightaway, into language that is more colloquial.

5.2   THE EFFICIENT MARKET HYPOTHESIS

The central tenet of EMH (Fama, 1965) is that, in markets that have access to all the relevant economic information, the speculative price of shares tends to be the one that provides a performance rate that is close to the reasonable and expected rate. Through backward induction it is easy to conclude that, if this is really the case, changes in prices around this rate are random – or a martingale – no matter what the interdependence of underlying economic variables in the formation of prices are, in other words, the *fundamentals*. Therefore, in markets with complete information, prices always reflect predictable changes in the relevant economic variables in the formation of these prices. Consequently, the only source of price fluctuations is the existence of unexpected changes in underlying economic variables.

To sum up, in less technical language, EMH has two postulates:

P1.   *Agents make their decisions in financial markets taking into account all the relevant information they have at their disposal.*

P2.   *Individual decisions are the result of a process of optimization in which agents try to maximize the performance of their financial investments taking into account their risk profile and level of wealth.*

It would appear to be beyond all reasonable doubt that the first postulate is the correct one. Agents make their decisions taking into account all the relevant information at their disposal, not only in the case of financial markets but also in all markets. Who does not consider how fresh fish is before deciding to buy it or not at the price at which it is being sold? Who does not consider all of the aspects of a technical report before deciding whether or not to buy a second-hand car? It would be absurd to think that agents omit part of the available information when they make their decisions because this would mean that they are acting deliberately and systematically against their own interests.

Another thing that EMH does not say is whether all of the relevant information exists for making fully informed decisions. If it does not exist, as happens in financial markets, since information is asymmetric and often incomplete, what happens is that the competitive equilibrium will not be efficient and that means poorer quality and a higher price – even the inexistence of certain markets – than if the information were complete and symmetrical. This is a well-known result from half a century ago subsequent to the seminal work of Akerlof (1970) on the second-hand car market. Consequently, EMH does not postulate against what its rather inadequate name could make one think, that financial markets are efficient.

The second postulate of EMH is more complicated to discuss. Technically, it implies that agents' behaviour can be modelled in the financial markets they perform in, like optimizers who try to maximize their profits – however, they are measured – subject to the restrictions implied by the availability of their savings, their financing needs and relevant personal traits, like their degree of aversion to risk, age, or level of initial wealth, and so on.

There is abundant evidence on individual, irrational behaviour in financial markets as a result of the advances in an area of analytical and experimental research known as 'behavioural finance' (see Shleifer, 2000). Agents frequently follow the rules of heuristic decisions and perform through force of habit given the newly available information, so that they foresee the future largely as a mere extrapolation of the past although they receive new information, which, if it were processed rationally, should lead to different forecasts. What's more, there is abundant evidence of herd behaviour having negative effects on the stability of financial markets. All of this calls for different improvements in the financial models in use – and I shall only touch upon this.

First, the abandoning of the principle of the representative agent since different agents interact in markets not only as far as information that is received is concerned, but also taking into account their knowledge, abilities and motivation.

Second, the emphasis that has been placed on the internal-logical consistency of financial models up to now should be complemented by a greater demand as far as its external-empirical consistency is concerned. A great amount of information is available on the behaviour of financial markets, which, if it were analysed on a descriptive level with powerful data-processing instruments, could shed a lot of light onto the weaknesses of the financial models in use and guide us in more fruitful directions of empirical research.

Finally, and from the perspective of stability, the growth in the interdependence of financial businesses has increased systemic instability. This is something well known in the theory of networks – greater instability when the number of nodes and the density of relations is higher – as well as in evolutionary biology – instability derived from herd behaviour.

Although the second EMH postulate has undoubtedly serious deficiencies, this does not mean that individual behaviour in financial markets is plainly irrational. Agents' behaviour when they buy some products that are in the eye of the storm in this crisis can be explained in terms of strictly rational behaviour. Here we are thinking of asset-backed trusts, for example. They are a complex product that packages up different assets, which can then be repackaged. For this reason, it is difficult to work out their value, to the point that even businesses who work with investments relied on the rating that rating agencies gave them.

Why do financial businesses (that is, banks) securitize assets such as mortgage loans? Because this allows them to take a part of the risk out of their balance sheets. In this way, they consume less regulatory capital and they can also use them as collateral in their demands for liquidity from central banks, which in turn allows them to give out more loans or to indebt themselves more. Why did other agents buy them? Because they offered profits that were some basic points higher than other products, which were also given an AAA by rating agencies. Basic points with which the issuing bank could pay for the advantages that it obtained from turning liquid assets into asset-backed trusts.

So, EMH has been found to be erroneous as far as the presumption that it is possible to explain the real behaviour of agents in financial markets in terms of absolute rationality, which has provoked weaknesses in the explanatory and predictive capacity of models that have been based on it. However, it gets it right when it points to the lack of information and the asymmetrical nature of information as the fundamental problem for attaining efficiency in financial markets. In other words, it justifies an increase in transparency as a crucial element of better financial regulation.

I believe it is necessary to add two points related to what EMH does *not* claim to this assessment although anonymous critics make it responsible for them. First, EMH does not postulate that financial markets are efficient, only that they could be if all of the relevant information was publicly available for the agents to make decisions and if they behaved with total rationality. Since neither of these two premises is true, the unquestionable conclusion is that EMH is compatible with the fact that financial markets are not and cannot be efficient. EMH wrongly postulates that if information problems were solved the efficiency would be guaranteed.

The second thing that EMH does not say, is that in the hypothetical case that financial markets were efficient, the resulting allocation would be desirable from the social point of view. Efficient financial markets can bring with them high instability, which can bring high systemic risk. External effects, as everyone has known for over a century, do not lead to efficient competitive equilibria.

We should highlight, as Samuelson did in 1965, that EMH does not postulate that the randomness of changes in share prices – the analytical root of this hypothesis – is a good thing; neither that speculation is good, nor that it constitutes any type of proof that competitive financial markets in the real word function correctly. In other words, EMH is not an empirical affirmation.

To sum up, EMH is compatible with inefficient financial markets because of the lack of distribution or asymmetric distribution of information and with efficient markets that are not socially desirable. Its basic weakness is to postulate that financial markets will be efficient only with complete information. Even so, it provides a fundamental guide for regulatory reforms on the need to increase transparency.

5.3 WHAT DID ECONOMIC ANALYSIS AND EMPIRICAL EVIDENCE SAY?

Besides EMH, the consolidated body of economic analysis at the end of the 20th century and accumulated empirical evidence allowed judgments to be passed on the problems that are at the source of today's crisis. As far as theoretical analysis is concerned, it should be pointed out, among other things (see Eichengreen, 2009), that:

- For decades, the agency theory has been pointing to the problems of coordinating the interests of portfolio managers and shareholders who, in the presence of incomplete contracts, needed an appropriate incentive system. The theory of the design of incentives had shown that short-term incentives did not lead to long-term efficiency, so that the coexistence of high bonuses and worthless shares was possible in the long term.
- The possibilities of regulatory capture (and, as I will expand on later, of academic capture) and its context have most probably been known since the 1950s.
- The problems of adverse selection in financial markets have been

known since the pioneering work of Akerlof. Among them, asymmetrical and incomplete information prevailing in financial markets led to competitive inefficient equilibria (high prices and poor quality) and also, to the inexistence of markets for certain financial assets.

- The theory of general equilibrium has shown that with incomplete markets – in other words, a market for every type of physical good, in every period and localization – the competitive equilibrium was inefficient in the presence of uncertainty. It is true that it can be attempted to 'complete' the structure of markets by creating new financial products, but having more markets without reaching a complete structure does not mean moving closer to efficiency.

It should be observed that the authors behind these theorems have won more than a dozen Nobel prizes for Economics. It is therefore difficult to hold that this type of finding is esoteric, irrelevant or unknown to the economic profession.

Then again, from an empirical point of view, it was well known, from research and the experience of earlier crises that:

- Excessive indebtedness, encouraged by a long period of low real interest rates and comfortable liquidity conditions and expectations of rising prices for all types of assets, would end up causing an unsustainable ratio of debt/liquid assets in many businesses when the inevitable revaluation of asset prices took place.
- Numerous empirical studies exist that showed that, at the very least, a high overvaluation of property assets would eventually lead to readjustment. Whether this adjustment would be a soft landing or a bursting bubble was debatable. However, after a decade of rising prices and two-digit rates of credit growth, with every day that passed, the risk of the second option happening was obvious.
- There was ample empirical evidence that when banks relax their requirements in exchange for the granting of credits, this is not immediately reflected in the financial and wealth situation. However, from the fourth or fifth year financial results would be affected, along with regulatory capital and as a result, this would have negative effects on solvency.
- It was known that the originate-to-distribute banking model, by virtue of which banks grant credits that they sell to other financial institutions that then package them up as ABS (asset-backed securities), transferred the risks from the regulated sector to the non-regulated credit entities – the final bearers of complex liquid assets.
- It was known that the conduits, which did not consolidate with the

bank where credits originated, were a way to avoid using up their own resources, and hence, the weakness of bank solvency.

- Conflicts of interests were known due to earlier crises with credit rating agencies and their debatable ratings and modifications, which, however, had gained weight as regulatory elements because, for example, the requirement of a certain credit rating to securitize assets or use assets as collateral to obtain liquidity in central banks.
- It is well known that models were being used – for example to calculate value at risk – that were fed with information corresponding to a long period of historically low volatility, so they were underestimating risks.

This was known when the process of spurious financial innovation destined not to consume its own resources was gaining momentum; when the Glass-Steagall Act that separated the activities of commercial and investment banks was repealed; when mortgages were valued by models that fed on data belonging to a long period of low indebtedness and prices that were rising tediously.

5.4   LOOKING FOR THE CULPRITS

If economic analysis was warning about (almost) all the risks that crystallized in the fall of 2007 and empirical evidence foresaw an ever sharper readjustment, what went wrong? It was the selective and biased reading of economic analysis encouraged by pressure groups in the financial and ideological industry and by social circles. In other words, what failed was a series of beliefs, not analytical hypotheses of political economy that used, as an apparent justification, a partial and self-interested interpretation of economic analysis that they themselves, managed to impose on public opinion.

The first failed hypothesis was that all financial innovation improves the efficiency in the assignation of financial resources. What is the analytical foundation of this belief?

As I have already said, the general competitive equilibrium is inefficient in the face of uncertainty if the structure of markets is incomplete. A complex structure requires as many markets as goods and this is impossible, simply because there are not markets for all of the goods during all the relevant periods. Economic analysis shows that if you manage to complete the structure of markets, the competitive equilibrium will be efficient and the increase in markets can be achieved through the appearance of new financial products. What the analysis does not say is that increasing the number of markets without completing the structure brings us closer to an efficient assignation. Therefore, to maintain that financial innovation improves the efficiency of competitive equilibrium is a belief that has no grounding in economical analysis.

Furthermore, it is true that a part of the innovation has allowed for the improvement of the sources of business financing and has increased the range of instruments for the final savers. Nevertheless, a no less despicable part of it has had as its aim the avoidance of the requirements of regulated capital, the consumption of its own resources, thus weakening the solvency of credit agencies and investment business services.

Finally, it should be pointed out that only in the financial world has innovation been considered uncritically as a synonym for efficiency. In energy, pharmaceutical, chemical or motor trades, innovations have to be assessed for their efficiency and many are rejected if they do not pass the test. We should also remember that part of the cost of financial innovation is a greater systemic instability.

It is worth noting that this belief has a corollary in economic policy: financial innovation should not be restricted or regulated at all. The recent crisis has shown, at a terrible cost, how mistaken this belief and its corollary have been.

The second failed belief was that all financial assets, in whatever condition, would have deep, liquid markets. With simple financial assets and comfortable liquidity conditions this is true, but when financial innovation multiplies complex and heterogeneous assets, they stop being so. It is such a complex task to value these assets that not even investment services companies are able to value them, so that they have to trust the ratings the rating agencies give them. As a result of this, they are acquired by institutional investors with the aim of keeping them until they mature so their liquidity is minimal.

The consequence of all this is that the valuation of these assets is highly deficient and the liquidity risk is as important as the credit risk. Therefore, when they are put on sale they have to be sold at an important discount, which added to their poor initial valuation by rating agencies, could lead to solvency problems for their holders and issuing banks – just what happened in the current crisis.

The third self-interested belief is that the transparency of the financial system was enough to minimize the problems of asymmetric information – its most important failure. Today's financial crisis has taken its course with one characteristic that had not occurred in the previous decades: the ineffectiveness of some price fixing mechanisms, in particular, the corporate debt markets. The disappearance of certain markets is the result of the lack of confidence in the financial system that insufficient transparency caused. The buyers of structured assets did not really know what they were buying and neither did the issuing banks – through successive repackaging of assets – know what the real value of the final asset portfolio was.

The crusade against the dangers of 'excessive' transparency (inferior competitive position, offshoring, the detection of strategies by competitors, etc.) has not only made regulating and supervisory arbitrage easier, but it has made the working of financial markets worse. Moreover, the crusade has reached the stage of trying, unsuccessfully for the time being, to turn international regulations related to financial information and accountancy into a solvency policy instrument rather than a transparency instrument.

The fourth belief that failed is that the financial world is capable of reaching the best assignations via competence and self-regulation, without public intervention. It is well known that, when there are conflicts of interest self-regulation cannot solve the problem, because there is no incentive to follow the norms of good behaviour and of voluntary acceptance when this affects profits negatively. In addition, it should be remembered that conflicts of interest are numerous in the financial world. To give a couple of examples: rating agencies that simultaneously value share issues and help to design and place them, banks who give out opinions and reports on assets that they charge for placing and that compete against others issued by them: banks that sell financial products amongst their clients or investment funds that depend on banks that issue the assets.

These are the type of postulates that failed: (pseudo)hypothesis, (pseudo) analytical, which concealed prior beliefs and very precise economic interests in the financial industry. Also, let's face it, an additional failure has been the permissiveness of many academics with partial and biased interpretations of their theoretical findings.

Users who are interested in economic analysis choose those partial aspects that provide an apparent scientific halo to their self-interested decisions. This appears less acceptable to me than academics – and even less so than teachers – who take part in this game, and it appears ethically reprehensible that they do not warn about the limitations of the models and condemn biased and hence erroneous interpretations of the analytical results. Although there are reasons that explain this behaviour, the cost of condemnation is high because academics have modest salaries that they make up for when they obtain research grants, elaborate reports and give conferences. The people who finance these activities are usually found in the area of users interested in economic analysis.

Those who are rightly convinced that there are risks of regulatory capture have to admit that those very risks are produced in the relation between self-interested users of economic analysis and academics. But asymmetrical short-sightedness is not infrequent, so that those who insist the most on pointing out the first danger are frequently more complacent with the second.

5.5   WHAT CAN BE IMPROVED?

It is not my intention to finish this paper with a totally despairing and pessimistic vision of things, so I shall briefly sum up some of the points and approaches that I believe should occupy a relevant place in the research agenda of financial economy over the next years (see Colander et al., 2009).

First, the emphasis of financial analysis has been aimed at logical consistency, in other words the internal consistency of the models, but in relative terms, less importance has been given to their empirical robustness. Let us take the example of models of general dynamic equilibrium.

They are very complex models (with many equations) that try to represent – in a stylized fashion – the essential characteristics of an economy, and that essentially contain different types of equations; technological restrictions, the endowment of resources, the behaviour of agents and of equilibrium. Their main asset is that they take into account the interrelationship among all the agents and sectors of the economy and since they are dynamic, they generate temporary paths of the relevant variables, at the cost of a great complexity and the existence of many parameters.

They are used, and this is what interests us, to simulate the temporary behaviour of a particular economy from the moment certain economic policy measures are taken. In other words, they are supposed to be used to accurately calculate the effects of different policy measures. Two aspects of the utilization of these models are unsatisfactory. The first is that their microeconomic foundations are very weak, essentially because they do not include heterogeneous agents, something crucial in financial themes. The second is that in their simulations, the parameters are given numerical values obtained from microeconomic research. However, this is not very satisfactory if the interactions are very relevant, because in that case, the aggregation of individual and heterogeneous behaviours is complex.

In other words, since we do not know what '*the*' good model is, the robustness of data and calculations is vital, so we can predict that the greater utilization of robust control techniques that produce temporary probability paths should be compatible with an ample range of specific models.

Also, and for the same reason that we do not know whether '*the*' superior model exists, it is possible to not take our starting point from the utilization of specific and totally specified models but rather to start by analysing data with techniques of data treatment and specification tests. In other words, give greater importance to the improvement of the model selection techniques (see Campos et al., 2005 and Rajan et al., 2008).

Another area where research should give greater weight is that of the design of early warning systems and early detection of bubbles. It is not easy to decide whether a particular dynamic of asset prices, financial as well as real ones, with expanding growth, constitutes an overvaluation. In that case, the return in the medium term to normal levels can be either smooth or lead to a bubble whose outcome will inevitably be explosive. But we should keep in mind the potential costs of a bubble against overvaluation, which means that monetary authorities would be more sensitive to the risks involved in keeping interest rates down and maintaining comfortable liquidity conditions during long periods of time. In addition, prediction systems and early detection of problems also require a type of information that, at this moment in time, financial supervisors do not have and the financial industry is reluctant to provide because of the costs it would involve.

To sum up, in my opinion there is a very important and wide agenda for economic academics, with implications in the regulatory and supervisory agenda of economic authorities, that involves a change in relative emphasis. On the one hand, the academic work in economics of the last 50 years has consolidated high standards of logical consistency in the models we use, and we should pay at least the same amount of attention to their empirical robustness and to the quality of forecasts and projections that arise from them. On the other hand, blind confidence in free financial markets plus self-regulation must be replaced by a new regulatory framework that must reduce the probability of the occurrence of a new crisis such as the present one, which means a better regulation of stability issues and more transparency.

NOTE

1. A version of this paper was presented at the Real Academia de Ciencias Morales y Políticas de España in March 2010.

REFERENCES

Akerlof, G. (1970), 'The market for "lemons": quality uncertainty and the market mechanism', *Quarterly Journal of Economics*, **84** (3), 488–500.
Campos, J., N.R. Ericsson and D.F. Hendry (2005), 'Introduction', in J. Campos,

N.R. Ericsson and D.F. Hendry (eds), *General-to-Specific Modelling*, Cheltenham, UK and Northampton, MA, USA: Edward Elgar, pp. xi–xci.

Colander, D., H. Föllmer, A. Haas, M.D. Goldberg, K. Juselius, A. Kirman, T. Lux and B. Sloth (2009), 'The financial crisis and the systemic failure of academic economics', Kiel Institute of the World Economy WP No. 1489, February.

Eichengreen, B. (2009), 'The last temptation of risk', *The National Interest*, **101** (May/June), 8–14.

Fama, E.F. (1965), 'The behaviour of stock market prices', *Journal of Business*, **38** (1), 34–105.

Rajan, U., A. Seru and V. Vig (2008), 'The failure of models that predict failure: distance, incentives and defaults', Chicago GSB Research Paper No. 08-19.

Robinson, J. (1962), *Essays in the Theory of Economic Growth*, London, MacMillan.

Samuelson, P.A. (1965), 'Proof that properly anticipated prices fluctuate randomly', *Industrial Management Review*, **6** (2), 41–49.

Shleifer, A. (2000), *Inefficient Markets: An Introduction to Behavioral Finance*, New York: Oxford University Press.

PART II

What does history tell us?

6. Does the current global crisis remind us of the Great Depression?

Sunanda Sen

As recently claimed by the present Fed Chairman, Ben Bernanke,[1] the intensity of the current global economic crisis, in terms of its damaging effects over a decade or more, will be far less than that of the Great Depression of the 1930s. Recalling the past, Bernanke reminds us that the Depression of the 1930s lasted for at least 12 long years and caused the unemployment rate to move up to 25 per cent. Also, it caused the GDP to drop by one-third, the banks to crash by about a third and stock markets to collapse by 90 per cent. Bernanke also points to the fact that, unlike today, there was no provision of social safety nets in the 1930s. However, he warned that the Wall Street crisis is the worst the nation has faced since the end of World War II and also urged Congress to take action on a proposed bailout package.

Confirming the fears of a more severe crisis, George Bush, the former President of the USA, came up with a warning that the current crisis could be even more serious than the one that took place in the 1930s.[2]

Of late there have been sharp differences among economists in comparing the current crisis to the days of the Great Depression. Thus, for Barry Eichengreen and Kevin O'Rourke, the world is already on the path to another global depression while for Romer it is still a far cry from the calamities of the Great Depression (Helbling, 2009; Eichengreen and O'Rourke, 2009; Romer, 2009; see also Bernanke, 1983). Economists, dealing with the current crisis, thus recall the severity of the past crisis, which may be comparable to the present one (Eichengreen and O'Rourke, 2009).

However, the above positions do not tell us much, given that the unfolding of the current crisis is not yet over. Its intensity in terms of the severe crash in the financial sector along with the output and job losses over a time span of nearly two years do not convey the message that the crisis is of a less serious nature, despite the slow process of recovery in the financial sector that has just started.

Incidentally, neither Bernanke nor Bush noticed that the Great

Depression also generated a revolutionary turnaround in economic theory, with Keynes offering a theory of underemployment in his 1936 classic *The General Theory* relating to output, employment and prices. We observe, however, a current revival of interest in what Keynes offered as policy proposals, especially in terms of expansionary policies.

History always unfolds more than what current events can offer. This makes it all the more important to compare the state of the Depression in the 1930s with what we are witnessing today. This requires first, a look at the build-up of the respective crises; second, an analysis of the set of policies that were adopted to address the failing systems at the respective points of time, and third, a look at the global spread of the respective crises, with their repercussions, not just on the macroeconomic aggregates but on policy changes at national levels, which include protectionism, exchange controls and the related moves. The following three sections of this paper deal respectively with the aspects mentioned above.

6.1   THE BUILD-UP OF THE CRISIS

Let us first look at the parallels between the two periods, in terms of the factors precipitating the crises. The crisis during the 1930s was preceded by uneven economic power among the major industrial nations; with disparate output growth rates and major imbalances in international trade and payments. Of these, the USA was the major industrial country, contributing respectively 42 per cent and 33 per cent of world output in the years 1928 and 1933. The USA was also the major provider of international loans and the chief source of import demand, especially for Europe. The country received large inflows of gold out of the trade surpluses earned during the (pre-WWI) years of the gold standard, and absorbed those flows within the country, without having much of an impact on domestic prices. At the other pole was Germany, subject to heavy reparations at the end of World War I, at a value that was 1.5 times its national income. Germany was also a major borrower from overseas, absorbing 50 per cent of all international loans while its economy was going through hyperinflation. Of the remaining industrial countries, the Allied Powers (which included Britain and France) were supposed to pay War Debt to the USA at the end of World War I; while the defeated nation, Germany, was subjected to reparation payments to the Allied Powers. To provide a solution to the imbroglio that arose due to Germany's inability to meet the reparations, the USA was providing loans to Germany (in terms of the Dawes Plan of 1924), thus aiming to avoid a disruption of the German reparations to the Allied Powers (which was needed to continue the repayments of the War Debt to the USA). In another move the USA launched a new scheme in 1929 with the launching of the Young Plan, providing loans to Germany. However, this plan failed with the October 1929 crash in the stock markets of Wall Street, which left the cross-border capital flows at a standstill.

As at present, during the 1930s, flows of finance were hardly contributing to growth in the real economy. These were effectively recycled, between the USA (with its currency afloat at an overvalued rate of exchange), the Allied Powers (the victorious countries) and Germany (the defeated nation), to make it possible that war-related claims on each other could be settled. None of those, in effect, were to be channelled to create productive assets that would contribute to growth.

Comparing recent events, the USA similarly ranks first among countries today in terms of GDP. It also happens to be a major importer. However, the USA now is a major borrower instead of being the chief lender as in the 1930s. In fact, the USA today remains the major international borrower while a new set of countries, in the developing area (China, and to some extent India) along with Germany and Japan are the major international lenders. All these countries, and especially China, have invested heavily in the past in the dollar-denominated US Treasury Bonds, given that the dollar is still rated as the most reliable store of value. China's growth rate, along with those for other emerging countries in Asia, continued to be high till 2008 when the crisis broke out, providing, between them, a large export market as well as sources of imports for countries in the rest of world. Current account surpluses and the official reserves held by these countries were effectively meeting the current account and fiscal deficits of the USA. Simultaneously, current account deficits of some advanced countries have also been huge, exceeding 6 per cent of GDP in the USA and 3 per cent in the UK in recent years. At the other extreme, current account surpluses of other advanced countries (primarily Germany and Japan), respectively exceeded 5 per cent and 3 per cent of GDP. While for China, the current account surplus in recent years has been over 7 per cent of its GDP. Thus, flows of external finance from China, Germany and Japan among others (like high reserve countries as India) have of late been flowing to the major international borrowers, the USA and the UK.

As in the 1930s, the current years have also witnessed the channelling of the flow of finance for unproductive pursuits. The use of those flows to meet loan charges during the 1930s has its parallel today in the pattern of their use, especially in the USA, to meet varieties of debt-financed consumer spending including those in the housing market, and also to finance speculation in stock markets. These provided conduits for uncertainty with speculation rife, along channels, both in stock market transactions as well as in the property market, where the debt-financed asset-backed securities (ABS) and credit default swaps (CDS) came up as major vehicles of leverages. Payment imbalances and capital flows sustained the high dollar rate, often in the interest of high finance in the global economy with stakes in dollar assets. It also reflects the dominance of finance in the world economy. The delicate balance of continuing cash flows between the surplus nations and those with deficits did not provide a lasting solution, especially with the flow of finance moving along unproductive and speculative circuits in the capital importing countries. One witnesses similar payment imbalances, with the financing of the US trade and fiscal deficit through the current account surpluses and reserve accumulations in China and other developing nations like Germany and Japan. As in the 1930s, these flows turned out to be insignificant in terms of their contribution to growth in the debtor country or in the world economy.

As for the capital importing countries, especially for the so-called emerging economies in the developing regions, these were receiving inflows of short-term finance from foreign institutional investors (FIIs). These funds were all directed to secondary stock markets where those were invested for quick returns. It should be pointed out that as in the earlier crisis of the 1930s, the current flows of finance have proved most useful to the dominant interests of finance in the global economy and least beneficial for the real economy. Current account imbalances among the major industrialized nations, preceding and/or during the crises, eventually proved unsustainable for both periods, however different the circumstances had been in the respective periods.

Thus, as in the earlier years of the 1930s, the current flows of finance have proved useful mostly to the dominant interests of finance in the global economy. There certainly exist strong parallels between the two periods in terms of aspects like major payments imbalances across nations and the dominance of finance over policies that contributed to the build-up of the latter. This confirms our argument that there exist strong parallels between the two periods in factors like major payments imbalances across nations and the dominance of finance over policies contributed to their build-up.

6.2   POLICIES IN RETROSPECT

We shall now draw attention to policies that proved wrong and eventually fatal in abetting the crisis in these two periods. For Britain and the USA in the 1930s, one can trace policies that actually had an active role in causing the Great Depression. These included the launching of an overvalued exchange rate for the British pound sterling and the implementation of a deflationary policy. The British pound was revalued in 1925 at the pre-war gold parity, with gold backing as in gold standard days. This move was matched by high discount rates along with a deflationary policy, with interest rates pitched high in a bid to attract capital from overseas. A reincarnation, as above, of the gold standard in Britain could continue only as long as inflows of capital to the country were coming. By 1931 the flow, already affected by the stock market crisis, had already dried up and Britain was off the gold standard for the second time. The package of policies (with a combination of an overvalued currency and deflationary policies) that followed, to revoke the gold standard, was ostensibly pro-finance, offering positive benefits to those holding financial assets that included the British pound. Moreover, such policies were clearly averse to the interests of the real sector, which included industrial capital and labour in the domestic economy.

In the USA during the 1930s, the stock market continued to boom till the onset of the crisis in 1929, and was largely fuelled by speculation and capital inflows. Regional banks in the country helped credit expansion with 'perverse flexibility', charging low rates during boom years and vice versa during slumps. Also, the Fed was continuing with a high interest rate policy, and, as held by Bernanke and endorsed by no less than the Chicago economist Milton Friedman, was responsible for the credit squeeze that resulted in the crisis during the 1930s![3] The credit boom in financial markets was also aggravated with holding companies operating on 'margins', which required little cash. However, the boom, largely fuelled by credit flows to stock markets, came to an end in 1929 and the market crashed along with the unfulfilled expectations of speculators. To arrest the free fall in the stock market the Federal Reserve Board of the USA raised interest rates, which, as can be expected, failed to have the desired effect. The chaos in the stock market also seriously disrupted the cross-border flows of capital. Following Britain's move to end the gold standard in 1931, the USA broke the links between the dollar and gold in 1933 and with that the exchange rates of nearly all the major currencies started floating. Attempts to achieve exchange rate coordination in the World Economic Conference of 1933 were also abandoned.

In a bid to revive the USA's ailing economy, President Roosevelt introduced the New Deal (1934–39). As has recently been held by Christina Romer, the current Chair of the US President's Economic Advisory Council, the New Deal helped to prevent the financial crisis for at least over the following seven decades or more.[4] Apart from providing subsidies to the ailing farm sector, reforms initiated by the New Deal were also responsible for the introduction of the Glass-Steagall Act, which prevented banks from speculation by investing in the security market. A number of regulatory devices were also introduced, including the setting up of the Federal Deposit Insurance Corporation (FDIC), the Securities and Exchange Commission (SEC) and a few others. However, the short-lived revival that took place in the US economy under the Roosevelt administration ended in 1937 when the economy collapsed again, largely due to the reimposition of fiscal austerity, with the expectation that those regulatory devices could be dispensed with.

Germany, which was the biggest debtor during the years preceding the Great Depression, was subject to hyperinflation by the mid-1920s. However, by imposing severe deflationary policies the country exper-ienced, by the 1930s, a drop in prices, output, employment and debt-deflation. This finally led Germany to default on reparations in 1932, which in turn was reacted to by the Allied Powers when they failed to pay the War Debt to the USA in 1934.

Comparing the events as above to the current global economic crisis, we notice, as with the causal factors discussed above, an underlying similarity in terms of the policies followed. Discarding the Keynesian policies that were in use in Europe and in Britain over the first two decades following World War II, policy-makers by the mid-1970s chose to go by neoliberal precepts of tight money policies and overvalued exchange rates, mainly to avoid the inflationary potential that harms finance. Thus, the Federal Reserve in the USA had pitched a high interest rate of 4 per cent to 5 per cent over the five years that preceded the crisis in 2008–09. Tight money policy was similarly followed in countries including Britain and the rest of Europe, in spite of the low or stagnating growth rates of output and employment. One notices tendencies to maintain the status quo, say with an overvalued dollar rate by the USA, which was contrary to any adjust-ment related to the country's current account deficits. Attempts at coord-ination were already ruled out by major industrial nations, with resistance rooted in national economic concerns. Those included the refusal by Germany as well as China to revalue their currencies against the US dollar, which thus was pitted against the USA's bid to continue with the prevailing dollar rate. In Europe, fiscal deficits had to be kept within the limits prescribed under the Maastricht Treaty.

Before the crisis, during the 1990s and later, the low output and employ-ment growth in these economies was hardly an issue in framing policies that continued to follow the course dictated by conservative macro-economic policies. A shock was felt after the fall of 2008, which, with a regime change in the USA, contributed to a temporary move in the direction of a Keynesian stimulus. A similar course of action is observ-able in other parts of the world, with fiscal stimuli, cuts in interest rates and especially with bailouts for major financial institutions. While these changes are still too early or inadequate in dealing with the magnitude of financial losses and real sector contractions, one can observe a pattern of corrective actions, which is distancing itself from the failed policies of the past. However, the stress on financial rescue packages and bailouts has not been matched by an equal emphasis on growth and employment in the real economy.

6.3   REPERCUSSIONS

The repercussions of the Great Depression included a sharp fall in world trade and international capital flows, and a stock market crash on 29 October, 1929 which led to a loss of nearly 40 billion dollars by shareholders. The banking system was ruptured with the emergence of investment and commercial banks, which led to the ascension of big industrial giants like Goldman-Sachs and Morgan-Stanley. Output in industrial countries fell by 9 per cent during 1927–33 and unemployment reached 25 per cent.[5] This was matched by significant declines in primary commodity prices, which hit developing countries like India and other colonies that faced the brunt of the Depression. Moreover, migration across nations also fell drastically in the process. The Great Depression of the 1930s also witnessed a revival of economic nationalism, neo-mercantilism and protectionism, which was matched by a rise in fascism in Germany (1934) and Italy (1936). All of the above meant a considerable loss in labour status in those economies.

On the economic front there were exchange control and payments clearing agreements in Germany during the 1930s; trade restrictions in the USA, with tariff barriers imposed in terms of the Smoot-Hawley Tariff Act (1930); and with the Ottawa Agreement (1932) with preferential tariffs across the Commonwealth nations, which were initiated by Britain. As economic nationalism was dominating policies of most industrialized nations, retaliations were not unusual.

Attempts to stall these moves started in 1933, especially by trying out an exchange rate coordination among nations. However, the attempt was soon abandoned due to lack of consensus. Similarly, Keynes's advocacy of debt cancellation at the end of World War I and later, at the end of World War II, his proposals for a clearing union and the instituting of bancor as the international currency both failed to get acceptance by the USA and other nations (Carabelli and Cedrini, 2009). The pace of trade and exchange restrictions continued along with the fluctuating exchange rates of the industrialized countries during the inter-war years. In the meantime, the major industrialized nations were embroiled in another

World War, which can be viewed as the political culmination of the unrest and disruptions in the economic front that were unleashed by the Great Depression. Discord among nations was pushed aside as the Allied Powers got together in 1944 to agree on the Charter of the Bretton Woods Agreement, which finally ended up in the setting up of the International Monetary Fund in 1945.

When we compare the current panorama, the immediate impact of the crisis has similarly signalled an end to the financial boom, which by the end of 2007 resulted in a collapse of the subprime loan market in the USA. With conceited norms for banking in the USA and the official low rate of inflation, official policy remained rather oblivious to the ongoing business cycle and excess liquidity in the economy that was chasing real assets. Losses for banks spilled over to the rest of the financial business in all advanced countries by October 2008. In the USA a large number of invest-ment banks and other financial institutions (including the mega insurance company AIG) felt the heat and were nearly at the point of collapse after the bankruptcy of the Lehman Brothers. Monetary and fiscal measures adopted in the post-crisis years to bail out and to instil liquidity into the system via banks have not so far worked as was expected.

The impact of the crisis has been pervasive, especially as one consid-ers the contractions in the real economy, with severe drops in output and employment all over the world. Thus, the GDP of the advanced nations have recorded a negative growth rate, while those for the fast-growing developing countries have also fallen drastically, both with domestic contraction and a drop in export demand from abroad.

However, as pointed out by some, the current crisis has features that are different from those during the 1930s (Folsom, 2008). While both have been precipitated by governments' mishandling these respective situations, in recent years it included the lowering of the interest rate, which, however, led to a reduction of the mortgage rate, from 8 per cent in 2002 to a range of 4 per cent to 6 per cent in 2006. As it is now clear today, the latter was a main factor behind the subprime crisis. The pattern, as held, was different during the 1930s when the interest rate was raised, despite a recession-ary situation. Other aspects that seem dissimilar between the two crises included tax hikes during the 1930s, with rates on big business pushed up from 24 per cent to 63 per cent during 1932 and the top income tax rate pitched at 79 per cent in 1935. This contrasts with the current panorama under the Obama administration, with the highest marginal tax rate at 35 per cent. Finally, no plans of bailing out banks were in vogue during the 1930s, despite the failure of the Bank of the USA (a major bank), in 1930. This contrasts with the massive financial packages to bail out the crumbling financial institutions that have been observed in recent times.

However, views on the comparability of the two crises do not end in unanimity. In terms of the alternative view, the current crisis is not only comparable but also has been subject to aspects that were more severe, relative to what happened in the past (Petrov, 2008). These aspects include the 'asset bubble' (which includes the stock and real estate bubbles), the domino effect of the securitization drive, excessive leverages and the lack of transparency in financial markets. According to the author, all of those indicators have been more severe in the current crisis compared with what it had been during the 1920s and 1930s. Thus, for example, while the S&P Case-Shiller index for housing prices hovered between 65 to 75 during the earlier crisis, it had shot up to 200 or more by mid-2007. Similarly, credit in the financial system today has been an astonishing 350 per cent of GDP in 2008 (and rising from 130 per cent in 1982). During the earlier crisis, it peaked at 250 per cent. Finally, it has also been pointed out that compared with the past crisis, the current one is more pervasive, and has already reached almost the entire world.

A direct response of the output and job losses that have followed the financial crisis has been the emergence of protectionism in the advanced countries. This had to happen in disguise, largely to cater to the formal compliance to the WTO regime. This includes the moves initiated in the USA to 'buy American', the scratching of H-1B visas for professionals, especially from India, and an end to tax breaks for US companies that out-source jobs. Clearly the WTO has been totally ineffective and even silent in terms of resisting these protectionist moves.

As a consequence of the crisis, most countries including the developing ones, are facing a sharp drop in exports, output and employment today. While many (including the advanced countries) are trying out a Keynesian mode with a fiscal-monetary expansionary path for the real economy, there has been no effective curb on speculation in any part of the world, including the widespread use of financial derivatives, hedge funds or flows of speculative short-term capital flows, and despite the most recent move by President Obama in the USA to introduce a bill against speculation by banks. Of late there is even a proposal to end the so-called expansionary fiscal moves and the stimulus packages, on the grounds that the recovery has started!

6.4 CONCLUSION

To conclude, despite the differences in terms of the relative dimensions of the two crises, one can detect strong parallels between what happened during the Great Depression of the 1930s and what the world is going through today. While the build-up of the crisis shared a similar pattern, both with payments imbalances and capital flows directed to channels, which in turn failed to contribute to real growth in the capital import-ing debtor nations, official policies that precipitated the crisis were also similar. These included Britain's move to reincarnate the pre-war gold standard in 1925 with the overvalued gold parity for the pound sterling and a tight monetary policy, both to attract funds from abroad; none of which finally worked. In the USA, free use was made of funds to stimulate the country's stock market transactions with a boom that finally came to an end in October 1929. In recent years Alan Greenspan's strategy of low interest rate fuelled credit expansion that continued with an overval-ued dollar in the years preceding the financial crash in 2008, all of which worked as factors in precipitating the collapse. Notwithstanding the acceptance of Keynesianism in post-war Europe, policy-makers swung back to pre-Keynesian neoliberal ideas of monetarist variety by the mid-1970s. The unprecedented boom in stock markets, leveraged finance supporting the securitized assets, and the continuing flows of capital to finance the trade and fiscal deficits of the USA gave way to unfulfilled expectations in the market leading to a collapse. Moreover, as for reac-tions, the protectionist wave has re-emerged in Europe and the USA, with economic nationalism ruling over notions of multilateralism and free trade. Racial discrimination, which led to fascist upheavals during the 1930s, remain very much camouflaged today, clothed in the language of economic nationalism. As for the magnitude of the loss in terms of output and employment, the current scene certainly overtakes the 1930s in terms of absolute magnitude. One can only hope that the duration of the slump will not be as long as what happened earlier during the 1930s and also that the world will witness the revival of progressive new ideas, as happened with the Keynesian revolution during those years!

NOTES

1. 'Bernanke says crisis "no comparison" to Great Depression', 1 December 2008, available at: http://www.breitbart.com/article.php?id=081201213246.v50zx9ik&show_article=1; accessed 6 September 2010.
2. 'Bush on financial crisis: It's a good thing I'm in charge', www.huffingtonpost.com, 11 October 2008, available at: http://www.huffingtonpost.com/2008/10/11/bush-on-financial-crisis_n_133842.html; accessed 6 September 2010.
3. 'Bernanke: Federal Reserve caused Great Depression. Fed chief says, "We did it. . . . very sorry, won't do it again"', www.worldnetdaily.com, 19 March 2008, available at: http://www.wnd.com/index.php?fa=PAGE.view&pageId=59405; accessed 6 September 2010.
4. 'Romer compares Great Depression and current crisis', www.wordpress.com, 25

September 2009, available at: http://mostlyeconomics.wordpress.com/2009/09/25/romer-compares-great-depression-and-current-crisis/; accessed 6 September 2010.

5. 'Great Depression 1929 vs current crisis', www.merinews.com, 27 November 2008, available at: http://www.merinews.com/article/great-depression-1929-vs-current-crisis/150846.shtml; accessed 6 September 2010.

REFERENCES

Bernanke, B.S. (1983), 'Nonmonetary effects of the financial crisis in the propagation of the Great Depression', *American Economic Review*, **73** (3), 257–276.

Carabelli, A.M. and M. Cedrini (2009), 'Shrinking policy space, global imbalances and world recession: a revisiting of our troubled times with an eye to Keynes', paper prepared for the conference 'The World Economy in Crisis – The Return of Keynesianism?', 30–31 October, Berlin, Macroeconomic Policy Institute (IMK) at the Hans-Boeckler-Foundation, Research Network Macroeconomics and Macroeconomic Policies (FMM), available at: http://www.boeckler.de/pdf/v_2009_10_30_carabelli_cedrini.pdf; accessed 6 September 2010.

Eichengreen, B. and K.H. O'Rourke (2009), 'A tale of two Depressions', VoxEU.org, 6 April, now available at: http://wallstreetpit.com/3689-the-world-economy-is-tracking-or-doing-worse-than-during-the-great-depression; accessed 6 September 2010.

Folsom, B.W. Jr. (2008), 'Financial crisis—yes; Great Depression—no', Ashbrook Center for Public Affairs, September, available at: http://www.ashbrook.org/publicat/guest/08/folsom/crisis.html; accessed 6 September 2010.

Helbling, T. (2009), 'How similar is the current crisis to the Great Depression?', VoxEU.org, 29 April, available at: http://www.voxeu.org/index.php?q=node/3514; accessed 6 September 2010.

Petrov, K. (2008), 'Current economic crisis worse than the Great Depression', www.marketoracle.co.uk, 2 November, available at: http://www.marketoracle.co.uk/Article7099.html; accessed 6 September 2010.

Romer, C. (2009), 'Lessons from the Great Depression for recovery in 2009', paper presented at the Brookings Institution, Washington, D.C., 9 March, available at: http://www.brookings.edu/~/media/Files/events/2009/0309_lessons/0309_lessons_romer.pdf; accessed 6 September 2010.

7. Innovation, growth, cycles and finance: three (or four or more) stories from the 1930s and their lessons

Catherine P. Winnett and Adrian B. Winnett

> Thus it is difficult to consider Keynes's solution to the investment problem to be satisfactory. The reason for this failure lies in an approach which is basically static to a matter which by its nature is dynamic.
>
> Michal Kalecki (1936)

7.1 INTRODUCTION

This chapter has two themes. First, *vide* the title, we discuss the messy interrelationships among innovation, growth, cycles and finance. Second, historically speaking, we focus on what might be termed the non- or even anti-Keynesian analysis of such issues. Thus, we discuss, in particular F.A. Hayek, Joseph Schumpeter and Michal Kalecki. We also give a nod to the 'Stockholm School' – well, more than a nod – and many others have walk-on parts – notably Nikolai Kondratiev. As the title suggests, the possible array of participants in the debates identified in this chapter is vast, so we are selective but cast our net wider as occasion demands.

Why turn back the clock? There are two reasons. First, although the *policy* prescriptions for the post-2008 recession are manifestly and successfully 'Keynesian', it is not at all obvious that the 'Keynesian model' – whatever that means – as opposed to the policy prescriptions supposedly derived from it, is at all helpful. We note, though, that some continue to dispute the success of the policies pursued, particularly very low central bank rates. This is, not surprisingly, the case with neo-Austrian commentators, for reasons that will become clear later in our discussion. In fact, somewhat contra our later assertion of neglect of non-Keynesian perspectives, there has been something of a revival of interest in Hayek.

Our line of argument in this chapter can be contrasted with Axel

Leijonhufvud's (1968) 'back-to Keynes' argument. Forty years on, in 2008, we economists did not necessarily misunderstand Keynes in Leijonhufvud's sense, but rather found that Keynes's model may well have missed some of the relevant points. This is to put it very roughly for now: the point will be refined in our conclusion. Second, the issues that were debated in the 1930s were of great relevance to the situation from 2008 onwards. Has there been preceding over-investment in new technologies? How is this related directly and indirectly to financial instability? And so on.

At the outset, we emphasize that this chapter is not a historiographical exercise, but makes very selective use of arguments from earlier literature in order to develop an understanding of the present conjuncture, as a Marxist might say. We are aware that we are 'having it both ways'. We are using history to berate some present interpretations of the crisis but playing rather fast-and-loose with history to make these points. So be it.

A couple of preliminary points: except for Kalecki, all of the authors we discuss to some extent derive from a Wicksellian tradition – Schumpeter somewhat marginally so. Kalecki made only slight reference to Knut Wicksell's cumulative process – interestingly immediately before the passage that is quoted at the head of this chapter – though it seems more than implicit elsewhere. Hence also our significant nod towards the Stockholm School. In the 1930s' context the Wicksellian tradition is inescapable – as incisively discussed by Leijonhufvud (1981). For all, money and finance were central. But – and a large 'but' – they differ from Keynes in adhering to the centrality of cycles (or, at least, dynamic disequilibrium) as contrasted with Keynes's central concept of persistent unemployment *equilibrium*. To a greater or a lesser extent, and not unrelated, cycles may have 'real' drivers such as innovation in a difficult-to-disentangle relationship with financial factors.

We emphasize repeatedly that obviously we do not buy into a 'real' versus 'money' dichotomy, but simply make the point that Keynes is neglectful of processes such as technical innovation – though undoubtedly it is present as background music in discussions of investment expectations and so on. But these processes are not central to Keynes's understanding of capitalist dynamics – if indeed his is a truly dynamic story at all: on which more in our later remarks.

Our argument in this chapter has resonance, we trust, for the current situation. The present woes have almost entirely and not unreasonably been blamed on the financial sector. However, there may be 'deeper' (note the quote marks) processes to do with innovation, in particular those associated with information and communications technology (ICT) – with which financial innovation is integrally related. And we should never neglect the ways in which the longer-run dynamics of growth present themselves in shorter-run situations. 'Blaming it on finance' is an easy option (pun perhaps intended) but the world is more complex and many drivers are present.

There is also a contemporaneous theoretical agenda. The so-called Schumpeterian species of endogenous growth models, notably that developed by Philippe Aghion and Peter Howitt (1998), have once again – after a long hiatus in the literature – focused on the interrelationship of growth and cycles. (This issue having been trivialized in modern macro-theory. In fact Aghion and Howitt's model is not strictly one of cyclical growth, but of stepwise growth that needs some modification to generate cycles.) Their analysis is, of course, an outstanding contribution to our recent understanding of economic growth processes, but to what extent is it historically well founded and, more importantly, are there aspects of the earlier literature that have been lost sight of? (In fact Lipsey et al.'s [2005] shamefully neglected contribution is far more historically informed, at least in terms of economic history if not the history of economic thought.) For example, to make a cheap point: Aghion's and Banerjee's (2005) later analysis of growth and financial volatility appears horrendously misguided in the light of recent events, with its assertion that financial innovation has decoupled the real and financial sectors, and thus damped volatility.

Anyway, to the positives: in order to develop its two themes, this chapter has three specific objectives: first, to compare and contrast competing inter-war perspectives on the nature of growth and cycles; next, to provide a critique and evaluation of these, especially in comparison with Keynes; and, last, very briefly, to thus provide an historically informed interpretation of the current situation.

These objectives may seem unduly ambitious, so we again emphasize our modesty: we interpret through a very selective and heavily nuanced reading of the literature. The key argument is that the current recession cannot be seen as a purely financial phenomenon but has 'real' roots, or more precisely, we need to intertwine financial and 'real' factors, more thoroughly. So, to repeat and emphasize, we need to pay rather more attention to the interrelations among innovation growth, cycles and finance than has been apparent in so-called 'Keynesian' (perhaps really Minskyian) commentaries on the 'crisis'. Here our non-Keynesian historical perspective may be of help. To avert criticism, we do not, in any way, reject 'Keynesianism' but wish merely to provide a viewpoint encompassing longer-run 'real' processes. (Contrary to some interpretations, these are present in Keynes, notably in Chapter 17 of *The General Theory* [1936], but the focus there is altogether different.) Again, we need to caution: obviously a key (post-) Keynesianism argument is that money is as omnipresent in the long as in the short run: we do not reject this, but argue that something has gone amiss in the way that this argument against neoclassicism has evolved. As this begins to indicate, in spite of our modesty our conclusions may be a little provocative.

7.2 OUT OF WICKSELL

Needless to say, what is now called macroeconomics was in a deeply unsettled state in the early 1930s. We have already signalled the centrality of Wicksell. Here we give a thumbnail sketch to set the scene. Leaving aside the irrelevance of Pigovian classicism, Keynes and Hayek were locked in a Cambridge–LSE controversy (with a key – but often overlooked – intervention by Sraffa. All this is now comprehensively and carefully documented in vol. IX of Hayek's *Collected Works*, 2009). Gunnar Myrdal, Bertil Ohlin, Erik Lundberg and others were driving forward their own process-analysis and would in due course engage with Keynes. Though Myrdal has had the lion's share of attention, Ohlin and Lundberg are especially interesting for our story; in fact much of what we have to say closely parallels their critiques of *The General Theory*. To cut short a long and complex story, three models emerged from the Wicksellian tradition: to label by cities these were, of course, Vienna, Stockholm and Cambridge. We mostly neglect the last, exemplified by Dennis Robertson (1932) and by Keynes in the *Treatise on Money* (1930).

However, the key developments in the theory of cycles *as such* lay, for the moment, outside these explicitly Wicksellian traditions: Schumpeter and Kalecki, especially the latter. Both were deeply Marx-inflected – obviously in very different ways. In this context we should also mention – more than mention – Nikolai Kondratiev.

Let us explore more closely what exactly was at issue in these debates. In a way this forms the central story of the present paper. Money and the short run *is* important but what about growth and its interrelation with cycles? Again, we emphasize current resonances: is something 'deeper' than financial instability happening? It is clear from recent discussions by Aghion et al. (cited above) that we are far from understanding this. So back to the sources and these forgotten or, at best, half-remembered vigorous even acrimonious debates.

The key determinant in Wicksellian analysis was the 'natural rate' and its relationship with the money rate in generating cumulative movements of the price level. This was most clearly analysed in the remarkable Chapter 9 of *Interest and Prices* (published in German in 1898, and in English translation by Richard Kahn in 1936) and later in the *Lectures on Political*

Economy (available in English in 1935, edited by Lionel Robbins). Much of the subsequent development of the Wicksellian theme is a transposition from price-level to output-employment cumulative processes. This development has been much analysed, but here we wish to direct our gaze in a rather different, although adjacent, direction.

As Myrdal painstakingly showed in *Monetary Equilibrium* (published in Swedish, German and English in 1931, 1933 and 1939 respectively), the natural rate can be defined in several ways, which may well not coincide out of equilibrium. Somewhat cavalierly, we use the terms 'natural rate', 'real rate' and 'profit rate' more or less interchangeably. In Keynesian discourse, the attention has fallen on the money rate, and, specifically on its determinants. In fact, via expectations the real rate is sometimes seen as ephemeral in (post-) Keynesian discourse, a bootstrapping phenomenon. However, the real rate is driven by factors such as innovation, well recognized by Wicksell. There are two blades of the scissors, to use the hackneyed phrase. The capitalist economy *does* have a rate of profit that flows from distributional relationships and responds to technological shifts and the like (*vide* the next section of our paper). As pointed out by John Presley (1978), Robertson was very attuned to this line of argument, perhaps due to his earlier study of industrial fluctuations (1915).

So that is one theme that distinguishes much Wicksellian-inspired analysis from the Keynes of 1936. The other, not unrelated, is that Keynes's analysis was basically static, driven by a concern to show that there could be a monetary *equilibrium* quite unlike those allowable by the classics. (Here we oversimplify wildly: for example, the multiplier is capable of a very 'dynamic', that is a periodized, interpretation as shown by Fritz Machlup in 1939). Both Stockholm and Vienna focused on dynamic process, as emphasized in Ohlin's famous critique of Keynes (1937). There is much fudging here of what constitutes 'dynamics', as, for example, in George Shackle's generally admirable work (1967). It is important to realize that privileging expectations does not make a theory dynamic. Keynes's unemployment equilibrium is conditioned on a *given* state of expectations.

There is also a final and important issue. Wicksell's brilliant, prescient fiction of a pure credit economy reduces financial issues to a very simple parameter: the money rate. It is therefore symptomatic, that so much ink has been spilt on his (correct) Tookean insight that this was the logical endpoint of the evolution of means-of-exchange, and not nearly enough on the reasons for adopting this extraordinary simplifying device, the purpose of which was precisely to focus on the ways in which the 'money' and 'real' sectors dynamically interact, without privileging either. However, this insight was not lost on Stockholm or Vienna.

The Stockholm economists, of course, developed Wicksell's cumulative process into something very elaborate indeed. Lundberg (1937) is especially interesting. (It is worth noting – without getting into the silliness of who discovered the concept of 'effective demand' – how early and independent of Keynes many of these very sophisticated contributions were.) As William Baumol pointed out so perceptively in his obituary of Lundberg (1990), Lundberg's numerical sequences show an appreciation of the difficulty and complexity of modelling the effect of various sorts of shocks on the time paths of prices and outputs. General models may not be available and this is anathema to modern modellers. This is also implicit in the earlier Stockholm work. Our interest is somewhat different, although related. Suppose innovation occurs. This drives the profit rate and expectations of it, and sets in motion a sequential cumulative process, which may – probably will – be cyclical. This may be amplified by the functioning of the financial sector. But the underlying process, irrespective, is of the sort described by Lundberg. This draws together our two preceding points for future reference.

In Vienna, the Bohm-Bawerkian capital theoretic element was omnipresent. Hayek's analysis in *Prices and Production* of 1931 (which, in fact, appeared in English after Hayek's arrival at the LSE – and this was all to do with the Robbins-inspired academic politics of challenging Cambridge dominance in economics) emphasized the ways in which investment in production processes could be over-extended and then suffer from severe contraction as the supporting credit shrank. There are many problems with his analysis, not least with the concept of 'forced-saving', and Hayek – confusingly – appeared to change it in somewhat contradictory ways, as Nicholas Kaldor (1942) pointed out. And the specific reasoning is very dependent on the lags assumed, as identified by John Hicks (1967), and can be interpreted rather more plausibly if these are realigned. All of this aside, the analysis contains some very basic insights, which can be freed from the specifics of Hayek's period-of-production triangles (Kaldor, 1939). Indeed Meghnad Desai (1991) has presented an interesting interpretation of Kaldor-on-Hayek, which emphasizes the importance of viewing capital in a more disaggregated way than became standard in mainstream macroeconomics but again, perhaps ironically, became the focus of attention in the so-called Cambridge capital controversies of the 1960s.

Hayek's central insight is that if the real rate rises above the money rate, over-investment in processes is inevitable. (We note that this conclusion was disputed by Kaldor.) Robbins used a somewhat simplistic version of this to ground his analysis in the *Great Depression* (1934). But although it has become common to identify the origins of the problem as monetary mismanagement, the driving factor may – probably will – be changes in the real rate, and the problem occurs due to lags in the financial sector. This is another key point that we hold for future reference. The Austrians were early on categorized as providing a 'monetary' theory of the cycle, and this has perhaps distorted understanding of the central issue.

Let us pull all this together. There are three key post-Wicksellian lessons. First, the 'real' or (perhaps better in this context) 'profit' rate is important. This sounds trivial, but it is not, for two reasons. The tendency has been, in much discussion, to say that the problem is that the money rate moves inappropriately, which is then magnified into 'the monetary sector is the problem'. And (post-) Keynesians too often seem to say that the profit rate is an entirely expectational construct. Obviously, projections of it are expectational, but to deny the reality (in both senses) of a profit rate in a capitalist economy is surely nonsensical: income gets distributed. There is a baby and bathwater here. (Whether or not in the very long run, the profit rate converges to a rule-the-roost money interest rate as in the Keynes [Sraffian] Chapter 17 of *The General Theory* is another issue, not pursued for now.) Second, is the importance of dynamic sequences. The lack of these was the main Stockholm gripe about Keynes, notably made by Ohlin in terms of the ex ante/ex post distinction. It is surely as relevant as ever, especially in understanding the ways in which growth and cycles are intertwined. It is no doubt important to understand unemployment as a possible equilibrium state contra the classics, but does this help in addressing the *dynamics* of the capitalist economy? Third, over- or mis-deployment of investment is important for all sorts of reasons. Investment expenditure is not simply a driver of effective demand: early on Harrod (1936, 1939) grasped its two-edged nature, but there has been a tendency to conveniently separate effective demand and growth between the short and long run. All of this we return to.

7.3   CAPITALIST DYNAMICS

All of the arguments we have so far looked at bear in various ways on the problem of the 'cycle'. We now centre our attention explicitly on this. There was a very wide range of theories of the trade cycle during the inter-war years, many of which are now mostly forgotten. (Comprehensive contemporary surveys were provided by Howard Ellis [1934] of the German-language literature and, of course, by Gottfried Haberler – first published in 1937 but later much expanded. The massive bibliography in the celebrated American Economic Association *Readings in Business Cycle Theory* [1950] – coordinated by Haberler – evidences the inter-war research in this area.)

However, the most thoroughgoing trade cycle analysis of the inter-war years was undoubtedly that of Schumpeter (1939); in fact the essential conceptual vision appeared in German before World War I in *The Theory of Economic Development* (1934). The central feature is that growth is *itself* a cyclical process, driven by the very nature of capitalist development as a dynamic process, and especially by the ways in which innovation takes place. Innovation is not a one-shot affair but a diffusive process. And innovations are not necessarily complementary with existing set-ups, but can be destructive of them: hence 'creative' destruction. Thus, Schumpeter's approach does not sit easily with the continuous incrementalism of the sort of 'augmenting' – the term is indicative – technical progress modelled in most Solowian growth theory. Its discreteness and cyclicality requires a different sort of modelling, which has only recently been attempted in mainstream economics. (But the pioneering and immensely important work of Richard Goodwin [1982] should not be forgotten, although indebted to Schumpeter, innovation is not central to his models. Some of his later versions focus heavily on distributional issues, relevant no doubt to some of what follows shortly in our discussion – but not pursued here.)

It also places it at odds with Paul Samuelson's (1939) influential multiplier-accelerator model, which dominated cycle theory for many years. As is well-known, the parameters of these models can either configure cyclical paths or smooth growth paths, but not both. Thus, as Hicks (1950, but see especially the 'Preface' to the Third Impression, 1956) for example, perhaps inadvertently, discovered it is very difficult to construct a consistent model with both growth and cycles using this approach. Harrod was more cavalier but perhaps more prescient. (The development of his thinking from cycles to growth over three years is particularly interesting.) This has always posed something of a dilemma: Schumpeter's *insight* has been lauded, but has apparently – at least until recently – lacked analytical tractability.

As is now recognized, the Schumpeterian approach, sits most naturally with large-scale innovations, often now termed (as, for example, by Lipsey et al. 2005 who pioneered much of this) innovations in 'general purpose technologies' (GPTs), which have widespread systemic properties. The leading current instance is obviously that of ICT. This is very much in the spirit of Kondratiev's long waves, although he is scarcely mentioned by Schumpeter. (The publishing history of Kondratiev's work is unusually tortuous; a version of his Russian work of the 1920s appeared in German soon after, but a somewhat misleading, partial English version only in 1935. Properly edited, complete versions [see Kondratiev, 1998] have only recently been made available.) Here it is important to caution against the accusation sometimes made against Schumpeter and Kondratiev (and before them Marx) that they are overly technologically deterministic in contrast to, say, Keynes, who emphasizes the centrality of human action and the often irrational springs of that action. There is plenty of scope for social action in all of these accounts of the dynamics of capitalist growth-cycles.

In terms of conciseness and mathematically precise modelling, Kalecki seems to be at the opposite pole from Schumpeter. Indeed, at the time, Kalecki was unusual in the explicitness and sophistication of his mathematical modelling of such processes, along with Frisch and his associates (Kalecki, 1933, 1935; Frisch and Holme, 1935). So we now, hopefully instructively, compare and contrast. Kalecki's approach is certainly different from Schumpeter's more historically grounded discussion, and was duly criticized by Schumpeter. Interestingly, Lundberg saw a strong affinity between Kalecki's and his own approach, but pointed out that Kalecki modelled partly in continuous rather than discrete periodic time – which Lundberg felt lost some ability to grasp certain crucial dynamic insights in terms of the sequencing of decisions. Kalecki's model went through various permutations, and the earlier publishing history is somewhat tortuous. (This has been carefully analysed, along with the intellectual influences on Kalecki, by the editor of vol. I of the *Collected Works* [Osiatynsk:, 1990]. Basically it was accessible to Western European audiences from 1933 onwards.)

On the surface, Kalecki's model is quite mechanistic and was indeed criticized (especially by Frisch) for picking parameter values to generate cycles of constant amplitude and periodicity. However, it has certain interesting features of wider import. The focus is on the determinants of fixed investment through the interplay of profitability and the size of the capital stock, but investment is carefully described as a time-phased process from orders though production and on to deliveries. Thus, as with all the authors we have discussed, time is of the essence – generally conceptualized as a wave-like process. There is an endogenous movement of the profit rate that generates cycles, which can be contrasted with Hayek's reliance on exogenous shifts in the money interest rate (Hayek, 1939) – although it could be argued that this is only exogenous if we fail to integrate the actions of financial institutions, especially public institutions, into the analysis of cycles – a point not without relevance to the situation centred on 2008.

More interesting still is the Marxian emphasis in Kalecki – filtered through M.I. Tugan-Baronovsky and Rosa Luxemburg – on the way in which capitalists' expenditures, whether on consumption or investment, generate profits. The same conclusion was famously arrived at via a very different route by Keynes in the *Treatise*: the well-known 'widow's cruse'.

What the routes *do* have in common is a two-sector capital and consumption goods industry model – a point referred to later in another context. So there *is* an historically informed social context in Kalecki, to be noted in relation to Schumpeter. In contrast to virtually all other writers on cycles, this gives it a very distinctive flavour, and probably helps account for the muted reception across the 'Western' profession. Thus, Kalecki's model, which superficially looks highly formal, is embedded in a vision of capitalism as a class system.

So whereas Schumpeter highlights the innovative dynamism of capitalism, Kalecki highlights the interaction between profits and accumulation within the capitalist class. Broadening out the latter into the relationship between capital accumulation and class, these are surely complementary perspectives. (We refer, again, to that maverick among Cambridge mavericks, Richard Goodwin [see Goodwin, 1982]. His growth-cycle models went though various permutations but the best known is perhaps the wage-profit version, which clearly fits into this Marxian mould.)

There is another point of comparison, and contrast, that pinpoints similar issues. Neither Schumpeter nor Kalecki had any truck with competitive assumptions, but identified monopoly as central to capitalism. Again, though, the contrast is present. Schumpeter, correctly saw that – as we would now say – the new information embodied in innovation was intrinsically not profitably marketable without some element of monopoly to secure the returns. Monopoly offers dynamic gains not the static allocative efficiencies of the competitive model. But the somewhat infamous 'degree of monopoly' distribution theory of Kalecki (1938) focuses instead on the monopoly profit-distributional issue in capitalist economies. Whatever the possibly questionable specifics of Kalecki's distributional model, Schumpeter and Kalecki are, once more, surely complementary perspectives. Capitalism is *both* dynamic and exploitative; and monopoly figures in both aspects in a complex interrelationship.

7.4   MONEY AND ALL THAT

As pointed out, in the Stockholm and Vienna models money and finance are central but are minimally elaborated in their modelling of cycles, at least. It is all subsumed into the money rate, with an occasional nod to constraints on the money supply, which may force movements in the money rate as expansion proceeds. This is in sharp contrast to the centrality of the complexities of money and finance in the Cambridge approach to cycles from Marshall onwards. In this, what we now call portfolio decisions are central. Keynes was firmly in this tradition, of course. But he radically changed the question to one of the nature of monetary equilibrium in 1936. Thus, in effect, the grounds of the question were shifted in ways inimical to a discussion of the roles and interrelations of monetary and real factors in cyclical instability. Indeed, the relative thinness of Keynes's notes on business cycles in *The General Theory* is symptomatic. As Bruce Caldwell, Hayek's recent editor, has argued (Hayek, 2009), Hayek was moving away from attempts to model monetary equilibrium towards a dynamic model of adjustments of capital structure in the progression from *Monetary Theory and the Trade Cycle* (which appeared in German in 1929, but in English translation only in 1933) to *Prices and Production* (1931). Keynes was moving in the other direction, away from emphasizing the two-sector model of capital and consumption goods industries in the *Treatise* (1930) towards a less dynamic, aggregate expenditure model in *The General Theory* (1936).

This is of basic significance for our argument in two respects. First, there has been a tendency to polarize discussion between 'money is a veil' and 'money drives all'. This is jejune and reflects the (post-?) Keynesian characterization of the question. Keynes argues that there could be unemployment equilibria in a competitive economy if money was essential (in the correct sense), and the classics had not understood its essentialness. That was a fundamental insight. But it is still possible to say that capitalist economies exhibit all sorts of inherent (the word is important) instability even if the role of money and finance is somehow off-stage but nonetheless crucial. We believe that this was the central insight provided by the authors on which we have focused. This whole agenda has drifted from view in Keynesian discourse, both theoretically and practically. As Frank Hahn once said 'money, in economic theory, brings out the worst in us': to say that money is 'essential' is not the same as saying that '*only* money is essential'.

To repeat and amplify, Keynes was engaged in a critical encounter with (neo)classical equilibrium – Say's Law and all that – but this was *not* an engagement with the dynamics of capitalist growth and cycles. Both perspectives are no doubt necessary, but neither should be necessarily privileged and the latter might even deliver more lessons for theory and practice in some instances. Delving a little further back into history, two points relevant to our discussion can briefly be made, both relating to Keynes's critique of Say's Law. First, situated in the context of a consideration of broader issues of economic development, 'supply creates its own demand' may be construed as a progressive insight in the classical vision of economic growth and not simply as a denial of the possibility of effective demand failures. This was superbly elucidated by Baumol (1977). Second, Keynes, of course, contentiously identified Malthus as his precursor in opposition to Ricardo. But Keynes does not mention Ricardo 'On Machinery' (1817), an analysis that explicitly relates investment in new technology to the possibility of unemployment within a context of ongoing growth – as pointed out, for example, by Hicks (1969).

Hence our wish to revisit the 1930s. There is now recognition of at least some of this via Aghion and Howitt (1998) especially, but it is very selective and loses much: whither the Stockholm and Vienna people, not to mention Kalecki. There now follows a little bit of provocation against Leijonhufvud. We might say that the 'bastardization' of Keynes is incredibly useful for policy, but – to overstate – the 'true' theory à la Leijonhufvud may be something of a detour, at least in its objectives. The authors we have looked at may possibly be more informative in *some* crucial respects.

Now we briefly revisit our chosen authors' views on money and finance. We have commented already on Stockholm and Vienna. Respectively, for one the money rate's discrepancy with the real rate drives cumulative processes and, for the other, 'distorts' investment. Though the former is more coherent in a formal sense, the latter is possibly more relevant, but we need to hold on to the process perspective, which is immensely valuable. Once again, the comparison of Schumpeter and Kalecki is instructive. Schumpeter regarded the operation of finance as interwoven with 'real' decisions on investment in innovation and so on, not some *deus ex machina* that seems often implicit in the Cambridge authors. This perhaps reflects the quasi-Marxian way in which the economy is conceptualized as what is now sometimes called a techno-social system in (some of) the 'continental' as contrasted with the Cambridge authors. There are big questions here to do with understanding apparently dysfunctional economic outcomes as products of individual irrationality as opposed to the workings of social institutions within which individuals are embedded. And, not unrelated, is the 'Cambridge' notion of policy-makers as disinterested manipulators of outcomes through fiscal and monetary interventions, as against that of them as embedded social actors – a vision shared, albeit in very different ways, by 'Austrians' and Marxists.

7.5 BACK TO THE FUTURE

Given its brevity, this chapter has attempted to cover much ground and open many agendas. So we now attempt to summarize the key points and draw conclusions – and suggest possible contemporary relevance.

First, dynamics matter: hence the Stockholm School. Second, capital (mis)investment matters: hence Vienna. Third, money and finance are self-evidently crucial but we should not neglect the underlying drivers of profitability: hence Kalecki. Last, growth is innovation-driven, monopolistic and intrinsically unstable: hence Schumpeter. These are the inputs into our argument. The Keynesian map, however read, is a pretty poor guide to most of this: it takes us to other important places, but not these destinations.

What does this tell us about the situation centred on 2008? The proximate cause of the 2008 crisis was obviously within the financial sector. So this has reinforced the argument that 'sorting out finance' is the issue: as we said earlier, a very Minskyian perspective and none the worse for that. Our longer view looks different. But – and, again, a large 'but' – we should not forget that preceding the current financial boom and crash was the investment boom in ICT, epitomized by the so-called 'dot-com' bubble. A point often forgotten is that what has remained is the upturn in growth rates that came from massive ICT investment. And the 'dot-com' boom underpinned this, providing cheap finance for ICT investment, both tangible infrastructure and intangible know-how. As Nicholas Crafts (2004, and elsewhere) perceptively pointed out, comparing the 19th-century railway boom with the ICT boom: financial bubbles look like bad news, but the infrastructure remains – a sort of positive gloss on the Austrian story. This is the classic Schumpeterian pattern. And, of course, it was associated with major distributional issues, of which 'bankers' bonuses' are a relatively small but exemplary part, the more important part being the overall distributional share of the financial sector. Hence the salience of both Schumpeter on innovation and of Kalecki on distribution: they are, as emphasized, complementary.

There is, though, a very specific linkage through the 2000s. To avert a recessionary feed-through into the real economy with the bursting of the 'dot-com' bubble, credit was eased in the USA and it can be reasonably argued that this fed (pun perhaps again intended) into the current boom-bust cycle. In broad outline, as Galbraith's classic account (1955) shows, this is not dissimilar to the sequencing of events in the 1920s, especially in the USA: for 'computer chips', read 'Model T' and for 'dot-com', 'suburban real estate'. Galbraith also tellingly emphasizes the unbalanced income distribution that developed in the 1920s.

Finally, in summary and conclusion we give some rapid generalizations and broad conjectures. There has been much talk as of 2010 of a 'double dip' but we suggest that it may have happened already – perhaps unnoticed *as such* – if we take a longer historical perspective. (Which is not to say that there may not be a triple or quadruple (. . .) dip.) The argument runs like this. The present recession is the aftermath of major innovation and investment in ICT that boosted growth, with an assimilative lag (the so-called 'Solow paradox'), especially globally, and thence led to inflated high profit-growth expectations within the financial sector supported by credit expansion.

All of this comes as no surprise to us from looking at the 1930s' literature. Kalecki and Schumpeter provide the systematic frame of capitalist innovation and distribution, and Lundberg, Hayek et al., the more specific tools from process-driven over-investment to understand the mechanism. So, here we have the trivial but important lesson for 2008 and beyond: a dramatic cycle ultimately driven by a major wave of innovation, amplified by the financial sector. And, additionally, the financial sector itself was more than partly driven in its unfortunate trajectory by its rapid absorption of the new technology that underpinned innovation in complex financial instruments.

There are long views and longer views. The message is that we need to take a long view, say, a decade, on the post-2008 situation, so as to anchor it in the context of a major Kondratievian long-wave of innovation, and to take the still longer view back to the debates of the 1930s to give us the road map through this. In short, our old 1930s' debates can give us the insights, and even the core of the analysis, to begin properly to find our way through the 'present conjuncture'. And we might not be well guided by the map drawn by Keynes.

REFERENCES

Note on referencing: original dates of publication are noted in the main text. We do not provide precise bibliographic references to sources in the body of the text, but all references are cited with full bibliographic details in these end-references. This is to avoid the anachronism of giving dates of publication that are often grossly at variance with those that are historically relevant and are appropriate to this chapter.

Aghion, P. and A. Banerjee (2005), *Volatility and Growth*, Oxford: Oxford University Press.
Aghion, P. and P. Howitt (1998), *Endogenous Growth Theory*, Cambridge, MA: The MIT Press.
American Economic Association (1950), *Readings in Business Cycle Theory*, London: George Allen and Unwin.
Baumol, W.J. (1977), 'Say's (at least) eight laws, or what Say and James Mill may really have meant', *Economica*, **44** (174), 145–161.
Baumol, W.J. (1990), 'Erik Lundberg, 1907–1987', *Scandinavian Journal of Economics*, **92** (1), 1–9.
Crafts, N. (2004), 'The economic impact of ICT: a perspective from the age of steam', Esmee Fairbairn Lecture, Lancaster University.
Desai, M. (1991), 'Kaldor between Hayek and Keynes, or did Nicky kill capital theory?', as reprinted in M. Desai (1995), *Macroeconomics and Monetary*

Theory. The Selected Essays of Meghnad Desai, Vol. I, Aldershot, UK and Brookfield, VT, USA: Edward Elgar, pp. 255–273.

Ellis, H.S. (1934), *German Monetary Theory 1905–1933*, Cambridge, MA: Harvard University Press.

Frisch, R. and H. Holme (1935), 'The characteristic solutions of a mixed difference and differential equation occurring in economic dynamics', *Econometrica*, **3** (2), 225–239.

Galbraith, J.K. (1955), *The Great Crash 1929*, New York: Houghton Mifflin (reissue 1997).

Goodwin, R.M. (1982), *Essays in Economic Dynamics*, London: Macmillan.

Haberler, G. (1937), *Prosperity and Depression*, London: George Allen and Unwin (revised 5th edition 1965).

Harrod, R.F. (1936), *The Trade Cycle*, London: Macmillan.

Harrod, R.F. (1939), 'An essay in dynamic theory', *Economic Journal*, **49** (193), 14–33.

Hayek, F.A (1931), *Prices and Production*, London: Routledge and Kegan Paul.

Hayek, F.A. (1933), *Monetary Theory and the Trade Cycle*, New York: Kelley (reprint 1966).

Hayek, F.A. (1939), *Profits, Interest and Investment*, London: Routledge and Kegan Paul.

Hayek, F.A. (2009), 'Contra Keynes and Cambridge. Essays, correspondence', reprinted in B. Caldwell (ed.), *The Collected Works of F.A. Hayek*, vol. IX, Indianapolis: Liberty Fund.

Hicks, J.R. (1950), *A Contribution to the Theory of the Trade Cycle*, Oxford: Clarendon (Third Impression 1956).

Hicks, J.R. (1967), *Critical Essays in Monetary Theory*, Oxford: Clarendon.

Hicks, J.R. (1969), *A Theory of Economic History*, Oxford: Oxford University Press.

Kaldor, N. (1939), 'Capital intensity and the trade cycle', as reprinted in (1960), *Essays on Economic Stability and Growth*, London: Duckworth, pp. 120–147.

Kaldor, N. (1942), 'Professor Hayek and the Concertina-effect', as reprinted in (1960), *Essays on Economic Stability and Growth*, London: Duckworth, pp. 148–176.

Kalecki, M. (1933), 'Essay on the business cycle theory', as reprinted in J. Osiatynski (ed.) (1990), *Collected Works of Michal Kalecki*, vol. I, *Capitalism: Business Cycles and Full Employment*, Oxford: Clarendon Press, pp. 65–108.

Kalecki, M. (1935), 'A macro-dynamic theory of business cycles', as reprinted in J. Osiatynski (ed.) (1990), *Collected Works of Michal Kalecki*, vol. I, *Capitalism: Business Cycles and Full Employment*, Oxford: Clarendon Press, pp. 120–138.

Kalecki, M. (1936), 'Some remarks on Keynes's theory', as reprinted in J. Osiatynski (ed.) (1990), *Collected Works of Michal Kalecki*, vol. I, *Capitalism: Business Cycles and Full Employment*, Oxford: Clarendon Press, pp. 223–232.

Kalecki, M. (1938), 'The determinants of the distribution of national income', as reprinted in J. Osiatynski (ed.) (1991), *Collected Works of Michal Kalecki*, vol. II, *Capitalism: Economic Dynamics*, Oxford: Clarendon Press, pp. 3–20.

Keynes, J.M. (1930), *A Treatise On Money*, London: Macmillan.

Keynes, J.M. (1936), *The General Theory of Employment, Interest and Money*, London: Macmillan.

Kondratiev, N. (1998), *The Works of Nikolai D. Kondratiev*, vol. I, *Economic Statics, Dynamics and Conjuncture*, ed. by N. Makasheva, W.J. Samuels and V. Barnett, London: Pickering and Chatto.

Leijonhufvud, A. (1968), *On Keynesian Economics and the Economics of Keynes*, Oxford: Oxford University Press.

Leijonhufvud, A. (1981), *Information and Coordination*, Oxford: Oxford University Press.

Lipsey, R.G., K.I. Carlaw and C.T. Bekar (2005), *Economic Transformations. General Purpose Technologies and Long Term Economic Growth*, Oxford: Oxford University Press.

Lundberg, E. (1937), *Studies in the Theory of Economic Expansion*, Oxford: Blackwell (1955 edition).

Machlup, F. (1939), 'Period analysis and multiplier theory', as reprinted in American Economic Association (1950), *Readings in Business Cycle Theory*, London: George Allen and Unwin, pp. 203–234.

Myrdal, G. (1939), *Monetary Equilibrium*, New York: Kelly (reprint 1962).

Ohlin, B. (1937), 'Some notes on the Stockholm Theory of saving and investment', as reprinted in American Economic Association (1950), *Readings in Business Cycle Theory*, London: George Allen and Unwin, pp. 87–130.

Osiatynski, J. (ed.) (1990), *Collected books of Michal Kalecki*, vol. I, *Capitalism: Business Cycles and Full Employment*, Oxford Clarendon Press, pp. 65–108.

Presley, J.R. (1978), *Robertsonian Economics*, London: Macmillan.

Ricardo, D. (1817), *On the Principles of Political Economy and Taxation*, 3rd edition (ed. by P. Sraffa as *The Works and Correspondence of David Ricardo*, vol. I, Cambridge: Cup, 1950.

Robbins, L. (1934), *The Great Depression*, New Brunswick: Transaction (reprint 2009).

Robertson, D.H. (1915), *A Study of Industrial Fluctuation*, London: P.S. King.

Robertson, D.H (1932), *Banking Policy and the Price Level*, London: P.S. King.

Samuelson, P.A. (1939), 'Interactions between the multiplier analysis and the principle of acceleration', as reprinted in American Economic Association (1950), *Readings in Business Cycle Theory*, London: George Allen and Unwin, pp. 261–269.

Shackle, G.L.S. (1967), *Years of High Theory*, Cambridge: Cambridge University Press.

Schumpeter, J. (1934), *The Theory of Economic Development*, Cambridge, MA: Harvard University Press.

Schumpeter, J. (1939), *Business Cycles*, New York: McGraw-Hill.

Wicksell, K. (1935), *Lectures on Political Economy*, vol. II, *Money*, London: Routledge and Kegan Paul.

Wicksell, K. (1936), *Interest and Prices*, New York: Kelly (reprint 1962).

8. Epic Recession and economic theory

Jack Rasmus

In a gathering a few weeks ago in Cambridge, UK, economists and financial practitioners met to begin the attempt to forge a new paradigm for economics. That gathering, the inaugural session of the Institute for New Economic Thinking, held 8–11 April 2010, reflected the view that ideas follow changes in real events – at least economic ideas and qualitative shifts in real events. The real change, of course, is the global financial crisis that, after nearly three decades of periodic, partial eruptions and temporary containment, imploded globally in late 2007. The implosion precipitated in turn a major contraction in non-financial sectors of the global economy in 2008. That contraction still continues to evolve in the wake of the cataclysmic economic events of 2007–09. However, prevailing mainstream economic theory continues to fail to predict the evolution of such events, just as it failed to predict their origins and eruption.

With a lag behind both the financial and real events, it has now become increasingly clear that the old post-1945 paradigm of economic thought has also collapsed. That paradigm collapse is not just a matter of the discrediting of 'efficient market hypothesis' (EMH). The collapse of EMH is just one expression of a more fundamental crisis at the root of contemporary economic theory in both of its major wings, which this writer has called 'Hybrid Keynesianism' and 'Retro-Classicalism'. The crisis is ultimately the consequence of that paradigm's faulty theory of price, a too narrow definition of investment, a misunderstanding of the nature of the relationship between savings and investment and a total failure to consider today's obviously critical variables of credit, debt and finance in general, in its economic modelling.

Arising in the wake of the World War II, the initially dominant wing of Hybrid Keynesianism had already begun fracturing more than three decades ago in the 1970s, spinning off intellectual detritus in the form of minor schools of thought (that is, real business cycles, supply-side theory, Post-Keynesian, and various 'Neo-Keynesian' offshoots) that attempted, but failed, to re-establish its foundations. In the 1970s it was the real crisis of the global economy, with the USA once again at the crisis centre, which produced a corresponding quagmire in economic thought equivalent to the stagnation of the real economy at the time. Hybrid Keynesianism – comprised of adaptations, fundamental revisions and deletions of key elements of Keynes's thought by John Hicks, subsequently simplified and restated further by Paul Samuelson, Robert Solow and others in the USA, and held together by a questionable theory of price called the 'Phillips Curve' – finally broke down in the early 1970s.

Its vacuum was filled in the 1970s to the early 1980s by Retro-Classicalists, initially by new quantity of money theorists like Milton Friedman. And when Friedman monetarism in turn failed the policy application test both in the USA and United Kingdom in the 1980s, Retro-Classicalists fragmented as well into minor schools of thought, like rational expectations theory and variations of 'New Classicalists'.

That both Hybrid Keynesians and Retro-Classicalists constitute merely two wings of the same paradigm is represented by the fact that both adhere in different ways to an erroneous theory of price, simplistic views about investment, crude notions about savings determining investment and a total disregard for the role played by credit and debt in financial and economic instability. Their debates and differences have turned largely around 'in-house' differences over the respective relative weight of money demand vs. money supply in interest rate (and thus investment) determination, the role of disposable income vs. future wealth in consumption and the relative effectiveness of fiscal policy action.

Hybrid Keynesianism was itself a reflection of the Treasury–Federal Reserve Accord of the early 1950s, reflecting a return of a joint role for fiscal and monetary policy, after the near complete discrediting of the latter during the 1930s and the Fed's relegation to the minor task of financing bonds in wartime and retiring the government debt in the 1940s. But Hybrid Keynesianism 'worked' in the 1950s because it had essentially little work to do. Changes in GDP were relatively shallow, short and dampened. Disruptions in the business cycle were largely 'external' to the system. There were no major financial crises events. A moderate rise in prices in the late 1950s was addressed by the addition of the aforementioned 'Phillips Curve'. The blunter tool of government spending was displaced with Fed manipulation of interest rates in the 1950s, and with the advent of government activist tax policy in the early 1960s. Fine-tuning of a combination of interest rate–tax policy was all that was needed, it was argued at the time, to adjust the economy to minor disruptions of price and output. This all began to break down, however, in the mid-1960s as price began to escalate beyond normal historical levels, capital account flows and balance of payments problems began to arise and financial instability in the domestic economy in the USA began to emerge and intensify once again.

The dominance of Hybrid Keynesianism collapsed in the 1970s, replaced by a more fundamental retreat (hence 'Retro') to pre-1930s' neoclassical economic theory in the form of quantity theory monetarism according to Friedman. Meanwhile, both wings of economic thought began to spin off variations. This intensified after the advent of Reaganism-Thatcherism in the 1980s and the failed experiments with Friedman monetarism based on crude money supply growth rules. It was in this context that EMH came into its own, as spin-offs from both wings of the paradigm – Hybrid Keynesianism and Retro-Classicalism – began to proliferate. Once both Hybrid Keynesianism and mainstream Retro-Classicalism (Friedman) were discredited by the late 1980s, centrifugal forces drove economic thinking in many minor directions. In other words, the fragmenting of economic thinking has been going on for decades and the decline and decay of the paradigm has been underway for decades. While that fragmenting continued, so too did financial instability from the 1980s, which continued through the 1990s to the present.

Put in 'Kuhnian' terms, economics pursued increasingly narrow 'normal science' while the great anomaly of the economic system's deepening financial instability continued to mature in parallel. When that great anomaly finally erupted in 2007, the final 'coup de grâce' was administered to the paradigm. The meeting of the participants in the recent inaugural session of the Institute for New Economic Thinking (INET) represents one of many efforts now underway to reconstitute the old failed paradigm in new form, or to begin creating anew.

This writer's theory of Epic Recession is an expression of the latter effort. It attempts to explain the current crisis not as a 'one type fits all' normal recession that the old paradigm in both its wings viewed post-1945 economic contractions, but as a fundamentally new form of economic contraction. A form not historically original, however, but a form that has occurred before in the 19th and early 20th centuries – in particular during the periods 1907–14 and 1929–31 (in the USA) and elsewhere globally as well.

8.1   LIMITS OF THE OLD PARADIGM

Both wings of mainstream economics have thus far failed to consider in their models the destabilizing role of speculative finance, the new forms of financial institutions, markets and products, and the growing relative weight of speculative investing in the overall capitalist investment process and business cycle in the closing decades of the 20th century. They both virtually ignore the role of asset price volatility and its origins in speculative debt-driven finance. All prices behave the same, according to the old paradigm, driven toward equilibrium by simple, discrete forces of supply and demand. The fact that asset prices do not respond in the same way to demand forces, and virtually not at all to supply over the cycle, is not recognized. Nor is the impact of asset prices on product and labour (wage) prices over the course of a down cycle in deep 'epic' contractions. The interrelationships between debt, price and defaults and the key influence of such on real economic indicators is also not factored into their models. Consumption and investment are narrowly conceived, devoid of all determination by debt levels, debt quality and terms of finance. The relationship between savings and investment is inverted. The distribution of income between investors and consumers is ignored, as well as between investors in real assets and in financial assets. And traditional fiscal-monetary policies are viewed as sufficient for generating sustained economic recovery whether or not the contraction has been precipitated by financial implosion. All recessions are 'normal', produced ultimately by external shocks to an otherwise equilibrium-oriented system. There is no endogenous instability at work within the system.

Retro-Classicalists believe the current crisis represents a mere temporary departure from an inherent stability within the global capitalist economic system. The current departure from stability is merely another temporary aberration that will correct itself. Just leave it alone and it will eventually return to stability. Specifically, let the bad assets and collapsed values on bank and business balance sheets simply work themselves off naturally over time. Let write-downs of losses occur, and even defaults if necessary. Don't bail out anyone – banks and non-bank businesses alike. And especially don't rescue homeowners facing foreclosure, local governments going broke, or consumers defaulting on loans or credit cards. Don't even bail out sovereign countries with ballooning public debt; that represents the transfer to public balance sheets of massive losses by banks and other business institutions. If enough assets, products and wages fall in price sufficiently, so the argument of Retro-Classicalists goes, then 'bottom feeder' investors eventually will enter the market and buy up what's left. Recovery will then follow. In other words, the crisis is not internal to the system – that is, is not endogenous, as they say. The crisis has nothing to do with the system's internal dynamics. It is simply due to government policy failures. The government should therefore avoid future bank and financial institution re-regulation, and just let the system heal itself, recover on its own.

The other camp of mainstream economics, the Hybrid Keynesians, also ignores the possibility of internal forces driving the system's instability.

Like their Retro-Classicalist cousins, they concur that the cause of the crisis is bad policy. But unlike the Retro-Classicalists, they believe bad policy can be replaced by good policy that in the past has been employed successfully to enable recovery from normal recessions. The current crisis may be more severe than past recessions, they admit, but in the last analysis it is essentially just another normal recession. Bailouts are not only ok but necessary, especially on the banking side. But the banking and finance system must be stabilized first, in order to 'get credit going again', as they say. Once bank lending returns and ample credit is once again available, investment and employment will eventually follow, according to this view. Fiscal policy – government spending and especially tax cuts – can put a temporary floor under the collapse of consumer spending while awaiting the return of bank lending. Together, financial bailouts and consumption subsidies – such as unemployment insurance assistance, medical insurance premiums subsidies, financial aid to states and local governments – will keep the real economy from also collapsing, until such time as market forces can recover and generate a sustained recovery. Once again, as with the Retro-Classicalists, Hybrid Keynesians ultimately believe true recovery is best left to the forces of the market. Government intervention is called for, but just to buy time until market-driven recovery takes hold.

Relying ultimately on the market for recovery means that, once again, there's nothing endogenously wrong with the system. There's no inherent destabilizing dynamic within the system itself. The dynamics of the current crisis are the same as during prior normal recessions. In the more severe current contraction, the costs of 'buying time' waiting for the market to recover are just somewhat higher. These views, however, are in error on all counts.

Neither of the two wings of mainstream economics are able to predict Epic Recessions, or suggest workable programmes for recovery, because their models do not consider the key forces driving such contractions. These forces include the key aggregate variables of financial and consumption fragility, which themselves incorporate secondary variables of debt, credit, speculative financing and income distribution. They also include processes and transmission mechanisms addressing how both forms of fragility determine each other, as well as how they both in turn determine, and are themselves determined by, processes of debt-deflation-default.

In contrast, mainstream economics does not distinguish between speculative and real asset investment, nor explain how and why the former has been growing in recent decades at the expense of the latter. There is no accounting of how financial crises transmit into real economic contractions or how they feed back upon each other. The role of debt and credit, and how they interact with the three price systems, is largely absent.

Investment is simplistically determined by levels and changes in interest rates. There is no accounting of the role of growing income concentration and inequality analyses of mainstream economics. The price system is seen as a force for basic stabilization and equilibrium, instead of a force tending toward system destabilization and disequilibrium.

Because mainstream economics does not understand the fundamental dynamics and forces above, it cannot suggest proposals that result in sustained economic recovery. Because it erroneously views 'Epic' Recessions as just another 'normal' recession, it holds that traditional fiscal-monetary policies are sufficient to generate a sustained recovery. But monetary and fiscal policies applied in situations of normal recessions do not effectively address either forms of fragility or processes of debt-deflation-default very well. Stabilizing the banking system with massive liquidity injections may temporarily contain banking insolvency but not resolve it, and simply offsets the bad debt to the government and/or household sectors of the economy. Fiscal policies that merely seek to place a 'floor' under consumption to prevent further collapse prove similarly insufficient. Normal fiscal policy does not resolve problems of continuing household debt load or stagnating income levels. Central bank liquidity injections cannot resolve insolvency problems. Fundamental structural changes are therefore necessary for a sustained economic recovery.

8.2 THE CURRENT CRISIS AS EPIC RECESSION

Epic Recession, in both its financial and non-financial dimensions, is a consequence of internal, endogenous forces within the economic system that develop long term over the course of a business cycle that result in a major destabilization of that system.[1] Epic Recessions are fundamentally different from 'normal' recessions, the latter of which are never precipitated by financial instability and crises. Normal recessions may be caused by external shocks, policy or non-policy induced. But Epic Recessions do not originate due to external supply or demand shocks or as a result of government policy errors. They originate ultimately as a consequence of a relative shift from real physical asset investment to speculative asset investing over the course of an extended boom phase that produces a financial crisis and implosion.

The speculative investment shift not only causes a relative slowing of real capital accumulation in the boom phase, but accelerates the relative shift toward speculative investment in the subsequent bust phase as well. As speculative asset investing accelerates in the boom phase, leading to excess debt accumulation and escalating asset price inflation, it subsequently 'crowds out' real asset investment as the cycle progresses. In the real economy's contraction that inevitably follows a financial system collapse, both real asset investment and speculative investment decline. However, speculative investment recovers more rapidly, thus further enforcing the relative shift at the expense of real asset investment in the recovery phase. Thus, both in the 'up' and 'down' phases of the overall cycle, investment shifts in favour of speculative forms. That shift has a long-run destabilizing effect on the financial system causing repeated (with growing intensity and global synchronization) financial implosions.

The fundamental theoretical point is that real asset investment, that is, capital accumulation, is influenced and even determined long term increasingly by speculative forms of finance and investment.

Epic Recessions are thus the consequence of major financial system implosions. The important question, however, is what causes the extreme financial implosions that result in exceptionally severe credit crashes that bring the economy to its knees? And why thereafter does the economy have such difficulty generating a sustained economic recovery in the wake of an Epic Recession once again?

If Epic Recessions are precipitated by financial implosion, then financial busts are in turn the consequence of prior speculative investing excesses, which drive debt and asset price inflation to dangerous levels. When financial bust occurs, it produces greater than normal debt unwinding that leads to deflation and defaults. During the boom-speculative phase of the cycle the financial system becomes more 'fragile' and prone to implosion while the rest of the real economy becomes correspondingly more consumption fragile. Both forms of fragility – financial and consumption – fracture when the bust occurs, setting in motion debt-deflation-default processes that drive the economy in a contractionary spiral.

The still more fundamental question is what produces the shift to speculative investment in the first place, thus causing the fragility and the subsequent downward spiral of debt, deflation and default? Underlying the speculative shift are forces of escalating global income inequality, exploding global liquidity and the expanding 'global money parade' of speculators, sustained by a global network of financial institutions, new financial markets and multiplying new financial instruments created for those markets (most notably derivatives). The global money parade of speculators, institutions and markets, with more than 20 trillion dollars on hand today, drives the speculative boom. In the process it creates a mountain of debt in the system. Following each financial bust, part of the debt is 'unwound' – but only part. Much of it remains, obstructing a return to normal lending, investing and household consumption. That remaining mountain of debt is what differentiates Epic Recessions from normal recessions. Policies designed for normal recessions do not address that debt overhang, and that is primarily the reason for the relative ineffectiveness of traditional fiscal and monetary policies in generating a sustained recovery in instances of Epic Recession.

To allow the 'log-jam' of debt to be slowly 'worked off' – as is the case in most advanced economies today – does not resolve the economic crisis, but instead results in an extended period of relative economic stagnation. To simply transfer the debt from banks and businesses to the public balance sheet (that is, government debt) does nothing to remove it, but only shifts the crisis to the public sector. Putting a 'floor' under bank and business debt in the private sector may prevent a meltdown of the banking system core for a while, but it does not remove the bad assets and debt or their effects on real economic recovery. The unwinding of debt load, in other words, must be accelerated and expunged, not simply shifted or transferred. However, that cannot be achieved piecemeal and incrementally. It must be done with major structural economic reforms, not with normal fiscal-monetary policies.

In the past century in the USA there have been two actual historical cases remarkably similar to what has been occurring in today's crisis – one we have chosen to call a 'Type I' and another a 'Type II' Epic Recession. The former occurred in the equally major 1907 financial collapse and years immediately following. Like today, the big banks were stabilized by massive government liquidity injections, while thousands of others were allowed to fail. Inestimable thousands of businesses failed. The unemployed rose to double-digit levels. Wages and incomes stagnated. Recovery after 1907 followed a trajectory of brief, weak growth of 12–18 months, followed in turn by similar economic relapses, by growth, and by relapse once again. Only massive government spending injections with the onset of World War I brought the stagnation to an end. The same thing occurred in the wake of the speculative boom and bust of the 1920s. Only this time the government failed to stem banking system collapses that followed the initial financial bust of 1929. Subsequent banking crises followed in 1930, 1931, 1932 and 1933. Debt-deflation-default processes worsened. Financial and consumption fragility deteriorated further and drove the processes to even greater extremes. 1929–30 may have been a Type II Epic Recession event – that is, one that was transformed into a bona fide depression.

Short of another financial-banking system implosion, which may originate anywhere globally given the now global nature of the capitalist financial system, the current economic crisis thus far shares many characteristics with a Type I Epic Recession. That is, a stubborn extended economic stagnation that may go on for years, with short, unsustainable recoveries and brief, equally unsustainable economic relapses. This can go on until massive fiscal spending in the form of major government public investment occurs and appropriate structural reforms take place. These structural reforms will almost certainly have to address the banking-financial system, the tax system and the serious income maldistribution problem today in the US economy.

8.3 CHARACTERISTICS AND PROCESSES OF EPIC RECESSIONS

What occurs in Epic Recessions is a dual, mutually reinforcing dynamic between financial collapse and the real non-financial sectors of the economy. This dynamic is reflected in the causal interactions between debt, deflation and defaults (business, household and public sector) following the financial bust. The excessive debt accumulation in the boom phase produces severe financial fragility that drives asset deflation and defaults in the contraction phase. Deflation and defaults in turn exacerbate real debt levels further. The dynamic of debt-deflation-default processes intensifies. Asset deflation continues and subsequently spills over to product price deflation, and in turn wage deflation, as businesses facing excessive debt loads and refinancing resort to reducing product prices, and turn to wage deflation in various forms, in order to raise revenue and cut costs. Financial fragility is represented by a growing ratio of debt-to-cash-flow and liquid assets for businesses, deteriorating terms of debt servicing and a growing inability to obtain credit to refinance debt. Financial fragility rises from either rising real debt loads and declining terms of debt payments, or a decline in cash flow, or both. Deflation in its three forms (asset, product, wage) are responses to raise cash flow as debt servicing strains increase as a consequence of the financial collapse. The attempt to 'unwind debt' is the initiating driver in the debt-deflation-default processes, but the latter reinforce the debt problem in the downturn.

But Epic Recessions are set in motion not only due to growing financial fragility in the boom phase and its intensification in the contraction phase, driving the debt unwinding and related deflation and business defaults. Epic Recessions are also the consequence of a corresponding consumption fragility that grows in the boom phase. That consumption fragility rises based on growing household debt and disposable income stagnation in the boom phase, which then deteriorates in the contraction phase further as real debt rises and real income falls as a consequence of layoffs, wage cutting and reduction in household credit availability.

Already deteriorating in the boom phase, financial and consumption fragility thus both deteriorate further in the wake of debt-deflation-default processes set in motion in the contraction phase. Moreover, both forms of fragility – financial and consumption – exacerbate each other, and are rendered more fragile by processes of worsening debt-deflation-default. The result of all this in real economic terms is that real asset business investment (that creates jobs and income) stagnates after the financial bust. Real investment is difficult to regenerate in the wake of an Epic Recession. Similarly, households are unable to work off (unwind) their debt loads in the post-financial bust period. Consumption therefore does not recover and real disposable income stagnates or falls. The failure to regenerate consumption holds back investment and business spending recovery.

Only the government sector is able to increase its level of spending. But that too has its limits, as in later stages of the Epic Recession cycle government's economic fragility rises as well. As a result of its efforts to bail out banks and financial institutions, to subsidize general corporate profits by tax cuts and other subsidies and to supplement household consumption, government debt levels rise. Government income levels simultaneously deteriorate as tax revenues lag as no sustained economic recovery occurs. Government debt-to-tax income ratios thus worsen, much as for financial and consumption fragility, albeit with a lag period once Epic Recession has begun. Financial and consumption fragility are, in other words, simply in part transferred from corporate and household balance sheets to government-public balance sheets. Fundamental debt and debt servicing problems are not resolved; just reshuffled around between various sectoral balance sheets.

The outcome of deterioration in the various forms of fragility (business, household, government) is an extended period of short, unsustainable, weak recoveries, followed by periods of short, moderate subsequent contractions in what appears to be a 'double dip' or 'W-shape' recovery, and even a double-double dip. In other words, at best an extended period of general economic stagnation that may last at minimum for seven to ten years. During that stagnation, should subsequent major financial implosions or general banking crises occur, the stagnation may well develop into a classic depression scenario.

8.4   ANALYSIS AT THE LEVEL OF PRICE

There are two basic approaches possible to explaining the origins, evolution and future direction of today's continuing economic crisis. One is to explain it from the perspective of value determination; the other is to explain it from the level of representations of value – that is, in terms of concrete price variables as those variables are reflected in forms of invest-ment, credit, debt, output and so forth.[2] This paper focuses primarily on analysis of the crisis at the level of 'price' categories. It is important to note, however, that it does so fundamentally differently from the manner in which mainstream economics argues in terms of price.

The Retro-Classicalist mainstream economics view rests upon an assumption that the price system in the capitalist economy is inherently stabilizing. In fact, price is considered the central stabilizing factor. The system will always return to a stable state (called equilibrium), the 'Retros' believe, because the price system will adjust supply and demand to ensure it does so. Given this assumption, in the long run there are no departures from instability – that is, economic crises (whether normal, Epic, or depression) – that will not eventually return to stability automatically, on their own, due to the workings of the price system. Given that assumption that the system is inherently stable, it follows that any departure from that stability is due to 'external' forces, which may be policy-based or other 'shocks' to the system causing it to depart from stability. If external shocks set the system on a path of instability (that is, disequilibrium), then any delay in its return to stability is due to something interfering with the workings of the price system performing its re-stabilizing function, according to the Retro-Classicalist view.

This view of price as stabilizer for the economy at large derives from a micro-view of how individual markets for products adjust to ensure stability between supply and demand and equilibrium – a micro-view that is then simply transferred to the macroeconomy at large. The Retro view also assumes there is only one kind of price system. A 'one price system fits all'. There are prices for products. For prices for labour – that is, 'wages'. For prices for money – that is, 'interest rates'. And price, according to the Retro view, behaves everywhere and always the same way; that is, adjust-ing to ensure balance between supply and demand and thus stability and equilibrium.

For the price of a specific product it works as follows: if there is an excess of demand for a product, then price will rise for that product. That rise will incentivize businesses to produce more supply. The additional supply will subsequently reduce the price. An iterative process will occur, shifting the price of the product back toward stability and equilibrium. Similarly, if there is insufficient demand for the product, lowering its price, supply will decline and cause price to rise back to equilibrium. The opposite occurs if supply initially rises or falls, provoking offsetting responses by demand.

Price is thus the great stabilizer and equilibrator. And it works in the same manner whether it is a price for a product, for labour (wages), for money (interest rates) or whatever. But for the 'Retros', one price system fits all. Moreover, this price behaviour scenario operates not only at the micro-level (products, wages, interest for an individual business) but for the economy at large (macro-) level as well. Macro-analysis is only micro 'writ large'.

But as our analysis of Epic Recession fundamentally argues, there is *not* only one price system. And the idea that market price is the great stabilizer is fundamentally in error. There are three distinct price systems and each operates differently at times: asset prices, product prices and labour prices (wages). And they interact with each other in a severe contraction – whether Epic Recession or depression – producing a mutually reinforcing downward spiral of contraction. Asset prices in particular do not respond in the assumed theoretical way, adjusting to changes in supply and demand, with a perpetual tendency toward equilibrium. Asset prices in particular follow an independent dynamic, and serve to drive product-wage-money prices in an economic contraction, and toward disequilibrium. Price in this view is thus actually a great destabilizer that drives the system toward increasing volatility and instability. Moreover, asset price system destabilization is endogenous to the system and plays a key role in the dynamic tendency of Epic Recession to potentially transform into bona fide depressions.

The logic underlying the Retro-Classicalist view of price as the great stabilizer is a simple but incorrect assumption. It is called the 'substitution effect'. For price to behave as described, whoever purchases the product, the Retro view assumes, has both a desire to obtain one more unit of that product as well as a desire not to obtain that one more unit. For each purchase there is a satisfaction in obtaining one more unit as well as a parallel dissatisfaction from obtaining it – that is, a utility and a disutility. The utility and disutility it further assumes are perfect substitutes for each other. When the trade-off in utility–disutility is equal, then adding one more of the product (or of labour, money, etc.) is all the same to the purchaser. The product's utility is perfectly substitutable by its disutility. The purchaser at that point, where utility–disutility are equal, therefore stops buying. At that point supply and demand are in equilibrium and stability occurs.

To employ another illustration, using the price for labour (wages), when the utility of one more hire is equal to its disutility then the capitalist won't hire any more workers. That is, when the cost of hiring one more worker is equal (perfectly substitutable) for the revenue that one more worker might produce, the utility and disutility of that one more unit of labour is equal. Equilibrium in labour supply and demand is achieved. The system is stable. No more hiring and no layoffs. The key point of all this is that without the assumption and application of the principle of the 'substitution effect', price cannot play the stabilizer role. There can be no equilibrium. Supply and demand no longer work to return the system to equilibrium and stability.

Retro-Classicalists today still preach this view. They then take this logic, expressed initially at the level of an individual business's output of products, hiring of workers, or borrowing of money, and extrapolate it to the level of the economic system itself at large. Thus, price becomes the great stabilizer for an economic system in crisis, not just a product or hiring of labour by an employer. It is the force and variable that can end a recession, Epic Recession and even a depression. External shocks to the economic system may indeed occur, according to the Retro view, but price adjustment via supply and demand will return the system to stability. If empirically, price fails to return the system to stability, the argument goes, that is due to interference with the price system's natural workings as described. Failure to achieve stability is the result of either government or workers and their unions refusing to permit the price system to adjust. The economy is like one big price system. Specifically, failure to recover from a recession or depression is due to workers refusing to lower their wages (that is, adjust wages-price downward) or even businesses failing to sufficiently reduce their prices (that is, adjust product prices downward). If they would only allow their prices to fall, it would stimulate more supply from producers that would result in more investment, more rehiring of workers and a rise in general demand that would end the recession or depression.

This is the famous 'real balance effect' (sometimes called the 'Pigou effect') that was so prominent among economists during the last Great Depression in the 1930s (Pigou, 1933). This view was thoroughly demolished by John Maynard Keynes in 1936, but was subsequently resurrected in new form by the Hybrid Keynesians following World War II.[3] And its vestiges still remain today among both wings of mainstream economists, who still argue that part of the problem of recovery from severe economic contractions is that prices and wages are 'sticky' downwards and interrupt the adjustment process. In other words, the victims of recession and depression – workers and their unions – are the cause of the recession or depression not ending in a quick, 'V-shape' -like recovery.

There is no single price system, behaving the same regardless of its forms (asset, product, wage), always moving the economic system toward stability. There are several price systems, not one. And they all don't behave the same way, with supply and demand working in consort to restore equilibrium. In fact, price may serve as a major force exacerbating disequilibrium, causing increasing instability in the economy at large, both at the level of finance and the real economy. This is especially true for asset prices in general, and for financial securities assets in particular. In the case of prices for financial securities, like mortgage, commercial mortgage and asset-backed securities (MBS, CMBS, ABS), collateralized debt obligation and loan obligation securities (CDO, CLO), and credit default swaps (CDS), price escalation is driven increasingly by demand over the boom phase of the cycle. Supply is a relatively minor factor. Speculative demand drives up prices for financial asset securities, which in turn brings in a flood of additional demand as prices rise. During a boom phase there are few supply constraints to rising financial asset prices – that is, no costs of goods, cost of sales, or distribution costs – for instruments that are largely electronic in form. Without supply constraints, inflation over the boom cycle continues unchecked until the inevitable financial implosion occurs. Thereafter, financial asset prices 'unwind', eventually driving product price deflation and subsequently wage deflation as business cost cutting and defaults take place to offset falling asset prices. Supply plays little role in this price 'race to the bottom'. Demand is the primary driver. All this is impossible in the Retro-Classicalist view of price as the great stabilizing and driver toward equilibrium, where demand and supply work as forces within the system in consort to ensure long-run stability and equilibrium.

Asset prices are inherently destabilizing both during the boom phase and in the subsequent bust phase. And in the contraction phase, it is asset price deflation that increasingly drives product price deflation, both of which in turn, drive wage deflation. It is not 'normal supply and demand' that determine price deflation, as Retro-Classicalist theories argue.

Like Retro-Classicalists, the Hybrid Keynesians also fail to understand the role of asset prices in producing financial instability and in exacerbating real economic contraction in the downturns following financial implosions. They do not argue as strongly that price is a stabilizer in the system. However, they have no accounting of asset prices in the system. Prices are limited to products, wages and money (interest rates). Asset prices are largely unaccounted for. Moreover, in a mechanical fashion, they envision an unrealistic 'substitution effect' between product price and wage inflation, on the one hand, and between money and product prices on the other.[4] Through a device called the 'Phillips Curve', Hybrid Keynesians maintain that rising product prices (due to either product costs and/or product demand – not asset price movements) can be 'traded off' (that is, substituted for) by lowering labour prices (wages) as a consequence of raising unemployment. Unemployment is in turn raised by raising interest rates (money prices). The opposite is also possible: lowering money prices results in more employment and higher wages and eventually more product price inflation. It all occurs in a very manageable manipulation by fiscal and monetary policies. And there are no financial variables, no speculative investment (only real asset investment exists), no excessive credit and debt accumulation and no asset price instability and volatility driving financial implosions (which also do not exist). Hybrid Keynesianism thus also misunderstands the role of price as a major destabilizer endogenous to the economic system itself.

What then lies behind the growing weight and influence of asset price volatility in the economy? Asset prices are driven by speculative forms of investing, by the increasing resort to debt, by multiplying and growing forms of leverage feeding that debt in the boom cycle, by the worldwide explosion of liquidity generated by growing income inequality and concentration among professional investors and by the institutions and professional investors that lay behind the speculative investing shift in the world economy. That body of institutions and investors, their multiplying forms of financial offerings, their speculative markets created to absorb those offerings and the explosion in global liquidity, credit and debt are the real material forces underlying the speculative investing shift and the system-destabilizing asset price volatility that has been spreading and growing rapidly in recent decades as a consequence of that shift.

Both wings of the old paradigm also fundamentally misunderstand the nature of the relationship of savings to investment. One still continually hears reference to the 'global savings glut' and 'global imbalances' as the cause of recurring crises and today's instability. If only global supply and demand were in 'equilibrium' once again, the argument goes, global financial instability would disappear. Both wings basically adhere to versions of what was called the 'loanable funds' theory of investment, in which money supply and money demand determine interest rates and interest rates in turn determine investment, in a narrow, simplistic relationship. Hybrid Keynesians give somewhat more weight to money demand in the explanation, whereas Retro-Classicalists emphasize money supply relative to money demand more heavily (or virtually deny the role of money demand). But the idea that savings determine investment is an inverted error of the relationship between savings and investment. Recognized as far back as Wicksell, and subsequently by Keynes as well, it is the obverse – investment determines savings not vice versa. This is particularly true of speculative forms of investment. Profits drive investment, and interest rates adjust in response to levels of investment driven by profits. However, this view was essentially deleted from Keynes in the post-1945 revisions undertaken by Hybrid Keynesians.

The foregoing analysis has focused on explaining the recent financial and economic crisis through the use of price variables. Price has been shown to play an important role, asset prices in general and financial asset prices in particular, in the growth in both scope and magnitude of

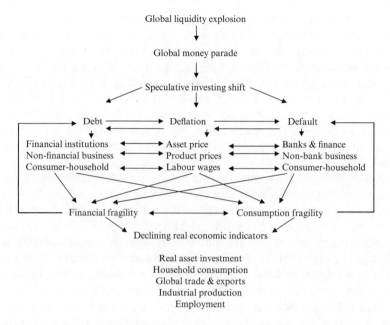

Global liquidity explosion

Global money parade

Speculative investing shift

Debt ——————→ Deflation ——————→ Default

Financial institutions ←——→ Asset price ←—————— Banks & finance
Non-financial business ←——→ Product prices ←—————— Non-bank business
Consumer-household ←——→ Labour wages ←—————— Consumer-household

Financial fragility ←—————————→ Consumption fragility

Declining real economic indicators

Real asset investment
Household consumption
Global trade & exports
Industrial production
Employment

Figure 8.1   Fundamental forces and relationships of Epic Recession

financial crises in the global capitalist system in recent decades. The key forces identified in the analysis at the level of price variables have included: the shift to speculative investing (enabled by the network of 'shadow' financial institutions, proliferation of new financial markets and products; explosion in global liquidity, credit and debt (business, household, government), financial fragility, consumption fragility, the interaction of debt with deflation in the three price systems (asset, product and wage) and defaults (business, consumer and government) and the interaction of debt-deflation-defaults with financial and consumption fragility.

The possible causal relationships between the foregoing variables may be overly simplified, but perhaps further clarified somewhat, by Figure 8.1.[5]

8.5   CONCLUDING REMARKS

It is necessary to distinguish between fixed asset investment and investment in speculative financial assets. Mainstream economics fails to make a sufficient distinction between the two, or explain how the two interact over the course of a business cycle and together contribute to economic instability. Mainstream economics considers only real asset investment as a variable, determined largely by changes in interest rates, which in turn are a consequence of money supply actions by central banks and money demand. In mechanical fashion, money supply changes determine interest rates, which in turn determine investment, according to Retro-Classicalists; whereas Hybrid Keynesians give token acknowledgement to money demand as well as money supply. But it is still a singular focus on real investment. Causal relationships and interdependencies between real asset investment and speculative forms of financial asset investment are ignored.

Additionally, for mainstream economics there is only one price system and all prices – whether asset, product or labour wages – behave the same. The price system always stabilizes the economic system and makes possible as a result the fiction of 'equilibrium'. This view of price fails to recognize the fundamentally destabilizing nature of asset prices in general and financial asset prices in particular. This failure prevents mainstream economics from properly understanding events like Epic Recessions and depressions. Nor is the ability of the banking system to create credit independently of the central bank acknowledged, and the role of debt in both consumption and investment is not addressed. Epic Recessions are not distinguished from normal recessions despite their profound qualitative differences. Epic Recessions are considered just normal recessions slightly writ large. (Just as depressions are viewed as normal recessions writ significantly large.) Consequently, mainstream economics can only suggest traditional fiscal and monetary policy measures as solutions to Epic Recession events, which is why they typically fail and result in either an extended stagnation or in limited instances in transitions to classic depressions.

NOTES

1. Rasmus (2010) analyses these endogenous forces at the level of priced variables – that is, wages, products, assets, constituent elements of GDP like consumption, fixed investment, government expenditures, net exports, cash flow, debt, disposable income and the like. However, the endogenous forces driving financial crises and Epic Recession may also be understood as the reflection of parallel causes at the level of value determination.
2. Value and price here are used in the Marxist terminological sense. That is, quantities of value in the long run are at the core of the dynamic of capital accumulation and reproduction, around which fluctuate in the shorter-term values of price in forms of investment, consumption, assets, wages, money and interest, and measures of general economic output like GDP.
3. Keynes (1936). Just about any introductory and intermediate macroeconomic textbook in the USA today refers to 'sticky wages and prices' as a cause preventing or inhibiting recovery from economic contraction. But the hypothesis of 'sticky wages', in the context of a severe contraction like Epic Recession or a depression, is a fantasy. In both,

wage deflation is a fact, taking numerous forms, not just hourly wage rate reduction. Furloughs, broad cuts in employer contributions to pensions, health care benefits, reductions in hours worked, cuts in paid leave (vacation, holidays, sick leave), shifts of tens of millions from full-time to part-time and temporary jobs paying 50–70 per cent of full-time rates, and direct layoffs themselves are all examples of 'wage deflation' for the class as a whole that is widespread during depressions and begins to occur in Epic Recessions.

4. This view of 'Hybrid Keynesians' is not to be confused with the view of Keynes himself, who saw the relationship between product and labour prices differently and who began to describe the unique character and role of asset prices in instability in his *General Theory*, but unfortunately did not pursue it more deeply in that work.

5. For a further, detailed clarification of the dynamic relationships – causal and feedback – between these variables, the reader is referred to Rasmus (2010, chapter 8).

REFERENCES

Keynes, J.M. (1936), *The General Theory of Employment, Interest and Money*, London: Macmillan.

Pigou, A.C. (1933), *Theory of Unemployment*, London: Macmillan.

Rasmus, J. (2010), *Epic Recession: Prelude to Global Depression*, London: Pluto Press.

9. Did asset prices cause the current crisis?

Edith Skriner

9.1 INTRODUCTION

There is evidence that economic relationships change over time and therefore many researchers focus on these topics. During the oil shock years, a large number of studies dealt with the links between oil prices and economic output. In non-oil-producing economies a clear negative relationship between oil prices and aggregate measures of output and employment was found. In the recent past, the US dollar has frequently been used as the invoicing currency of international crude oil trading. Therefore, fluctuations in the US dollar exchange rate may be considered as one reason for the volatility of crude oil prices. In fact, researchers have identified a significant response of the oil price to an exchange rate shock. While the main concern of central bankers, the inflation rate, is now low and stable in the main developed economies, financial instability has become one of the most discussed issues.

Recently, Austrian Business Cycle Theory, with Ludwig von Mises and Friedrich von Hayek as its main proponents, has gained much attention, as the 2008–09 crisis shows certain similarities with the Great Depression. Austrian theorists propose that the key cause of the Depression was the expansion of the money supply in the 1920s that led to an unsustainable credit-driven boom. Capital resources were misallocated into areas that would not attract investment at higher rates of borrowing. Prices increased and a correction occurred when the exponential credit creation could not be sustained. Then the money supply suddenly and sharply contracted when markets finally cleared. Resources were then reallocated towards more efficient uses.

In credit-driven booms asset prices increase; Bagus (2008) considers psychological phenomena like universal optimism and herding behaviour as important determinants of asset market developments. A policy issue often emphasized in theoretical literature is whether central banks should include stock prices in their reaction functions. Many researchers have addressed the measurement of the effects by means of vector auto-regressions.

Underlying research deals with the structural relationships of key world indicators like aggregate exports, asset prices, non-energy commodity prices, interest rates, the oil price, oil production and the USD/EUR exchange rate and how these relationships have changed over time. For this analysis, structured vector auto-regression methodology is applied. The observations, ranging from 1974 to 2009, have a monthly frequency. The full sample is split into 253 smaller sub-samples (windows), where each window consists of 180 observations. In the rolling window analysis the first window is placed at the beginning of the time horizon. This window is then moved forward by monthly increments. For each window the vector auto-regression and the structural relationships are newly estimated. The results are a sequence of accumulated impulse responses for all combinations of variables.

The study starts with a brief description of the methodology. In section 9.3 the data is described. Results are discussed in section 9.4. In section 9.5 conclusions are drawn.

9.2   METHODOLOGY

Economic relationships can be explained by theory-based models or any kind of empirical modelling. From an econometric point of view the two approaches are fundamentally different. Theory-based modelling starts from a mathematical (static) formulation of a theoretical model and then expands the model by adding stochastic components. Empirical modelling refers to observations and is a summary description of the historical data based on sample correlations. Unrestricted vector auto-regressive models typically relate a dependent variable to its past and to the pasts of other variables with random errors that may be serially correlated. However, for policy analysis a structural model that generates predictions of results given various kinds of actions is needed. Due to the feedback inherent in the system, these equations cannot be estimated directly.

Structural vector auto-regression (SVAR) methodology allows explicit identification[1] to isolate estimates of policy and/or private agents' behaviour and its effects on the economy while keeping the model free of the many additional restrictive assumptions needed to give every parameter a behavioural interpretation. To achieve an interpretation for a policy choice it is necessary to assume that a policy variation can be identified with the residual in one of the model's equations. In that case, policy projections can be made in the standard way – by quantifying the effects of changes in the policy (exogenous) variable on the endogenous ones in a linear implicit system. This way of achieving identification is exactly what underlies the usual use of econometric models to project the effects of policy, whether they are explicitly SVAR models or not.

Introduced by Sims (1980), SVARs have become a widely used tool for policy analyses. In Sims (1986) a six-variable dynamic system was set up, considering real economic growth, real business fixed investment, inflation, the money supply, unemployment and the treasury-bill rate. The results on the structural relationships of the variables appeared to be consistent with the notion that money supply shocks affect prices, income and interest rates. This example made it clear that small-scale systems can be sufficient for testing economically meaningful hypotheses. In the last 20 years many policy analyses based on the SVAR methodology followed; these documented the effects of money on output, the relative importance of supply and demand shocks on business cycles and the effects of fiscal policy.

As the goal of the underlying analysis is to find the important relationships among a set of global indicators, SVAR methodology is employed here. The ordering of the variables in the SVAR may be based on theory or on the Granger causality (block exogeneity) test. However, when the cross-correlations of the residuals are insignificant, no particular ordering is required. The right-hand side of the set of equations contains only predetermined variables and the error terms are assumed to be serially uncorrelated with a constant variance. In the estimation procedure the appropriate lag order is determined by the multivariate generalization of the Akaike information criterion. The block exogeneity test tells whether lags of one variable have an influence on any other variables in the system. The Cholesky method is used for the identification of the structural relationships. The impulse response function allows the time path of the various shocks on the variables contained in the SVAR system to be traced out. The accumulated impulse responses show the structural relationships of variables.

9.3   DATA

The empirical analysis is based on the variables world trade (*wdexm*), world asset prices (*wdfcf*), the world production of crude oil (*wdpro*), world non-energy commodity prices (*wdpri*), the oil price (*brent*), world short-term interest rates (*wdirst*) and the USD/EUR exchange rate (*exruseu*). The time series of world exports is regularly published by the International Monetary Fund (IMF) as *International Financial Statistics*. It is reported in billion USD at current prices and has a monthly frequency. The world aggregate consists of all countries that report their export performance to the IMF. The calculation of the world totals takes into account the problem that data for some countries are not current and may have gaps. World estimates are made when data is available for countries whose combined weights represent at least 60 per cent of the total country weights.

The time series of world asset prices is an aggregate equity price index that is accomplished by Datastream on a daily basis. The index covers publicly quoted companies in 70 countries that are constituents of targeted global indices like the FTSE All World, Dow Jones Global, MSCI World, MSCI EMF, S&P Global and S&P Citygroup. There is full market coverage of all listed companies trading equity securities for developed markets and a selection of emerging markets. In the underlying analysis daily data has been transformed into monthly averages.

The world production of crude oil is reported as 1000 barrels per day. The US Department of Energy (DOE) calculates the aggregated time series, which is published every month.

The world interest rate series is a weighted average of short-term interest rates (three-month bank rates) of the major trading blocs, namely the USA, Japan and the euro area. The data sources for all variables are national statistics, available on a daily basis. Since the eurozone was only established in 1999, German short-term interest rates were used for the preceding years. In the underlying analysis the daily data has been transformed into monthly averages.

The time series on world commodity prices is an index that consists of non-energy world spot prices. The price index is US-dollar based, is calculated by Standard & Poor and has a daily frequency. The index is a benchmark for investment performance in the commodity markets and is widely recognized as the leading measure of general commodity movements and inflation in the world economy. The commodity basket consists of industrial metals, agricultural products and livestock. It is calculated on a world production weighted basis and is designed to reflect the relative significance of each of the constituent commodities in the world economy. In the underlying analysis the daily data has been converted into monthly averages.

According to the Energy Intelligence Group there are about 161 different internationally traded crude oils. They vary in terms of characteristics, quality and market penetration. While the West Texas Intermediate (WTI) is the major benchmark of crude oil in the Americas, the Brent blend forms the benchmark for the European and African markets. These two crude oils are traded and their prices are reflected in other types of crude oil. Brent blend is generally priced at about a USD 4 per-barrel premium to the OPEC basket price or about a USD 1 to 2 per-barrel discount to the WTI, although on a daily basis, the pricing relationships can vary greatly. The price of the Brent blend is reported in USD per barrel. Datastream provides its daily quotations. In the underlying analysis the daily data has been converted into monthly averages.

The exchange rate between the US dollar and the euro is reported by Datastream on a daily basis. In the underlying analysis the daily data has been converted into monthly averages.

Figure 9.1 shows how the observed variables evolve over time. The shaded areas indicate the periods of economic downturns. Some features can be readily spotted from the plots. The time series *wdexm*, *wdfcf* and *wdpro* have the typical shape of a macroeconomic time series, as they increase over time. Also, the time series on prices (*wdpri* and *brent*) exhibits an increasing growth path during the observation period. The oil price declined from the early 1980s until 1999. However, from then on, a strong upward movement is observable and it is very likely that oil prices will continue to increase. One can expect that, due to limited resources, raw material prices will also increase in the long run. In contrast, interest rates may have a non-trending development. In fact, world interest rates increased from 1960 to 1980 and fell thereafter, reaching a historic low in 2009. Since 1984, the euro has gained strength compared with the US dollar.

One way of handling non-stationarity in time series is to compute first differences. Therefore, the time series *wdexm*, *wdfcf*, *wdpri*, *brent*, *wdpro* and *exruseu* are converted into year-on-year differences, while *wdirst* remains in levels.

The observations of the stationary data set start in January 1974 and end in December 2009. The full sample is split into 253 sub-samples, where one sub-sample consists of 180 observations. The estimation of the structural relationships based on one sub-sample comprises the following steps: the estimation of the vector auto-regression, the block exogeneity test, the identification, the accumulation of the impulse responses and the re-basing of the innovation to 1, so that a one-unit shock of one variable causes a response of *x* units by the other variables. The same procedure is carried out for all sub-samples. In the rolling window analysis the first window (sub-sample) is placed at the beginning of the time horizon. This window is then moved forward in monthly increments.

In a vector auto-regression each variable should be explained by the lagged values of the other variables of the system. However, the status of being either endogenous or exogenous may have changed over time. Therefore, a block exogeneity test has been carried out, considering all windows. The results of the test show that world trade and also world oil production have been endogenous variables throughout all windows.

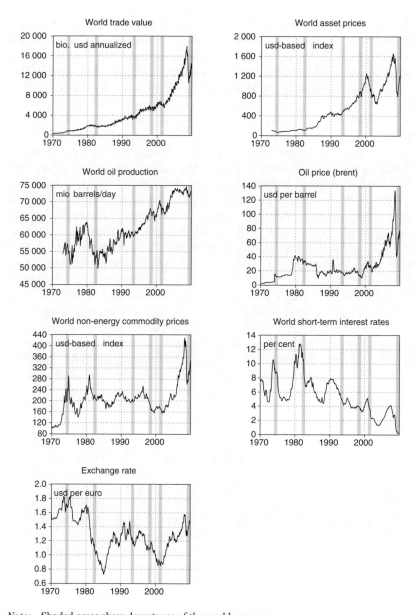

Note: Shaded areas show downturns of the world economy.

Figure 9.1   Observed data set

Also, in the case of the USD/EUR exchange rate there has been a low probability of exogeneity, and since 2005 the probability has even declined to zero. The development of asset prices is determined by the set of the other variables; however, there are periods in which their explanatory power is weak. Particularly in the fourth quarter of 2008 the probability of exogeneity shot up strongly when the world observed a sharp decline in asset prices. Non-oil commodity prices occasionally went through periods with a higher probability of exogeneity. In the second half of the 1990s, interest rates might have been determined by other factors than the set of variables under consideration. The results suggest that 40 per cent of the development is attributable to external factors.

The block exogeneity test shows that in the windows 1976–90 up to 1990–2004 oil prices were exogenous in the system, due to their large fluctuations.[2] During the 1970s and 1980s the oil price was primarily determined by political actions, like the decisions on the quantity of oil to be produced or military conflicts in the Middle East (Hamilton, 2003). Such an exogenous cut in the supply of energy pushes up prices. However, the determinants that can influence the development of the oil price have changed. Meanwhile the block exogeneity test suggests that in the windows 1991–2005 up to 1995–2009, the oil price can be considered as an endogenous variable of the system. It points to the fact that the oil price is now driven by key indicators of the world economy. Hamilton (2009) reviewed a number of theories explaining the high price of oil in summer 2008, including commodity price speculations, strong world demand, time delays or geographical limitations on increased production, OPEC monopoly pricing and an increasingly important contribution of the scarcity rent. The three key factors of these are the low price elasticity of demand, the strong economic growth of China, in the Middle East, and in other newly industrialized economies, and the failure of global production to increase. These facts explain the initial strong pressure on prices that may have triggered commodity speculation in the first place.

As the underlying analysis refers to a number of different windows, in which the relations of the set of variables change, the ordering of the variables in the SVAR is based on the block exogeneity test. The test suggests the following ordering of variables: *brent* → *wdpri* → *wdirst* → *wdfcf* → *exruseu* → *wdpro* → *wdexm*.

9.4   RESULTS

A strong structural relationship was found between an asset price shock and the response of interest rates. In the windows 1980–94 to 1984–98, a 1 per cent rise in asset prices led to a 6-basis-point increase in interest rates. The magnitude of the multipliers and their significance level increased strongly in the windows 1988–2002 to 1995–2009. In these years a 1 per cent rise in asset prices led to a 12-basis-point increase in interest rates, with a likelihood of around 90 per cent. The significance level of the other structural relationships is low in general. There are only a few episodes in which the estimated impact multipliers have a probability of more than 50 per cent. For example, the windows covering the years of major oil price shocks show that an increase in the oil price led to an increase in interest rates and also to a decline in oil production; and in the windows 1976–90 to 1986–2000 interest rates responded positively to commodity price shocks. However, in the subsequent windows the impact of the responses faded. This might be due to multiple structural breaks that occurred at unknown dates in each system of equations.

9.4.1   Impact of an Asset Price Shock

As financial markets become more and more closely integrated, investors benefit from the opportunity to choose between domestic and foreign financial assets. Capital flows are directed to the economies with the best growth prospects, generating large wealth effects. Movements in the stock market can have a significant impact on the economy and are therefore likely to be an important factor in the determination of monetary policy. The impact of the stock market on the macroeconomy comes primarily through two channels. First, movements in stock prices influence aggregate consumption through the wealth channel. Hence, stock price movements have a significant effect on household wealth. Second, stock price movements also affect the cost of financing to businesses. Because of their potential impact on the macroeconomy, stock market movements are likely to be an important determinant of monetary policy decisions. However, little is known about the magnitude of central banks' reactions to the stock market, in part because the simultaneous response of equity prices to interest rates makes it difficult to estimate. Rigobon and Sacks (2003) used an identification technique based on the heteroskedasticity of stock market returns to measure the reaction of monetary policy to the stock market and found a significant policy response, with a 1 per cent rise (fall) in the S&P 500 index increasing the likelihood of a 5-basis-point tightening (easing) by about a half. The sample 1985–99 had a daily frequency. With the same methodology and a smaller sample size ranging from 1985 to 1995, Furlanetto (2008) found a similar positive reaction; however, the probability reached 95 per cent.

Although the underlying analysis refers to global asset prices and

Table 9.1   Long-term response of interest rates to a 1 per cent asset price shock

Windows	Relation	Basis Points	Probability
1980–94	+	6	50
.	.	.	.
.	.	.	.
.	.	.	.
1984–98	+	6	50
1988–2002	+	12	90
.	.	.	.
.	.	.	.
.	.	.	.
1995–2009	+	12	90

interest rates, the results are very similar to the previously mentioned studies as monetary policy also responds positively to an asset price shock (see Table 9.1).

This result as shown in Table 9.1, which has been tested for its robustness, suggests that the strong positive structural relationship between asset prices and interest rates might be responsible for the 2008–09 crisis. Therefore, there is evidence that this crisis follows the path of the Austrian Business Cycle. The strong long-term response of interest rates to an asset price shock also explains why the crisis turned out to be much more severe than the 2001 crisis.

Figure 9.2 shows the sequence of long-run responses of interest rates after a one-unit shock of asset prices with the two standard error bands. Each data point of the bold plot shows the accumulated impulse responses estimated for one window. Each data point of one of the two thin plots is the aggregate standard error. The date that is associated with each data point is the first date outside the respective window.

9.4.2   Other Relationships

9.4.2.1   Impact of an exchange rate shock

The USD/EUR relationship is the most widely used currency pair in the world. The US dollar is frequently used as the invoicing currency of international crude oil trading. Hence, fluctuations in US dollar exchange rates may be considered as one reason for the volatility of crude oil prices. In Fan et al. (2008) a significant long-term equilibrium co-integrating relationship was identified between the USD/EUR exchange rate and the oil price. This implies that the US dollar's depreciation from 2002 to date was

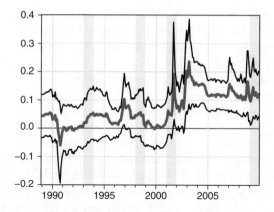

Note: Right axis percent. Bottom axis last data point of window. Shaded areas show downturns of the world economy.

Figure 9.2 Long-term response of interest rates to an asset price shock

a key factor in driving up international crude oil prices. In the underlying analysis the changes in the exchange rate did not have any impact on the oil price until the 1985–99 windows. However, in subsequent years, some structural relationship between these two variables is observable. In the 1995–2009 window a 1 per cent depreciation of the currency usually led to a 1 per cent increase in the USD quoted oil price.

9.4.2.2 Impact of an oil price shock

Since the early 1970s fluctuations in crude oil prices have been a major concern of monetary authorities, as for non-oil-producing economies a clear negative relation between oil prices and aggregate measures of output and employment has been reported. The underlying study suggests that a one-time increase in the price of oil has a permanent impact on the key indicators of the world economy. During the 1970s and 1980s, interest rates increased following a rise in oil prices. The positive relationship of the two variables became negative in the windows 1981–95 to 1995–2009, when interest rates remained unchanged, or they even declined after an oil price increase. In these years, monetary authorities no longer reacted to inflation purely resulting from oil price increases. Some have argued that recessions that followed big oil shocks were caused not by the oil shocks themselves, but rather by the monetary authorities' contractionary response to inflation concerns attributable to the oil price shocks. Bernanke et al. (1997) presented key evidence supporting this view, demonstrating that, if one shuts down the tendency of the federal funds rate to rise following an oil shock, or simulates an SVAR subsequent to the big oil shocks under the condition that the federal funds rate could not rise, it appears that the economic downturns might be largely avoided.

9.4.2.3   Impact of a non-energy commodity price shock

A key characteristic of the development of commodity prices is their cyclical behaviour, as prices tend to increase when demand is above its natural level and to decrease when demand is low. These cyclical movements in prices have important implications for many developing countries that depend on commodity exports, as booms and slumps in prices can induce wide fluctuations in earnings from commodity exports. Until the window 1988–2002 interest rates went up, responding to an increase in commodity prices; however, the positive relationship of these two variables became negative in the following years. Up to the window 1982–96 a shock in commodity prices caused a decrease in world trade. In the following years this negative relationship turned positive. A possible reason for this change could be that rising commodity prices lead to an increase in earnings, which in turn increases the emerging markets' demand for investment goods from abroad.

9.4.2.4   Impact of an interest rate shock

Monetary aggregates tend to move in the same direction as the aggregate economic activity. This co-movement accounts for the passive response of the money supply to changes in the level of activity that are not directly related to monetary policy. In some countries, this endogenous feedback is interrupted by interventions by the monetary policy authorities. However, most changes in monetary policy reflect macroeconomic conditions, since monetary authorities are committed to macroeconomic stabilization. Economists closely connected with policy tend to view the monetary authority as capable of controlling nominal short-term interest rates and thereby of strongly influencing the level of aggregate activity. Many authors have addressed the measurement of the effects of monetary policy by means of SVAR methodology, for example, Sims (1992) or Bernanke et al. (1997). The results of this analysis suggest that interest rates have a dampening impact on economic growth. World oil production, which also reflects global demand, shows a negative response to an interest rate shock; however, the impact declines over the years. The negative response of world trade to an interest rate shock has been fading since the 1986–2000 windows.

9.4.2.5   Impact of an oil production shock

A large body of researchers, for example, Hamilton (2003), has found that energy supply disruptions have a significant impact on economic activity.

In this context, one can clearly identify military conflicts in the Middle East that have significantly disrupted world petroleum supplies. An exogenous decrease in the supply of energy pushes up prices and reduces economic output directly by lowering productivity and indirectly – to the extent that lower wages include movements in the labour supply scheme – by inducing changes in business mark-ups, or capacity utilization rates. If the magnitude of supply disruptions is used as an instrument for oil price changes, the predictions of a linear regression become very similar to those of the nonlinear specifications. However, since the 1992–2006 windows the emergence of a structural relationship between oil production and oil prices is observable, as an increase in production leads to lower oil prices. In the preceding years this relation only held occasionally and the impact was very low.

9.4.2.6   Impact of a trade shock

International flows of goods are considered as the major factors for sustainable development. In Edwards (1998), open economies experience faster productivity growth than others. In order to maintain competitiveness, countries have to specialize, which leads to increased cross-border trade flows. Trade linkages generate both demand and supply-side spillovers across countries. Through these types of spillover effects, stronger trade linkages can result in more highly correlated business cycles. During the windows 1982–96 and 1988–2002, the cross–border trade flows had a positive impact on interest rates. However, in the following years the impact declined again.

9.5   CONCLUSIONS

Underlying research focuses on the structural relationships of key world indicators like aggregate exports, asset prices, non-energy commodity prices, interest rates, oil prices, oil production and the USD/EUR exchange rate. The analysis is based on SVAR methodology. The observations range from 1974 to 2009 and have a monthly frequency. A smaller date range, or window, whose width is fixed, is placed at the beginning of the selected date range. This window is then moved forward by monthly increments. For each window the model was estimated again and its structure was identified again. The results are a sequence of long-term impact multipliers for each variable for the windows 1974–88 to 1995–2009.

A strong structural relationship of variables was found between an asset price shock and the response of interest rates. In the windows 1980–94 to 1984–98, a 1 per cent rise in asset prices led to a 6-basis-point increase in interest rates in the long run. The magnitude of the multipliers and their significance level increased strongly in the windows 1988–2002 to 1995–2009. In these years a 1 per cent rise in asset prices led to a 12-basis-point increase in interest rates, with a likelihood of around 90 per cent. This result suggests that the strong positive structural relationship between asset prices and interest rates might be responsible for the 2008–09 crisis. Therefore, there is evidence that this crisis follows the path of the Austrian Business Cycle. The strong long-term response of interest rates to an asset price shock also explains why the crisis turned out to be much more severe than the 2001 crisis.

In contrast to the asset price/interest rate relationship, the significance level of the other relationships of variables is relatively low. There are only a few episodes in which the estimated impact multipliers have a probability of more than 50 per cent. For example, the windows covering the years of major oil price shocks show that an increase in oil prices led to an increase in interest rates and also to a decline in oil production; and in the windows 1976–90 to 1986–2000 interest rates responded positively to commodity price shocks. However, in the subsequent windows the impact of the responses faded. This might be due to multiple structural breaks that occurred at unknown dates in each system of equations.

NOTES

1. The process of recognizing a possible appropriate model is called identification.
2. For example, Cashin et al. (1999) state that the historical behaviour of oil prices does not allow predictions of future oil price cycles.

REFERENCES

Bagus, P. (2008), 'Monetary policy as bad medicine: the volatile relationship between business cycles and asset prices', *Review of Austrian Economics*, **21** (4), 283–300.

Bernanke, B.S., M. Gertler and M. Watson (1997), 'Systematic monetary policy and the effect of oil price shocks', *Brookings Papers of Economic Activity*, **1**, 91–157.

Cashin, P.A., J.C. McDermott and A.M. Scott (1999), 'Booms and slumps in world commodity prices', IMF Working Paper No. 155.

Edwards, S. (1998), 'Openness, productivity and growth: what do we really know', *Economic Journal*, **108** (447), 383–398.

Fan, Y., H. Tsai, Y. Wei and Y. Zhang (2008), 'Spillover effect of the US dollar exchange rate on oil prices', *Journal of Policy Modeling*, **30** (6), 973–991.

Furlanetto, F. (2008), 'Does monetary policy react to asset prices? Some international evidence', HEC Lausanne and Norges Bank Working Paper.

Hamilton, J.D. (2003), 'What is an oil shock', *Journal of Econometrics*, **113** (2), 363–398.

Hamilton, J.D. (2009), 'Understanding crude oil prices', *Energy Journal*, **30** (2), 179–206.

Rigobon, R. and B. Sacks (2003), 'Measuring the reaction of monetary policy to the stock market', *The Quarterly Journal of Economics*, **118** (2), 639–669.

Sims, C.A. (1980), 'Macroeconomics and reality', *Econometrica*, **48** (1), 1–48.

Sims, C.A. (1986), 'Are forecasting models usable for policy analysis', *Federal Reserve Bank of Minneapolis Quarterly Review*, **10** (1), 2–16.

Sims, C.A. (1992), 'Interpreting the macroeconomic time series facts: the effects of monetary policy', *European Economic Review*, **36** (5), 975–1000.

10. The role of the history of economic thought in the development of economic theory and policy

Steven Kates

Since the onset of the Global Financial Crisis (GFC), the question that has been before the economics community of the world has been, first, how to explain what brought on deep recession during the latter months of 2008 and the first few months of 2009, and then, more importantly given the nature of these problems, how to reduce the impact of the recession and return our economies as quickly as we possibly can to rapid rates of non-inflationary growth and acceptable levels of unemployment.

There is, as it happens, a textbook answer to the second question and in many ways it is also the answer to the first. The answer to the second question, so far as policy is concerned, is to stimulate aggregate demand through a vast public expenditure programme. As to the first, explaining why it has happened revolves around explaining why there had been a fall in aggregate demand across the world. It is this fall in demand that is seen to have lowered economic growth and caused unemployment rates to rise.

The analysis and policy response come from the bedrock Keynesian model found in virtually every macroeconomics text in the world. They come in a number of different forms, but no economist is unfamiliar with the C+I+G Keynesian-cross-approach, IS-LM curves, or models built around aggregate demand-aggregate supply. All of these were first constructed to illustrate Keynes's argument that recessions are a result of too little demand and to show how an increase in public sector spending could hasten an economy's return to full employment and higher levels of economic activity.[1]

The best known of the world's stimulus packages was the programme introduced in the United States. This was a $US787 billion spending plan that was passed by the US Congress almost immediately after Obama's inauguration. There was no effort made to ensure value for money in the spending. It was the spending itself, basically on anything at all, that was considered sufficient. In this, the approach taken followed the prescription laid out in Keynes's *The General Theory* (1936) which essentially suggested that it is always better to spend funds productively but if it proves impossible to do anything else, then unproductive spending would be better than doing nothing. To quote Keynes in one of his most famous passages:

> If the Treasury were to fill old bottles with banknotes, bury them at suitable depths in disused coalmines which are then filled up to the surface with town rubbish, and leave it to private enterprise on well-tried principles of laissez-faire to dig the notes up again (the right to do so being obtained, of course, by tendering for leases of the note-bearing territory), there need be no more unemployment and, with the help of the repercussions, the real income of the community, and its capital wealth also, would probably become a good deal greater than it actually is. It would, indeed, be more sensible to build houses and the like; *but if there are political and practical difficulties in the way of this, the above would be better than nothing.* (Keynes, 1936, p. 129; italics added)

Given the haste with which such expenditure programmes were designed and put into place, the virtual certainty is that no genuine efforts were made to ensure that the funds were used in ways that earned a positive return.

Nor was the US stimulus package even the largest. The following is a discussion of the approach taken within China to deal with the effects of the fall off in export demand that had major impacts on economic activity:

> Faced with the dramatic fall of GDP growth, the Chinese Government took action swiftly. In November 2008, the Government introduced a Rmb4 trillion stimulus package for 2009 and 2010. The prescribed dosage of the stimulus is very large, at 14 per cent of GDP in 2008. (Yu, 2009, p. 9)

Here, too, there is no mistaking the underlying Keynesian approach. The Chinese government, in an attempt to reverse the recessionary effects of the fall in exports, launched a massive domestic expenditure programme. The proper response to a downturn in economic activity was seen by the Chinese government as an increase in the level of aggregate demand driven by higher levels of public spending.

10.1   CONTRAST WITH CLASSICAL POLICY

The Keynesian approach to policy is almost the reverse of the policies that were put into place in accordance with the economic theories that prevailed during the Great Depression. As Keynes made clear in *The General Theory*, the core issue was whether demand deficiency was a proper explanation for recessions, and therefore whether stimulating demand was the proper response. And within this discussion, the pivotal issue was the validity of a principle that Keynes referred to as 'Say's Law' and that he famously defined as 'supply creates its own demand'. According to Keynes, because they had accepted Say's Law as valid, classical economists had denied not only that deficient demand was the cause of recession, but had also denied, according to Keynes again, that it was possible for recessions even to occur. By ignoring the effects of aggregate demand on the level of output, Keynes wrote that the economics profession of his own time had 'neglected to take account of the drag on prosperity which can be exercised by an insufficiency of effective demand' (Keynes, 1936, p. 33). The consequence has been that economic policy since Keynes has been directed towards ensuring that recessions are dealt with through efforts to increase the level of effective demand.

But what is noteworthy is that by the time that *The General Theory* had been published, the Great Depression was in most places a thing of the past. The one economy in which recessionary conditions lingered was the USA, which had employed what would later be described as a Keynesian policy; it attempted to bring the Depression to an end through high levels of public spending. Yet the US maintained exceptionally high rates of unemployment until its entry into World War II at the very end of 1941. Elsewhere, and most notably in the UK, the policy employed was strictly classical. Most importantly, the aim was to reduce public spending and return the budget to surplus, which the UK was finally able to do in 1933. And while recovery remained slow and difficult, the UK had returned to more or less normal times by the end of the 1930s.

Within this, Australia is a particularly interesting case study. Australia entered the Great Depression with the rest of the world in 1929. In 1931, following a report to the government on what needed to be done, there was a massive cut in public spending and a 10 per cent cut in wages across the board. The result was that Australia was one of the first economies to emerge from the Great Depression with continuing improvement year by year right up until Australia's entry into World War II in 1939. Thereafter, labour shortages were, as would be expected, the general experience.

The following data on the unemployment rates in the United States, the United Kingdom and Australia provide some indication of the relative success of the policies that had been pursued at the time.

Given these historical parallels, it is therefore of quite some interest to recognize that the policies that were introduced to deal with the GFC provide a potentially decisive test in which Keynesian policies can be assessed. A Keynesian model is just one model amongst many possible models. It is a product of human thought. It is an attempt to identify the important variables that determine growth rates and the level of

Table 10.1   Unemployment rates in the USA, the UK and Australia,
1929–38

Year	USA	UK	Australia
1930	8.7	16.1	12.7
1932	23.6	22.1	23.0
1933	24.9	19.9	21.0
1934	21.7	16.7	17.9
1935	20.1	15.5	15.5
1936	16.9	13.1	12.6
1937	14.3	10.8	10.9
1938	19.0	12.9	8.9

Source: Australian data: Withers and Pope (1993); United States data: US Bureau of
Labor Statistics; UK data: Garside (1990).

unemployment. But even though it is the model that is now familiar
to every economist, and provides the framework for almost all policy
analysis, it is still only one way of looking at things.

What the history of economics can do is bring into contemporary
debates over the appropriate response to the GFC an understanding of
the models of the business cycle that had existed prior to the publication
of *The General Theory*. These were models based on an acceptance of
Say's Law. They therefore took a different approach to explaining recessions and large-scale unemployment, with such theories based around
structural questions. It was not the level of demand that mattered in a
classical model, but rather the structure of demand relative to the structure
of supply. It is now possible to examine the effects of the policies adopted
as a response to the GFC and an indication of their validity as a means to
bring coherence to our understanding of the events that took place and as
a guide to policy.

But there is an additional issue that is the practical usefulness of the
study of the history of economic thought (HET) itself. One cannot
compare Keynesian theory with the theories of the past unless one knows
what those theories of the past actually were. The role of the history of
economics is to ensure that economists retain an active knowledge within
their discipline of the different ways of understanding real world phenomena. Whether all economists understand the singular importance of the
history of economics in the development of economic ideas is very much
in doubt. One of the tasks of HET specialists, therefore, is to ensure that
the entire profession comes to understand the relevance and importance of
the study of the history of their own discipline.[2]

10.2   HISTORY OF ECONOMICS AND ECONOMIC POLICY

In this regard, there was a quite instructive correspondence on the history of economic thought website dealing with the role and significance of HET within economic theory that should not be allowed to disappear into the ether without comment. What that correspondence highlighted was the very different views of the role and significance of the history of economic thought held within the discipline by specialists in HET. And what makes this correspondence so significant is that two of the most influential members of the history of economics community joined in the debate and gave their own views on the role they believe HET ought to play.

The correspondence was initiated by a posting of my own on 13 March 2009. This was in the early stages of the GFC when the level of economic uncertainty was at its most intense. It was posted because *The Economist* was at the time running an online debate about whether a Keynesian stimulus package would make economic sense given the difficulties that the world's economy was in. What I found worth noting was that part of the discussion took up the issue of Say's Law and therefore explicitly dealt with an issue well within the realm of the history of economic thought. Or so I believed.

This posting brought forward a number of responses, but the following from Roy Weintraub was highly significant. Professor Weintraub is a former President of the History of Economics Society in the United States and Associate Editor of the *History of Political Economy*. He is Professor of Economics at Duke University specializing in the history of economic thought. And on 25 March he wrote the following brief post: 'I'm confused. What does this have to do with the history of economics? Why would an historian of science care about which kind of reserve requirement is "best"?'

This brought directly into focus the issue to the question that was central to my original posting. From the perspective of Professor Weintraub, economic policy questions are of no concern to historians of economics when acting as historians of economics. This was beyond whether an historian of economics would have any additional insights to contribute to such a debate. This was whether an HET specialist should even care about economic policy, which took the discussion back to the original point I was trying to make. The mainstream thinks there is no role for HET in the development of economic theory and policy, but that we have known for a long time. Weintraub's question meant that, in essence, he agreed with the mainstream but in the reverse direction, by asking what role does a discussion of contemporary issues have in HET? A very interesting issue indeed over which reasonable people might well disagree.

Amongst the many subsequent postings was one from Steve Medema. Medema had been the editor of the *Journal of the History of Economic Thought* from 1998 to 2008 and was not only on the executive committee but was also President-elect of the History of Economic Society in the USA at the time he made his own contribution to the discussion. There was a great deal of food for thought in Medema's posting but of particular significance was his division of the uses that HET could be put to into three broad classifications:

1. studying the history of ideas and disciplines as just a thing in itself with no other motivation other than to know what had happened;
2. using that history of ideas and disciplines toward a particular end – whether it be to prop up what passes as the mainstream at any given point in time, or to attack it;
3. using the ideas of the past to help us understand the present – without passing judgment.

The first and third he had sympathy for; 'not so much' as he put it for the second. In writing as he did, although superficially he appeared to be taking issue with the use of HET in debates over policy, the real question in his mind seemed be whether debates on policy ought to take place amongst HET specialists in HET journals.

In my reply to Medema, I noted that discussions amongst historians of economics are where economists clarify amongst themselves those ideas that have descended to us from the past. Perhaps the history of economic thought is not the place for such discussion. But if such discussions are not to take place amongst historians of economics, then where should they take place? Who would be able to conduct such an inquiry if not specialists in HET?

My reply to Steve Medema led to a further response from Professor Weintraub. His core point was that in regard to the usefulness of HET, 'an overwhelming majority of modern economists find HET of no use whatsoever in their own projects. Attempting to valorize that belief, that choice, is simply a waste of time'. My reply to Professor Weintraub closed off the correspondence on this topic. The core point I tried to make was that while there is too little understanding of the role and usefulness of HET amongst the wider profession, it would be a mistake for HET to retreat into the history and philosophy of science. Such a descent would not only be a mistaken judgment for historians of economics, it would be a mistaken judgment for economists generally were they to allow it to happen.

10.3   SOME COMMENTARY

We who study the history of economics approach our own researches with different motivations. One can study Adam Smith, say, for entirely historical reasons unrelated to contemporary policy issues. Or one might study Smith for historical reasons but suddenly find that the insights gained have a contemporary policy relevance. Or one might study Smith specifically because of the insights that might be offered in regard to the economic issues of our time. One might even be interested in Smith for entirely philosophical reasons unrelated to any economic purpose whatsoever. The aim of the researcher is whatever it might be but is basically personal and has little to do with the subject itself.

However, one of the most important issues in a discussion of the role of the history of economic thought is to identify whether HET has an important role to play in the development of economic theory and policy. To return to Professor Weintraub's question, 'why would an historian of science care about which kind of reserve requirement is "best"?' But supposing not a single historian of economics cares about any of this, the question still remains, given the research that HET specialists have undertaken into the history of monetary theory, where they have examined and written on the works of monetary economists of the past, whether that research has been guided by an invisible hand of a different kind to add value to the study of economics even though that may not have been the intent of the person doing the research.

Partly through contact with HET specialists, partly through personal research of their own, economists dealing with practical policy questions have their answers informed by studies that are undertaken into the history of economics. Economists who have studied the works of Thornton, Ricardo, Tooke and Fisher will have insights useful to others. Thinking about Fisher, it might well be asked whether studying Friedman today is part of modern economic theory or is part of the history of economics. When do the insights provided by an economist transfer into HET and disappear from mainstream economic consideration?

The mainstream of the profession at the moment is of the belief that investigating the views of earlier generations of economists provide them with less value than the cost of discovering what those views had actually been. If this were the case, there would be virtually no value in HET being taught to economists. Nor would it much matter whether it was taught and studied by economists within economics departments or was, instead, taught as the philosophy of science to students of cultural studies. But it is not the case as Steven Medema's posting should make clear. To repeat, Medema argues that there are three possible reasons for studying HET:

1. studying the history of ideas and disciplines as just a thing in itself with no other motivation other than to know what had happened;
2. using that history of ideas and disciplines toward a particular end – whether it be to prop up what passes as the mainstream at any given point in time, or to attack it;
3. using the ideas of the past to help us understand the present – without passing judgment.

The first of these is what might be described as 'the Weintraub approach'. It is HET as a scholarly activity undertaken with no particular intent in mind other than a desire to know. This is a purist's version of HET, and may indeed, represent the approach of the majority of those engaged in HET. Most academics are not involved in policy questions. They pursue areas of interest to themselves for personal reasons, which are largely of no extrinsic interest. Whether or not such individuals have economics training is irrelevant nor does it much matter who their readership is. It is a study undertaken only for its own interest with no wider concerns about relevance to the rest of the world. It is the classical picture of an academic and of an academic pursuit.

Medema believes that the Weintraub approach is completely valid as a direction for HET scholars to take (as do I) but also accepts the third, 'using the ideas of the past to help us understand the present – without passing judgment'. Let us call this third possibility 'the Medema approach' since this is what he has done himself in relation to the GFC. As he wrote, 'an understanding of the history of ideas is of no less import for dealing with the present than is understanding the history of events' but in providing such understanding, one should not use the research one undertakes to attempt to pick and choose between different policy directions. So far as policy is concerned, one should remain agnostic; one should not pass judgment based on these studies in HET on the policy choices made by governments and other decision-making bodies.

There is then the second possibility listed above, which I will call 'the Adam Smith approach' following Smith's use of HET in the *Wealth of Nations* where he contrasted his own theories with the mercantilist doctrine of Thomas Mun who had written more than a century before Smith (1776, vol. I, p. 453).

What I take from the distinction made by Medema between his own approach and the Adam Smith approach is that if one follows the Medema approach, one should not then use the knowledge one has gained in studying this area in the history of economics to undertake research on these issues within HET nor should one apply any of the conclusions reached to form a judgment about policy. Because if one does, an economist is shifting into that second category, 'using that history of ideas and disciplines toward a particular end – whether it be to prop up what passes as the mainstream at any given point in time, or to attack it'. It is this option that Medema has little sympathy for. This is not, in his view, what scholars in HET really ought to be doing.

Yet if someone has a comparative advantage in a particular issue, which they have gained through mastery of an area of economic scholarship, the community loses the value of what that scholar has discovered. Since such self-discipline would seldom if ever be exercised by scholars with a depth of knowledge in an area of public debate who are also able to find their way into the public square should they so desire, it is not likely to lead to a loss of policy advice. To the extent that it did, it would be a net loss to society.

But in reality, the question is not whether individual scholars within HET should be involved in discussing public issues. The core issue is whether the subject area of the history of economic thought is a necessary part of the study of economics and therefore should help inform policy debates. The question is not whether there are other uses for HET, but whether the subject area of economic theory and economic policy are diminished without the history of economic thought being an integral part of the subject. This is the issue that matters.

What drives the research into HET is irrelevant to recognizing that research into HET is an important component of the study of economics itself. Economic theory and policy development require that the study of the history of economic thought takes place alongside. The uses that are made of the research into HET are separate and apart from the research itself. My issue is not with what historians of economics do but with what economists do. Historians of economics are merely the means by which policy-makers and their economic advisors come into contact with historic ideas beyond the mainstream. That is why I wrote: 'You do not become a better physicist by reading Newton, Rutherford and Einstein, but you do become a better economist by reading Adam Smith, Marx and Hayek'.

As I read Weintraub's reply, my understanding is that there is no point in arguing from authority about any of the economic issues that divide us. Since one can only argue from one's own perspective, in going back to earlier generations of economists all one is doing is finding a genealogy for one's present beliefs. As far as he is concerned, HET should not be the feedstock of ideas for contemporary debates, with the most important reason being that if you do not believe some argument in the first place, having an ancient economist quoted at you will make no difference.

This enters quite deep currents of epistemological truth. Bringing

Thornton, Ricardo, Tooke or Fisher to the discussion may not win an argument purely on weight of authority. But if their arguments are sound, or if their arguments can be developed in ways that capture important aspects of an issue, their contributions can be valuable. Such grounds for belief will, of course, seldom be decisive but the acuteness of so much of the economics written in the past does help to clarify issues before us in the present.

In his conclusion, Weintraub adds that 'an overwhelming majority of modern economists find HET of no use whatsoever in their own projects'. But even if most, at present, find no direct use in HET in their economic work, even on Weintraub's assessment some clearly do and all benefit from living amongst a pool of economists, some of whom are well versed in the history of their subject. The aim amongst historians of economics, not all but at least for some, is to remind the mainstream of the profession that there are valuable insights that exist amongst our forebears. And while it may be that there will never come a time when the majority of economists make any use whatsoever of the economists of the past, it is in their interests to ensure that those economists and their ideas remain alive within the economics communities in which they work. The result is a deeper, richer tradition upon which they can draw, even if they themselves are only reading the most recent papers or the latest texts.

NOTES

1. See Schneider (2010) for a discussion of the origins of these curves following the publication of *The General Theory* (1936).
2. One of the reasons I take seriously the role of HET in the development of economic theory and the formation of policy is an earlier experience in 2007 during which the Australian Bureau of Statistics attempted to remove HET from the 'Economics' classification within our national statistical collection. This re-classification would have effectively ended the study of HET in Australia. (For a discussion of this episode see Kates and Millmow, 2008a, 2008b, 2008c.)

REFERENCES

Garside, W.R. (1990), *British Unemployment 1919–1939: Study in Public Policy*, Cambridge, UK: Cambridge University Press.

Kates, S. and A. Millmow (2008a), 'The history wars of economics: the classification struggle in the history of economic thought', *History of Economics Review*, **47**, 110–124.

Kates, S. and A. Millmow (2008b), 'A canary in the coalmine: the near death experience of history of economics in Australia', *History of Economic Ideas*, **16** (3).

Kates, S. and A. Millmow (2008c), 'A canary in the coalmine: a rejoinder', *History of Economic Ideas*, **16** (3).

Keynes, J.M. (1936), *The General Theory of Employment, Interest and Money*, as reprinted in D.E. Moggridge (ed.) (1973), *The Collected Writings of John Maynard Keynes*, vol. VII, London: Macmillan.

Schneider, M. (2010), 'Keynesian income determination diagrams', in M. Blaug and P. Lloyd (eds), *Famous Figures and Diagrams in Economics*, Cheltenham, UK and Northampton, MA, USA: Edward Elgar.

Smith, A. (1776), *An Inquiry into the Nature and Causes of the Wealth of Nations*, as reprinted in E. Cannan (ed.) (1976), Chicago: University of Chicago Press.

US Bureau of Labor Statistics (various years), *Historical Unemployment Data*, Washington: BLS.

Withers, G. and D.H. Pope (1993), 'Unemployment statistics – historical series', The Australian National University (internal document).

Yu, Y. (2009), 'China's policy response to the global financial crisis', Richard Snape Lecture, 25 November 2009, Melbourne: Productivity Commission.

Societies for the History of Economics (SHOE) Postings

The entire correspondence can be viewed at: https://listserv.yorku.ca/cgi-bin/ wa?A1=ind0903d&L=shoe for weeks 2, 3 and 4 of March 2009; all accessed 9 September 2010.

The specific postings discussed in this article are found at the following addresses within the SHOE archive:

First Steve Kates posting:
https://listserv.yorku.ca/cgi-bin/wa?A2=ind0903b&L=shoe&T=0&P=1127

First Roy Weintraub posting:
https://listserv.yorku.ca/cgi-bin/wa?A2=ind0903d&L=shoe&T=0&P=2531

Second Steve Kates posting in reply to Roy Weintraub:
https://listserv.yorku.ca/cgi-bin/wa?A2=ind0903d&L=shoe&T=0&P=2911

Steve Medema posting:
https://listserv.yorku.ca/cgi-bin/wa?A2=ind0903d&L=shoe&T=0&P=4125

Third Steve Kates posting in reply to Steve Medema:
https://listserv.yorku.ca/cgi-bin/wa?A2=ind0903d&L=shoe&T=0&P=5238

Second Roy Weintraub posting:
https://listserv.yorku.ca/cgi-bin/wa?A2=ind0903d&L=shoe&T=0&P=5997

Fourth Steve Kates posting in reply to Roy Weintraub's second posting:
https://listserv.yorku.ca/cgi-bin/wa?A2=ind0903e&L=shoe&T=0&P=659

PART III

Country cases in a global crisis

11. Testimony to the Financial Crisis Inquiry Commission by Alan Greenspan[1]

Editorial note

On 7 April 2010, Alan Greenspan, former Chairman of the Federal Reserve, appeared before the Financial Crisis Inquiry Commission of the USA. The editors have considered it useful to reproduce the nine sections of his speech where Greenspan scrutinizes the origins of the crisis in the financial system of the USA, the institutions that must bear the blame and the remedies to avoid similar crisis.

11.1 THE INTERNATIONAL ROOTS OF THE FINANCIAL CRISIS

It was the global proliferation of securitized US subprime mortgages that was the immediate trigger of the current crisis. But its roots reach back, as best I can judge, to 1989, when the fall of the Berlin Wall exposed the economic ruin produced by the Soviet system. Central planning, in one form or another, was discredited and widely displaced by competitive markets.

China, in particular, replicated the successful economic export-oriented model of the so-called Asian Tigers, and by 2005, according to the IMF, 800 million members of the world's labor force were engaged in export-oriented, and therefore competitive, markets, an increase of 500 million workers since 1990. Additional hundreds of millions became subject to domestic competitive forces, especially in Eastern Europe. As a consequence, between 2000 and 2007, the rate of growth in real GDP of the developing world was more than double that of the developed world.

The developing world's consumption restrained by culture and inadequate consumer finance could not keep up with the surge of income and, as a consequence, the savings rate of the developing world soared from 24 percent of nominal GDP in 1999 to 34 percent by 2007, far outstripping its investment rate.

Whether it was a glut of excess intended saving, or a shortfall of investment intentions, the result was the same: a fall in global real long-term interest rates and their associated capitalization rates. Asset prices, particularly house prices, in nearly two dozen countries accordingly moved dramatically higher. US house price gains were high by historical standards but no more than average compared to other countries.

The rate of global housing appreciation was accelerated beginning in late 2003 by the heavy securitization of American subprime and Alt-A mortgages, bonds that found willing buyers at home and abroad, many encouraged by grossly inflated credit ratings. More than a decade of virtually unrivaled global prosperity, low inflation, and low long-term interest rates reduced global risk premiums to historically unsustainably low levels. (They remained 'unsustainably low' for years, however.)

11.2   GROWTH OF THE US SUBPRIME MARKET

For years, subprime mortgages in the United States had been a small but successful appendage to the broader US home mortgage market, comprising less than 2.5 percent of total home mortgages serviced in 2000. The market served a relatively narrow part of the potential US homeowner population that could not meet the 20 percent down payment requirement of prime mortgages, but could still support the monthly payment amounts and less stringent loan origination requirements of a subprime loan. In the 2000 time frame, almost 70 percent of such loans were fixed-rate mortgages, fewer than half of subprime originations had been securitized, and few, if any, were held in portfolios outside the United States. From its origins in the early 1990s to 2003, it was a well functioning market. I supported such lending, which increased access to homeownership for minorities and other traditionally underserved populations, an important goal in a capitalist society.

With the price of homes having risen at a quickening pace since 1997, subprime lending was seen as increasingly profitable to investors. Belatedly drawn to this market, larger financial firms, starting in late 2003, began to accelerate the pooling and packaging of subprime home mortgages into securities. The firms clearly had found receptive buyers. Foreign investors, largely European, were drawn to the above-average yield on these securities and the seemingly below-average risk reflected in a foreclosure rate on the underlying mortgages that had been in decline for two years. At the peak of demand in 2006, according to trade reports at the time, a significant part of subprime securities were sold abroad (largely in the form of collateralized debt obligations), a fact confirmed by the recent heavy losses on US mortgages reported by European investors.

11.3 THE ROLE OF THE GSEs

Of far greater importance to the surge in demand, the major US government-sponsored enterprises (GSEs), Fannie Mae and Freddie Mac, pressed by the US Department of Housing and Urban Development[2] and the Congress to expand 'affordable housing commitments', chose to meet them in a wholesale fashion by investing heavily in subprime mortgage-backed securities. The firms purchased an estimated 40 percent of all private-label subprime mortgage securities (almost all adjustable rate), newly purchased, and retained on investors' balance sheets during 2003 and 2004.[3] That was an estimated five times their share of newly purchased and retained in 2002, implying that a significant proportion of the increased demand for subprime mortgage-backed securities during the years 2003–04 was effectively politically mandated, and hence driven by highly inelastic demand. The enormous size of purchases by the GSEs in 2003–04 was not revealed until Fannie Mae in September 2009 reclassified a large part of its securities portfolio of prime mortgages as subprime.

To purchase these mortgage-backed securities, Fannie and Freddie paid whatever price was necessary to reach their affordable housing goals. The effect was to pre-empt 40 percent of the market upfront, leaving the remaining 60 percent to fill other domestic and foreign investor demand. Mortgage yields fell relative to ten-year Treasury notes, exacerbating the house price rise which, in those years, was driven by interest rates on long-term mortgages.

In testimony before the Senate Banking Committee in February 2004, the Federal Reserve expressed concern:

> about the growth and the scale of the GSEs' mortgage portfolios, which concentrate interest rate and prepayment risks at these two institutions. Unlike many well-capitalized savings and loans and commercial banks, Fannie and Freddie have chosen not to manage that risk by holding greater capital. Instead, they have chosen heightened leverage, which raises interest rate risk but enables them to multiply the profitability of subsidized debt in direct proportion to their degree of leverage.

The testimony goes on to say that, '[t]hus, GSEs need to be limited in the issuance of GSE debt and in the purchase of assets, both mortgages and nonmortgages, that they hold.' I still hold to that view.

11.4   CONCERNS ABOUT THE UNSUSTAINABLE HOUSING BOOM

In 2002, I expressed concerns to the FOMC [Federal Open Market Committee], noting that 'our extraordinary housing boom . . . financed by very large increases in mortgage debt – cannot continue indefinitely.' It did continue for longer than I would have forecast at the time, and it did so despite the extensive two-year-long tightening of monetary policy that began in mid-2004.

By the first quarter of 2007, virtually all subprime originations were being securitized, and subprime mortgage securities outstanding totaled more than $900 billion, a rise of more than six-fold since the end of 2001.

The large imbalance of demand, led by foreign and GSE investors, pressed securitizers and, through them, mortgage originators, to reach deeper into the limited potential subprime homeowner population by offering a wide variety of exotic products. The newer products (most visibly, adjustable-rate mortgages (ARMs), especially payment option ARMs, lowered immediate monthly servicing requirements sufficiently to enable a large segment of previously untapped, high-risk, marginal buyers to purchase a home.

The securitizers, profitably packaging this new source of paper into mortgage pools and armed with what turned out in retrospect to be inaccurately high credit ratings, were able to sell seemingly unlimited amounts of subprime mortgage securities into what appeared to be a vast and receptive global market. Subprime loan underwriting standards, as a consequence, rapidly deteriorated. Subprime mortgage originations accordingly swelled in 2005 and 2006 to a bubbly 20 percent of all US home mortgage originations, almost triple their share in 2002.

The house price bubble, the most prominent global bubble in generations, was engendered by lower interest rates, but, as demonstrated in the Brookings paper I previously provided to the Commission, it was *long-term* mortgage rates that galvanized prices, not the overnight rates of central banks, as has become the seeming conventional wisdom. That should not come as a surprise. After all, the prices of long-lived assets have always been determined by discounting the flow of income (or imputed services) by interest rates of the same maturities as the life of the asset. No one, to my knowledge, employs overnight interest rates – such as the Fed Funds rate – to determine the capitalization rate of real estate, whether it be the cash flows of an office building or the imputed rent of a single-family residence. As I note in the Brookings paper, by 2002 and 2003 it had become apparent that, as a consequence of global arbitrage, individual country long-term interest rates were, in effect, delinked from their historical tie to central bank overnight rates.

11.5   THE DEFLATION OF THE BUBBLE

The bubble started to unravel in the summer of 2007. All asset bubbles, by definition, deflate at some point. But not all bubble deflations result in severe economic contractions. The dot-com bubble and the stock price crash of 1987 did not. Leverage, as Reinhart and Rogoff data demonstrate, is required to set off the serial defaults that foster severe deflation. Thus, unlike the debt-lite deflation of the earlier dot-com boom, heavy leveraging during the housing bubble set off a series of defaults that culminated in what is likely to be viewed, in retrospect, as the most virulent global financial crisis ever. The withdrawal of private short-term credit, the hallmark of severe crisis, on so global a scale, I believe, is without precedent. (The unemployment rate in the Great Depression, of course, was far higher, and economic activity far lower, than today.)

11.6   THE INADEQUACY OF EXISTING RISK MANAGEMENT SYSTEMS TO ADDRESS INCREASINGLY COMPLEX FINANCIAL INSTRUMENTS AND TRANSACTIONS

For almost a half century, we have depended on our highly sophisticated system of financial risk management to contain such market breakdowns. That paradigm was so thoroughly embraced by academia, central banks, and regulators that by 2006 it became the core of global regulatory standards (Basel II).

The risk management paradigm nonetheless harbored a fatal flaw. In the growing state of euphoria, managers at financial institutions, along with regulators including but not limited to the Federal Reserve, failed to fully comprehend the underlying size, length and potential impact of the so-called negative tail of the distribution of risk outcomes that was about to be revealed as the post-Lehman Brothers crisis played out. For decades, with little to no data, almost all analysts, in my experience, had conjectured a far more limited tail risk. That led to more than a half-century of significantly and chronically undercapitalized financial intermediaries, arguably the major failure of the private risk management system.

The financial firms counted on being able to anticipate the onset of crisis in time to retrench. They were mistaken. They believed the then seemingly insatiable demand for their array of exotic financial products would enable them to sell large parts of their portfolios without loss.

Only modestly less of a problem was the virtually indecipherable complexity of a broad spectrum of financial products and markets that developed with the advent of advanced mathematical models to evaluate risk and the large computation capacity to implement them. In despair, an inordinately large part of investment management was subcontracted to the 'safe harbor' risk designations of the credit rating agencies. But despite their decades of experience, the rating agencies proved no more adept at anticipating the onset of crisis than the investment community at large.

Even with the breakdown of private risk-management and the collapse of private counterparty credit surveillance, the financial system would have held together had the second bulwark against crisis – our regulatory system – functioned effectively. But, under crisis pressure, it too failed.

US commercial and savings banks are extensively regulated, and even though for years our largest ten to 15 banking institutions have had permanently assigned on-site examiners to oversee daily operations, many of these banks still were able to take on risky assets that brought them to their knees. The heavily praised UK Financial Services Authority was unable to anticipate or prevent the bank run that threatened Northern Rock. The venerated credit rating agencies bestowed ratings that implied Aaa [sic] smooth-sailing for many a highly toxic derivative product. Even the IMF noted as late as April 2007 that 'global economic risks have declined since . . . September 2006 . . .. [T]he overall US economy is holding up well . . . [and] the signs elsewhere are very encouraging.' The Basel Committee on Banking Supervision, representing regulatory authorities from the world's major financial systems, promulgated a set of capital rules that failed to foresee the need that arose at the height of the crisis for much larger capital and liquidity buffers.

Bubble emergence is easy to identify in narrowing credit spreads. But the trigger point of crisis is not. A financial crisis is descriptively defined as an abrupt, discontinuous drop in asset prices. If the imbalances that precipitate a crisis are visible, they tend to be arbitraged away. For the crisis to occur, it must be unanticipated by almost all market participants and regulators.

Over the years, I have encountered an extremely small number of analysts who are *consistently* accurate at discontinuous turning points. The vast majority of supposedly successful turning point forecasts are, in fact, mere happenstance.

In my view, the recent crisis reinforces some important messages about what supervision and examination can and cannot do. Regulators who are required to forecast have had a woeful record of chronic failure. History tells us they cannot identify the timing of a crisis, or anticipate exactly where it will be located or how large the losses and spillovers will be. Regulators cannot successfully use the bully pulpit to manage asset prices, and they cannot calibrate regulation and supervision in response to movements in asset prices. Nor can they fully eliminate the possibility of future crises.

11.7 CAPITAL- AND COLLATERAL-BASED SOLUTIONS TO SUPERVISORY INADEQUACIES

What supervision and examination can do is promulgate rules that are preventative and that make the financial system more resilient in the face of inherently unforeseeable shocks. Such rules would kick in automatically, without relying on the ability of a fallible human regulator to predict a coming crisis. Concretely, I argue that the primary imperatives going forward have to be (1) increased risk-based capital and liquidity requirements on banks and (2) significant increases in collateral requirements for globally traded financial products, irrespective of the financial institutions making the trades. Sufficient capital eliminates the need to know in advance which financial products or innovations will succeed in assisting in effectively directing a nation's savings to productive physical investment and which will fail. A firm that has adequate capital, by definition, will not default on its debt obligations and hence contagion does not arise. All losses accrue to common shareholders.

I believe that during the past 18 months, there were very few instances of serial default and contagion that could have not been contained by adequate risk-based capital and liquidity. I presume, for example, that with 15 percent tangible equity capital, neither Bear Sterns nor Lehman Brothers would have been in trouble. Increased capital, I might add parenthetically, would also likely result in smaller executive compensation packages, since more capital would have to be retained in undistributed earnings.

In addition to the broad issues of capital and liquidity, I also argue that the doctrine of 'too big to fail' (or, more appropriately, 'too interconnected to be liquidated quickly') can not be allowed to stand. The productive employment of the nation's scarce saving is being threatened by financial firms at the edge of failure, supported with taxpayer funds, designated as systemically important institutions. I agree with Gary Stern, the former President of the Federal Reserve Bank of Minneapolis, who has long held the position that 'creditors will continue to underprice the risk-taking of these financial institutions, overfund them, and fail to provide effective market discipline. Facing prices that are too low, systemically important firms will take on too much risk.'[4] These firms absorb scarce savings that needs to be invested in cutting-edge technologies, if output per hour and standards of living are to continue to rise.

One highly disturbing consequence of the taxpayer bailouts that have emerged with this crisis is that market players have come to believe that every significant financial institution, should the occasion arise, would be subject to being bailed out with taxpayer funds. Businesses that are bailed out have competitive market and cost-of-capital advantages, but not efficiency advantages, over firms not thought to be systemically important.

The existence of systemically threatening institutions is among the major regulatory problems for which there are no good solutions. Early resolution of bank problems under the Federal Deposit Insurance Corporation Improvements Act of 1991 (FDICIA) appeared to have worked for smaller banks during periods of general prosperity. But the notion that risks can be identified in a sufficiently timely manner to enable the liquidation of a large failing bank with minimum loss has proved untenable during this crisis and I suspect in future crises as well.

The solution, in my judgment, that has at least a reasonable chance of reversing the extraordinarily large 'moral hazard' that has arisen over the past year is to require banks and possibly all financial intermediaries to hold contingent capital bonds – that is, debt which is automatically converted to equity when equity capital falls below a certain threshold. Such debt will, of course, be more costly on issuance than simple debentures, but its existence could materially reduce moral hazard.

However, should contingent capital bonds prove insufficient, we should allow large institutions to fail, and if assessed by regulators as too interconnected to liquidate quickly, be taken into a special bankruptcy facility. That would grant the regulator access to taxpayer funds for 'debtor-in-possession financing.' A new statute would create a panel of judges who specialize in finance. The statute would require creditors (when equity is wholly wiped out) to be subject to statutorily defined principles of discounts from par ('haircuts') before the financial intermediary was restructured. The firm would then be required to split up into separate units, none of which should be of a size that is too big to fail.

I assume that some of the newly created firms would survive, while others would fail. If, after a fixed and limited period of time, no viable exit from bankruptcy appears available, the financial intermediary should be liquidated as expeditiously as feasible.

11.8   THE FUTURE OF SUBPRIME LENDING

It remains to be seen what type of private subprime market emerges from the ashes of the old. There have been virtually no private subprime originations or securitizations since the beginning of 2008, despite the recovery during the past year in other less-than-investment-grade debt. It is an open question whether investors will be attracted back to a private subprime market anytime in the foreseeable future. The new subprime lending rule initiated by the Fed in 2007 appears reasonable to address future prudential problems when, and if, private lending resumes.

Between 1994 and 2003, when subprime lending was still a niche business and before the explosion in subprime securitization that began in late 2003, minority homeownership increased by approximately 14 percent, a rate of increase not quite double that of whites.[5] A substantial part of that increase was financed with subprime mortgages. Increased foreclosure rates have erased some of those gains, particularly those achieved late in the cycle, but homeownership rates for minorities remain well above their 1994 levels.[6] The withdrawal of affordable housing finance, including for borrowers with subprime credit histories, will surely lower the minority homeownership rate still more. Many recent consumer protection laws in such an environment become moot.

Aside from the setting of the federal funds rate and the management of its investment portfolio, the Board has always had a responsibility to address systemic risk. But recognizing that neither regulators nor economists can predict the timing of future crises or their severity, it is important to have authorities in place to mitigate their impact. In 1991, Congress, at the urging of the Board, modernized section 13(3) of the Federal Reserve Act that granted virtually unlimited authority to the Board to lend in 'unusual and exigent circumstances.' Section 13(3) is the legal authority for much of the actions taken by the Federal Reserve during this crisis.

11.9 CONCLUSION

In closing, let me reiterate that the fundamental lesson of this crisis is that, given the complexity of the division of labor required of modern global economies, we need highly innovative financial systems to assure the proper functioning of those economies. But while, fortunately, much financial innovation is successful, much is not. And it is not possible in advance to discern the degree of future success of each innovation. Only adequate capital and collateral can resolve this dilemma. If capital is adequate, by definition, no debt will default and serial contagion will be thwarted.

We can legislate prohibitions on the kinds of securitized assets that aggravated the current crisis. But investors have shown no inclination to continue investing in much of the past decade's faulty financial innovations, and are unlikely to invest in them in the future. The next pending crisis will no doubt exhibit a plethora of new assets which have unintended toxic characteristics, which no one has heard of before, and which no one can forecast today. But if capital and collateral are adequate, and enforcement against misrepresentation and fraud is enhanced, losses will be restricted to equity shareholders who seek abnormal returns, but in the process expose themselves to abnormal losses. Tax payers will not be at risk. Financial institutions will no longer be capable of privatizing profit and socializing losses.

I thank the Commission for the opportunity to submit these thoughts, and look forward to answering your questions.

NOTES

1. Reproduced with kind permission of Alan Greenspan: Greenspan, A. (2010), 'Testimony to Financial Crisis Inquiry Commission of the USA', speech presented at Washington DC, 7 April 2010.
2. In October 2000, the US Department of Housing and Urban Development (HUD) finalized a rule 'significantly increasing the GSEs' affordable housing goals' for each year 2001 to 2004. In November 2004, the annual housing goals for 2005 and beyond were raised still further (Office of Policy Development and Research, Issue Brief No. V and others).
3. FHFA Annual Report to Congress (2008) (Revised) Historical Data Tables 5b Part 2 and 14b Part 2. (Originally published 18 May, 2009, updated to include a significant reclassification effective 3 September, 2009.)
4. Statement before the Committee on Banking, Housing, and Urban Affairs, US Senate, Washington, DC, 6 May, 2009.
5. Georgetown University Credit Research Center Seminar, 'Ensuring fair lending: what do we know about pricing in mortgage markets and what will the new HMDA data fields tell us?', 14 March, 2005, available at: https://www.chase.com/ccpmweb/chf/document/HMDA2_Staten_Intro.pdf; accessed 11 September 2010.
6. Rakesh Kochhar, Ana Gonzalez-Barrera, and Daniel Dockterman, 'Through boom and bust: minorities, immigrants and homeownership', 12 May, 2009, available at: http://pewhispanic.org/reports/report.php?ReportID=109; accessed 11 September 2010.

12. Long-term depression and new markets: economists and the 2008 recession

Davide Gualerzi

12.1 INTRODUCTION

A cyclical pattern is a well-known aspect of long-term growth. A crisis cannot last forever. However, to get out of the crisis the economy will have to settle into a new growth pattern. The length and severity of the slump are of course important, but so is the new pattern that will emerge. It inevitably implies one of two things: a step forward, or a step backward, an improvement or a deterioration with respect to the previous situation. Our paper focuses on this rarely discussed aspect of the crisis, thus on its relationship to long-term depression. The analysis focuses on the US economy, so that it may not apply to other countries, and developing economies in particular. Still, the main thrust of the argument has a general significance and seems highly relevant for most industrialized economies and especially the EU.

Nobel Prize winner Paul Krugman argues that economic theory is brought again to task by the crisis, suggesting that a return to Keynesian ideas is necessary. But is a rehearsal of the debate between Keynesian and non-(or less) Keynesian economists telling the whole story of the current crisis? Or is it leading the way to a larger set of questions for the history of economic analysis?

We attempt to argue that there is indeed more on the table. Keynesian interpretations of the crisis focus on unpredictable behaviour, market imperfections and the 'human' element. However, it is precisely the characteristics of the current crisis that suggest a more serious question. It concerns the long run and in particular the creation of new markets. Even if the short-term crisis is overcome, without too great a deficit, the long-term contains a different set of problems, and they are not being faced in the debate.

12.2   CRISIS AND LONG-TERM DEPRESSION

During 2009 the debate has been: will the crisis have a V shape (sharp down, sharp up), a U shape (plunge, then flatten out, followed by a sharp recovery), or an L shape (sharp down and stay down)? Or perhaps a W shape (a false recovery in the middle)? Underlying this debate is the long-run question, which seems appropriate since a comparison of today's crisis is often made with the Great Depression.

The real crisis affecting the USA and all the advanced industrial economies appears to be a failure of aggregate demand, itself the consequence of the financial crisis, which caused credit to dry up. With credit simply not available, household consumption slumped and business investment collapsed. This alone is not uncontroversial but it is widely accepted. To counteract the recession, governments increased spending. As a result there has been a considerable amount of debate around the 'stimulus packages' approved by the Obama administration, as well as those of other countries. According to some, these measures are working and will get the US economy out of the slump. Evidence comes from improvements in the banking industry, new profits in investment banking and the rebound of the stock markets from the lows of March 2009. But bringing down unemployment appears to be very difficult.

While the debate between economists focuses on the merits of deficits,[1] there has been a deafening silence on the nature of the crisis and the way fiscal stimulus might kickstart the economy. Underlying all of this is the idea that deficits will re-establish a reasonably stable growth process. But very little is said on such a growth process.

12.3   THE CRISIS AND ECONOMIC THEORY

Parallel to the debate on policies is the debate among economists. With a few exceptions economists were mostly caught by surprise by the eruption of the crisis. The problem has been with the approach of mainstream macro-theory and with the overwhelming role that financial economists have come to play, argues Paul Krugman (2009). Ultimately both have their roots in two hypotheses: agents' rational behaviour and market perfection. The idea that theory had it all under control, including the tools to overcome economic depression, completes the picture.

Since Adam Smith the message had been 'trust the market'. And precisely this was questioned by the Great Depression. Keynes challenged the idea that market economies could work without supervision. In particular, Keynes was sceptical about financial markets that, Krugman recalls, he compared to casinos. That stands in sharp contrast to the leading role played by the theory of financial markets, according to which markets operate efficiently, correctly pricing assets on the basis of the information available. The rational investor would evaluate risk and returns; the CAPM (Capital Asset Pricing Model) has become the basis not only of portfolio decisions but also for the pricing of derivatives.

The hypothesis of efficient markets gained dominance despite the periodical collapses of the stock market, such as those of 1973–74 and 1987. So by the 1970s, irrationality, bubbles and disastrous speculation were virtually cancelled in the theory of financial markets. In macroeconomics Keynes's response to the Great Depression was also almost completely forgotten. It focused on the possibility of an insufficient level of demand driving a depression. The neoclassical purists (Lucas), Krugman argues, would simply call that nonsense; there cannot be a failure of effective demand and so there is not one. Those Krugman calls pragmatists (G. Mankiw, O. Blanchard and David Romer) to some extent did accept the Keynesian notion of a failure in demand, making government intervention desirable. However, they too were fascinated by the notion of rational individuals and perfect markets and did not want to depart much from orthodoxy. These differences were played down by the fact that policy intervention was focused on monetary policy. As long as fiscal policy was not called on to fight recession, the purists were willing to let it go.

This had a lot to do with the fact that between 1985 and 2007 recessions were mild and inflation was under control.[2] The current crisis has changed all of that. It brought down the purists' edifice based on rationality and perfect markets and left the pragmatists to observe that whereas lowering short-term interest rates had been successful in 1990 and 2001, it is not working this time, since at the end of 2008 rates had already reached the 'zero lower bound'.

The crisis forced a change of policy. The Obama administration returned to the fiscal stimulus, re-establishing a Keynesian orientation.[3] According to Akerlof and Shiller (2009) the main point is that Keynes thought that much economic activity is driven by animal spirits. Ultimately these account for economic fluctuations and involuntary unemployment. Government intervention is required to counteract the negative effects of animal spirits, and in particular episodes of exuberance and panic. So the difference between classicism and Keynesian theory is blind trust in rationality as the key to economic decisions. Akerlof and Shiller elaborate on the effects of the 'irrational' component and argue that it affects trust, equity, corruption and antisocial behaviour, monetary illusion and finally the story that is told about what influences economic behaviour and is rooted in who we are and what we do. Through these channels animal spirits can explain phenomena like depression, unemployment, volatility in financial prices and investments, and cyclical patterns in the real estate market.

They argue that the current financial crisis is not just a shortfall in demand, which is customarily addressed by a mix of monetary policy and fiscal stimulus. The problem is the shrinking of credit. Its causes can be found in the change introduced by the 'new finance'. So the story went, in the years of its rise new financial products were tools to manage risk, which they were, at least at an initial stage. As these products spread and grew more complex and complicated, the story began to change; it was suggested that these financial products were ways to sell false remedies. As the new story about the nature of Wall Street's financial transactions took hold the demand for these 'exotic' products collapsed and the credit crunch began. Reconsidering Keynes's notion of animal spirits is then fundamental to manage what are indeed imperfect markets.

According to Akerlof and Shiller this approach is part of an emerging field of studies called behavioural economics, which attempts to explain the real functioning of the economy when the human element is taken into account.

There is a remarkable similarity with the conclusion reached by Krugman. Economists, he argues, should accept the fact that financial markets are far from being perfect. Macroeconomics should incorporate the reality of financial markets and accept that the Keynesian theory is still the best framework for the analysis of recessions. That has a price: giving up the 'clarity, completeness and sheer beauty that characterizes the full neoclassical approach' (Krugman, 2009). In other words, economists must refocus attention on 'mistakes and tensions', trading elegance for relevance. What is relevant are the limitations of human rationality and economic institutions, the shortcoming of markets and the dangers created when regulators do not trust regulation. Behavioural finance stresses that investors are prone to exuberance and panic. Herd behaviour dominates their choices and it is reinforced by problems of trust, credibility and limited warranty. Indeed, there is an entirely new approach, called behavioural economics, trying to explain investors' irrational behaviour and how that leads to instability in financial markets.

In Krugman, the reconstruction of the fading away of the recollection of the Great Depression's mass unemployment and the idea that financial markets are efficient concurred with the re-establishment of an idealized view of the economy. However, there is not much of a criticism of the Federal Reserve monetary policy.

According to Talbott,[4] one of the problems of the crisis is precisely Bernanke's analysis of the Great Depression (see, e.g., Bernanke, 2005). They are both seen as liquidity crises, so injecting enough liquidity would cure the problem. This was certainly done and it might have stopped the collapse of the banking system. However, the remedy may not stretch to what is really necessary for a sustained recovery. The reduction in the money supply and the liquidity crisis, Talbott argues, was a result of the depression, not its cause. The problem is not so much liquidity per se, but the danger of bank failure and that has deeper roots in finance, the real economy and lack of regulation. He singles out the wages standstill, despite continuing productivity growth, as one of the fundamental factors of the crisis. That, and not innovation, new markets and good management, drove the boom in the stock market. Preventing wage inflation was almost an obsession for Alan Greenspan. But success here is the reason for the imbalances experienced by the economy.

12.4 THE MAKING OF THE CRISIS

To fully understand the seriousness of the challenge posed by the crisis we ought to take a step backward and look at the way it developed out of the collapse of the 1990s' expansion. Indeed, the recovery that followed precipitated the crisis of the second part of the 2000s.

12.4.1 Slowdown and Resilience: 2000–03

The collapse of the growth scenario of the 1990s and the burst of the hi-tech bubble at the beginning of 2000 determined the turning around of the cycle.[5] But the downturn was not as bad as the collapse of investment and the 'correction' of stock markets would have suggested.

Critics of the 1990s' expansion who had focused on the piling up of household debt, such as Wynne Godley (2000), would argue that when families hit the bedrock of debt and stop consuming, with little help coming from the government budget, then the economy was bound to slow down.[6] That did happen. Still, the economy as a whole did not crash. At least not in the first part of the 2000s. Why not? Fiscal policy has a role, although here we must probably use an extra amount of caution.

As pointed out by Stiglitz (2003), changes in fiscal policy were already taking place in the 1990s, but they took a decisively harder turn with the Bush administration. The two major features of fiscal policy were military expenditure and tax cuts on dividends. As a result of more spending and less revenues, and declining income since the downturn began, the government deficit went up. Indeed, as in most of the world, right wing politics is not afraid of deficit, certainly less than the moderate left. However, it is not indifferent to how money is spent. The deficit in the Bush administration is mainly the result of cutting taxes for the rich and waging war. The expansionary effects, giving the transmission channels, are weak, (except perhaps contracts given to industries working for the military). So the overall expansionary effects of the deficit were weak, certainly much less than the stimulus required after the retreat of private spending.

While the stock market went into a long, deep correction phase, real estate prices were instead sustained and provided a powerful channel to back household debt. This was facilitated by the 'easy money' policy of the Federal Reserve and the lower than ever interest rates. That, however, shifted the burden of driving growth to the real estate market. And that did not last very long either.

Real estate values, which had been rising throughout the 1990s, were an important element of economic expansion. The mechanism through which they contributed to growth is essentially the possibility of contracting cheap mortgages, because of low interest rates, and then borrowing against rising home values. This had a positive influence on consumer spending, regardless of personal income dynamics.[7] Demand sustained houses prices, and real estate values worked to ensure credit to households that had accumulated debt to unprecedented levels on their credit cards (Manning, 2000). This had an important role in preventing the stagnation of the early 2000s from becoming a more severe slump. In fact, the positive effect continued while the house market remained strong and house prices stayed high. Sustained by consumption spending and house sales, overall aggregate demand showed a remarkable resilience. Then, of course, one should not forget the stimulus coming from the finally enacted tax cuts and the jump of military spending, which as pointed out above are the backbone of the Bush administration economic policy. Though part of a fiscal policy subject to severe criticism, they can have an expansionary, although short-lived and relatively weak, expansionary effect.

To sum up: consumer spending remained relatively vigorous in the middle of such a serious downturn, which, combined with other reasons, contributed to keep the economy afloat. However, considering other major facts affecting the US economy in the 2000s, such as a war and rising oil prices, it was still unclear at the end of 2003 whether there was going to be any kind of expansion at all. The growth scenario was a combination of weaknesses found in GDP growth, employment, wages and the stock market. The US economy had gone from a boom to a phase of uncertainty and stagnation, which it was still experiencing, despite the signs of having reached the bottom.[8]

12.4.2 Recovery and Crisis: 2004–08

The economy did go back to more solid growth and the idea of a new phase of expansion did take hold. The new Fed Chairman Bernanke, at the beginning of his tenure, focused on inflation, in fact core inflation.[9] Despite rising energy costs and the hurricane(s), economic growth was back and inflationary pressures were not so bad. Nonetheless, all of this overlooked the fact that the recovery depended fundamentally on the expansion of credit to households willing to buy homes, with little else – contrary to the 1990s – contributing to aggregate spending. That exacerbated the problem that had been building up over the years. With no new leading sectors driving growth, consumer spending could be sustained only through debt lying in the real estate market. The problem was going to surface soon with the burst of the real estate bubble.

Manning (2005) argues that the real estate bubble in the 2000s was a substitute for the 1990s' hi-tech bubble. All bubbles must burst, and this one did too. However, this one took a few years to materialize. Despite weakness in wages and income growth, rising real estate values continued to provide credit for consumers who had already reached the limit on their credit cards. Indeed, they prevented a wave of personal bankruptcies. Real estate values kept rising because a larger and larger number of buyers were attracted into the market by the combination of low interest repayments, especially for the first two or three years, and a relaxation in the conditions required to obtain mortgages. Attracting low-income, risky clients into the market kept the mechanism running. But this was the last phase of the bubble, and the beginning, in 2006 heralded the turn around in the real estate market.[10]

When interest payments went up, these buyers could not meet their obligations. Banks repossessed properties, but these could not be sold and their prices fell. This brought about the crisis of 2007. Manning argues that it was only a first act in the real estate bubble drama. A second one would involve more wealthy home owners finding themselves with an unsustainable debt in the face of sliding real estate values. Unless, of course, the market rapidly improved.

It becomes clear that in the 2000s the recovery prepared the crisis of the later years. The subprime loans crisis started a generalized debt and liquidity crisis, threatening the banking system and the real economy. It prompted the Federal Reserve, together with other major central banks, and the US Treasury to intervene on a massive scale, setting aside worries about deficit and inflation. That has not prevented the economy from entering into a severe recession. Observing the dramatic reversal of the policy stance that had argued and almost preached against government intervention and supported an increasing deregulation of financial markets, economists and commentators have spoken of the end of a phase. For a new one to begin it must articulate a strategy that, while getting the economy out of the recession, re-establishes prospects for long-run growth.

12.5   FISCAL STIMULUS AND NEW MARKETS

12.5.1   The Stimulus and the Deficit

The real estate bubble was an almost necessary outcome of the 1990s' latest technology-driven stimulus to productivity, growth and structural change (Gualerzi and Nell, 2010). Its burst was a coming to terms with a number of imbalances and especially an accumulation of private debt that had gone on throughout the 1990s.

It is not hard then to see a return to a fiscal stimulus consensus. Although it is unclear whether this is a fundamental reorientation of policy or just a way to cope with a tremendous blow dealt to the economy, this stimulus appeared to be the only way out. However, while one side calls for more stimulus, the other worries about driving up the deficit. A stimulus might cure a crisis, a deficit could interfere with future monetary and fiscal policy. Indeed, a common critique is that even if the stimulus/ bailout package works temporarily, it will fail in the long run because of the burden of debt it will create. A short boost comes at the price of a long-term drag. The doctrine of fiscal austerity, preached for decades, was set aside for a time through fear of economic depression, but it is already making a comeback. Paul Samuelson (2009) has argued that spending and spending now is the only remedy, not the recuperation of finance, as Treasury Secretary Geithner seems to think. Engulfing the market with new sophisticated instruments, financial innovation destroyed market transparency. It is not the time to worry about deficit. We have to worry about the real economy and employment. The New Deal taught us, he says, that only with a resumption of consumer spending will the economy overcome the crisis.

But, let's suppose that the stimulation package works. Even more, let's suppose that Samuelson's advice is fully accepted, that is, assume a massive stimulus, can we expect that to result in a new boom and sustained expansion? Even if fiscal austerity is set aside, that should not overlook the different circumstances in which the stimulus takes place. That ultimately accounts for its long-term consequences. More than the burden of debt we should pay attention to the ways in which the stimulus may restart the economy, sustaining consumer spending and investment. The bulk of the argument about the burden of debt is that it will affect interest rates negatively, therefore discouraging private investment. But this is precisely the point; what does it take to bring investment back into the picture? Focusing on new markets, a better (happier) story about investment can be told, beyond the one customarily focusing on the interest rate.

12.5.2 Deficits and Markets

The alleged dangers of deficits can be seen in a different light looking at history. One example from the past is the war economy in the period 1943–45. Another is the 'golden age' of the 1960s.

The stimulus of World War II, based on a deficit of more that 25 per cent of GNP for three years running, and accompanied by massive planning, price controls, export controls, control over financial markets, and labour directives, decisively ended the depression. The deficit did not have any impact during the war because interest rates were held down, and finance was planned, but it did not matter later either, because growth was really on solid ground. By the 1960s, growth had been so strong and so steady that the ratio of debt to GNP was back to the normal range. Those were certainly exceptional circumstances.

Circumstances were also dramatically different in the 1960s. Those expansion years were marked by the maturity of mass consumption and they were combined with the boom of new industries such as air transportation and television. Electronics was in its infancy, but the markets for durable goods indeed came of age with a large growth in sales and income in the industries producing automobiles and electric appliances. Besides, there was a boom in real estate. The GI Bill had created an enormous market for buying houses and distributed income on a massive scale. The government provided guarantees on mortgages and that encouraged the housing market. But the government also provided support for automobile purchases and college tuition. In general, a full employment macropolicy and union pressures that raised wages led to a large redistribution of income.

Circumstances were then positive from the point of view of a large spending capacity, pinned on the side of demand, and new markets were sustained by the products of rapidly expanding new industries. Both the development of mass consumer industries and new industries in the stricter sense of the word, providing new products and new services, were made possible by the massive use of new technologies. Part of this came with the adaptation of war technology for civilian uses. The effects of new technologies on new markets were driven by investment that contributed to create the modern industry dominated by large corporations. The whole process was intertwined with the rise of the middle class, initially based on war veterans, but soon encompassing families that moved into the cities and the suburbs. This new class saw income and possibilities for spending growing in step with the upgrading of consumer habits and lifestyles.

Is there anything like that on the horizon today? For one thing on the income distribution side, there is a process going the opposite way, with large numbers being pushed out of the middle class into a situation just above or barely keeping up with subsistence level that is not favourable to expansionary consumer evolution. Samuelson observed that we have been deregulating everything, from labour markets to financial markets, to an extent never seen before, and deregulation has a negative effect on income distribution.[11] There is, then, hardly any basis for a mass upgrading of consumer habits and lifestyles. More fundamentally, new products and new industries seem incapable of affording the kind of virtuous cycle going from technology to large investment and innovation, transforming the consumption patterns of the majority of the people. That was the basis of the boom of the 1960s. Its crisis is the background of the stagnation tendencies revealed in the 1970s. Growth slowed down to replacement level and a new pattern emerged where the fundamental problem was the slow growth of the market.

12.6 CAN WE COUNT ON NEW TECHNOLOGIES FOR EXPANSION?

12.6.1 ICTs: The Technology, Investment, New Markets Relationship

The underlying issue is that there were no longer any positive circumstances left in post-war technology, investment and new market relationships. The new pattern was articulated differently in the 1980s and 1990s; it was combined with a rising globalization that, although not a new phenomenon in itself, was changing the relationship of economic and political power between the centre and the periphery of the world economy (Gualerzi, 2007).

The expansion of the 1990s compares favourably to the slow growth of the 1980s. Indeed, one can argue that the 1990s witness a coming of age of information technologies that were finally felt in a massive way creating an investment boom and (admittedly overblown) expectations of a large transformation leading to new markets (Gualerzi, 2010). ICTs in the 1990s well illustrate the fundamental problem with technology-driven development. The problem is not the pace of technological change, which actually accelerated considerably in those years, and it did stimulate a boom, but it lasted only a few years, and fed right into the current crisis. The substitute for the technological bubble was the real estate bubble, and it left the economy in its current precarious state marred by the prospects of a weak and slow recovery. In fact, it cannot fully recover unless it finds a new expansion path.

Two traits of ICTs need to be recalled. It is widely known, although often played down, that new technology – and productivity growth – can cause technological unemployment. Computerization with its effects on automation raises indeed the problem of job loss.[12] ICTs, however, do more than create technological unemployment; they can also destroy markets. Of course, innovation has always had a destructive side.[13] But this appears to be different. New information technologies create extensive externalities, and it is these externalities, which are by definition *free*, that can undermine whole industries.[14]

This only stresses the fact that ICT-driven transformation results in new jobs only if their labour displacement and market-destruction effects are more than compensated by the growth of demand and the formation of new markets. That explains the 'exuberance' while an Internet scenario of development (Gualerzi, 2001) was maturing in the second part of the 1990s, but also the collapse that followed, as the prospects of further market creation appeared badly overestimated. The point is that to become a new engine of growth a technology must create new markets on a large enough scale. The key factor is not the speed of diffusion, with its inevitable delays and accelerations, but rather the prospects of market creation it raises, that is, finding a new field of customers. But that fundamentally depends on a transformation of consumption patterns sufficient to validate the initial investment in innovation and sustain a long-term investment expansion. This in turns calls for an examination of the barriers that a fundamental transformation of consumption patterns may encounter. This is about changing the character of consumption in an advanced economy, a question little investigated as yet but crucial for the question of new markets and investment. One aspect of this bigger picture is precisely the diffusion of ICT products and the Internet.

New consumers' electronics, cell phones and computer networks – including hardware and software for network access – are the most identifiable items of ICT-driven consumption transformation, affecting entertainment, the 'culture industry', education, journalism and the media, tourism and domestic life, but also developing new markets concerning information, communication, access and mobility. These are critical consumer markets in advanced industrial economies. Transformation was sustained by the rapid diffusion of ICT products and the Internet, combined with constant technical improvements, which added new features to successive new generations of these products. From status symbols and/ or items for limited specialized communities (the scientific community) or technology freaks, these innovations have become, in a few years, established consumers items, following a diffusion path that is typical of mass consumption.

12.6.2   Barriers to Consumption Transformation and New Markets

The ICT-driven transformation of consumption patterns, however, has also shown numerous peculiarities and difficulties, which highlight why the diffusion process may not result in the same rapid growth of the market as we have seen in the past. Some important factors can act as a constraint on this development process.

12.6.2.1   Computer literacy and skills acquisition

Users' familiarity with advanced technology and services is fundamental, especially for the spread of computers and the Internet in the home. An important prerequisite is, then, a certain degree of education and computer literacy. Computer literacy and users' familiarity depend on three factors. First, an 'age' factor, which closely relates a higher level of keyboard literacy to younger generations. We might say that in the 1990s a first generation of people developed the capacity to use the Internet and Internet services effectively. Second, experience in the early years, conceivably transferring to the teens and the twenties what had been learned in their thirties and forties by an earlier generation, leaves a mark, both on lifestyle development and consumer decisions, influencing the pattern of need development. Notice that older generations might be, and in many cases have been, completely cut off from this kind of development. Here we get to the third aspect, which is precisely that of skills. There are severe constraints imposed on those who are not capable or willing to acquire the skills necessary for an effective use of technology and that involves an array of new possibilities of consumption.[15] Unlike more traditional skills, learned on a mass basis, for example typing, or driving a car, these new basic skills must be acquired at an early age. But, these are more complex than before. Typing requires visual and manual coordination, keyboard proficiency adds cognitive and planning skills to those. We further observe that this development is contingent on time allocation and fees for access. (Note that time is involved in acquiring skills, but then skills may reduce the time needed to perform certain operations.)

Computer literacy and familiarity, depending on age, early experience and skills acquisition, works then as a limiting factor on the Internet-based transformation and 'virtual reality' as a viable notion for economic development. But the true limitations may have an altogether different nature.

12.6.2.2   Time in the home and domestic capital

The Internet affects the allocation of time between the production-consumption activities (a typical example might be that of cooking meals) that take place in the private, domestic sphere. All too often the shift of certain functions away from the market to private time and the home setting (which by the way can be of a very different quality and 'capital intensity') is treated as a shift at zero cost. Saving the financial and time costs of physical mobility, as well as the fees imposed by service companies, the access provided by Internet to services appears a net gain. The most typical example might be reserving an airplane ticket or organizing a holiday. This shift has, however, several critical aspects.

For one thing it gives a new angle to the fact that 'consumption takes time'. The way time is used has been discussed as part of the traditional consumer choice problem (Steedman, 2001). Here the point is that new technologies enter the home and the 'production' of services requires time that was previously available for other things. Home computerization and the Internet make it very clear that technology also affects consumption through this channel.

Access is an empty notion without the time it requires. This is often overlooked, in so far as it is assumed to be negligible, per se and/or with respect to the time it saves. It must be noted that time spent on simple operations may be, and often is, longer than expected, given the lack of availability of the central units or the failure of the connecting link. This may pose a further constraint on time allocation, since the operation needs to be repeated according to some kind of individual day timetable. Indeed, saying that 'information is available on the Web' spells out another subtle form of technological determinism. Information is available only in principle, the real issue being its accessibility, depending on quality of the interface, Web design and search engines, which can, and have been, improved.[16] Nevertheless, the quality and improved management of websites is unlikely to solve the problem easily. In any case, accessing information on the Web becomes a domestic operation, being fitted into the time spent at home, through planning and changes in lifestyle.

If time use is a 'hidden cost', other costs, which are also overlooked, are quite tangible. The most obvious concern is the fact that neither the equipment nor Internet access are free; they have simply been added onto what has become a higher 'domestic capital', like electric appliances and household bills. Second, these home-based activities rely on a fundamental capital that is the house itself.

The shift to domestic production of services, made possible especially by the Internet, is not a shift without cost, but rather a trade-off between costs, and towards costs (the free time of individuals in their own home) that are hard to quantify, but nevertheless exist. Both the capital costs and the time costs involved in this trade-off are often ignored, whereas they affect both the experience and the economic impact of ICTs.

12.6.2.3　The notion of home and place

This acquires a further connotation when considered in light of a general pattern of transformation. In the theory of transformational growth (Nell, 1998), one of the main sources of demand growth is the industrialization of domestic production, moving the production of goods and services outside the home. We now observe that ICTs and the Internet are partially reversing this tendency, reimporting some functions within domestic production. Hence, the necessity to observe the often neglected costs of transformation and the way that they affect the consumption sphere through changes in domestic life. But we can take the analysis a step further, observing how ICTs have changed the very notion of home. The home is now the base for accessing virtual reality; the place par excellence, as such full of personal history and projections, is filled by information, images and contents available on the Web. It is therefore immersed in virtual reality, becoming part of a virtual space. To that extent it loses the sense of place and identity that is typical of the private domestic sphere.[17] How this change in meaning and definition of the domestic sphere might affect consumption activities and the development process is a matter of elaborating on its social and economic implications. However, we can certainly suggest that it might raise new constraints connected to the anthropological transformation it implies.

Finally, we would like to note that there are still other limitations, coming from negative externalities. The domestic use of ICT products and access to virtual reality, in particular, may have costs that are more social rather than strictly economic. There are indications that these costs may lie, for instance, in the phenomena of addiction that have been observed by clinical research.[18]

12.6.3　Why New Technologies Do Not Breed Strong Expansion

Admittedly this is only an initial analysis of the limitations engendered by a growth pattern centred on ICTs. It doubtlessly requires further development.[19]

However, these barriers have been underestimated even when they were perceived at all. While we can interpret the boom and the exuberance of the stock market in the 1990s as an instance of rushing in to be the first (Hobijn and Jovanovic, 2001), we can explain the bust in terms of the more sober consideration of the limitations that ICTs encounter in the creation of new markets after the initial promise. The technological, economic and social bottlenecks made an Internet scenario of development unrealistic, with the withdrawal of investment spending in this area, leading to the collapse of the expansion.

The fundamental limit of another step in ICT-driven development appears to be a deeper transformation of production and consumption. But a deeper transformation might depend on changes in economic and social organization and institutions that are hardly in sight, in fact difficult even to delineate. What the 1990s have shown are the complexities and the difficulties that stand in the way of ICTs becoming a new engine of growth like other general-purpose technologies (or epoch-making innovations) have done in the past. With this in mind, the end of the 1990s' boom appears to be more than an adjustment in a continuing growth path; rather, a grinding halt and precisely because of its capacity to create new markets.

The above-mentioned barriers to consumption transformation highlight this difficulty. Underneath is the question of the economic feasibility and social desirability of a much deeper transformation capable of creating new markets. Despite mass diffusion, the effects of computerization and the Internet on consumers' markets is constrained by new barriers that are specific to the particular path of transformation they drive. This explains why technological change did not and is not having the same results as it had in other cycles of expansion. Cell phones and the Internet are not cars or television sets, precisely because they require a much deeper social adaptation to fully exploit their potential – nor is it clear what that might require in terms of social life and required institutional change. Ultimately, ICTs might have a much weaker expansive effect. We might say we have now a first clear picture of the limits on the Information economy and society.

12.7   NEW MARKETS IN THE 2000s

The limiting factors, together with the balance of costs and benefits, put in perspective the question of the transformation of consumption and new markets (expected demand growth), shedding a negative light on the prospects of ICT-driven development. It is not a matter of pessimistic determinism, rather of focusing on technology diffusion in the perspective of new market creation. Indeed, paraphrasing the title of David's well-known article (1990), we could say that networks are not computers; they have a different impact on growth and structural change. Nor does the time-lag argument seem sufficient; it inevitably leads to the question: how much time is enough time? (Gualerzi and Nell, 2010).

The argument can be corroborated observing what happened to the ICT sector and to the economy as a whole in the 2000s. The diffusion of ICT products and the Internet together with some trends of transformation have continued unabated, sustained by the same forces of computerization and access. Still, there has not been a new expansive phase. Rather, a consolidation of the ICTs' research-industrial complex. In this respect, we can note the retreat of investment and recall that restructuring is not in general favourable to market creation. Technology development – and productivity growth – continued, in directions that were already articulated in the 1990s. However, the positive aspects of the boom dissipated into a new slowdown of the economy. The recovery after 2003 was pulled forward by a booming household debt sustaining consumption, eventually collapsing in a liquidity crisis that triggered a recession. This strongly suggests that there has not been an alternative to the leading role played by ICTs in the 1990s.

At the same time, some trends of development have returned to the fore in the 2000s, shifting the attention away from hi-tech and further complicating the question of what might be the future directions of market creation. These developments centre on energy and the environment, which appear to be closely related issues, both reaching a new critical stage. In this respect, one notices, on the one hand, the pressure created by the rise in oil prices[20] and the uncertainties about oil reserves and market prospects; on the other hand, the new step forward of the alternative energy industry, a rapidly growing market indeed. The developments in the areas of energy and the environment are causing mounting pressure on the transportation and automobile industries. The latter is going through an even deeper process of crisis and consolidation, while the search for an alternative to the internal combustion engine and/or to the automobile as the master of private transportation is an open door.

This sparse observation suggests that we should think of new markets in broader terms and beyond the association with hi-tech.[21] At the same time, we ought to note that, despite their importance, these developments have not so far been sufficient to establish a pattern of growth centred on these (potential) new markets.

This should be seen as a warning in the current discussion on the stimulation package and the return to fiscal policy as a way to getting back to solid economic growth. It reminds us that even a strong stimulus is not likely to have the same effects it might have had in profoundly different circumstances than those facing the US economy at the end of the 2000s. This is not to say that there are no possible new industries and new markets. As mentioned above some alternatives did take hold in the 2000s. Although, so far they have been unable to give a decisive impetus to growth, they might do so in the future as the oft-mentioned prospects of a green revolution suggest.

So the real trap in which the economy is caught is that while new technologies are not mobilizing enough resources (arguably because they are not creating enough of a structural transformation), there are no other well-articulated directions of transformation creating prospects for new markets and large investment. While the effects of technological change are not comparable to those experienced in other phases, income distribution and social polarization tend to discourage a push into the middle class, which had a tremendous impetus in creating markets in the 1960s.

This is indeed a major question that was not discussed here. The long-term stagnation of wages and an increasingly uneven income distribution have clearly negative effects on new markets, although the focus here was on technology and investment. We have argued elsewhere that the rising income of the wealthy and the emerging social classes can drive a divergent pattern of consumption biased towards 'glamorous consumption'. That was one of the distinguishing features of the 1980s' recovery in the USA (Gualerzi, 2001). The 1990s are noteworthy for a change in that pattern, with the resumption of more vigorous growth and a modest rise in wages, at least in the second part of the decade. But that was reversed during the 2000s (Gualerzi, 2010). So, income distribution must be fitted into the picture for a more complete view of the current recession.

Similarly, one should not overlook the differences considering the issue of new markets in developing economies. The most striking example might be comparing the USA and China. The Chinese government also enacted a stimulation policy in 2009. Looking at its more than 8 per cent growth rate one should conclude that it was successful. But this is precisely the point: it depends on the overall circumstances and structural characteristics of the economy. Which brings us to our second point. Although very successful, Chinese growth has been largely driven by world demand and industrialized economies' demand in particular. That is not to say that the internal market is unimportant. However, one can recognize that market growth so far depends on the mass diffusion of the consumption patterns already established in the West. In this case technology does in general have positive effects, but follows a well-established pattern; it does not reflect any major novelty or innovation in consumption. In other words, the economy is not yet confronting the problem of market saturation. But it may encounter other obstacles, notably arising from low wages, social constraints, the deterioration of the environment. This should suggest caution in discussing the shift of economic power at the world level.

12.8 CONCLUDING REMARKS AND RESEARCH QUESTIONS

The current crisis does bring the analysis of expansion of market economies back to the fundamentals. This is the real challenge posed to economic theory and it is not too well addressed in the debate among economists. Krugman and Akerlof-Shiller outline what economists should do to bring back Keynesian ideas into theory and policy. Is behavioural economics – which is by no means a complete novelty – the main alley to develop the Keynesian insight into depression and effective demand? There seems to be room for more than asserting irrational behaviour and market imperfections as the key to economic fluctuations. (Notice: we are not dealing with short-term, relatively mild fluctuations, but the possibility of long-run stagnation.)

The particular angle from which this paper pursues that goal is bringing into focus the way fluctuations and depression are intertwined with the rise (rather the creation) of new markets. That needs to be approached in light of the overall economic development process, as our few observations on China suggest. Investment decisions find clear foundations in the prospects of new markets. While leaving room for a number of influences, such as those contained in the notion of long-run expectations, that spells out a perfectly rational reason to proceed or delay investment spending. That does not do away with the notion of an uncertain future and therefore implies no deterministic view of the market operation.[22]

The second element of the return to Keynesian ideas brought about by the crisis is the attention given to government intervention and in particular to fiscal policy. Krugman highlights the importance of the latter as opposed to monetary policy or laissez-faire. The effects of a stimulus might depend on its intensity and how it is subdivided between income support, tax reduction and public investment. Still, what ultimately determines its effectiveness are the circumstances of the economy. A rapid look at history and to references to the New Deal suggest that public intervention and public investment will have limited effects unless the prospect of new markets is created. This is an 'independent' question to be raised; it cannot be answered referring to the prospects of new technologies or the power of market mechanisms. Equally important is to assume that the stimulus will operate through the channel of aggregate demand and that it will trickle down to the entire economy. That might not be sufficient, unless the economy settles into a new growth pattern. The key questions are that of effective demand in the long run, autonomous investment and new markets.

To be brought up to the task of confronting the risk of long-run depression the Keynesian legacy needs a major rethink, given that conditions are far different from those faced by Keynes himself.[23] In the end, the long run *does not* take care of itself and a reformulation of a growth scenario is necessary.

NOTES

1. Many alleged 'dangers of the deficit', widely brandished by opponents, are subject to much criticism.
2. The very success of the Federal Reserve in overcoming the 2001 recession after the burst of the technological bubble seems to have contributed to the rejection of the possibility of a new bubble developing in the real estate sector. Both Greenspan in 2004 and Bernanke in 2005 ruled out such a possibility. House prices were simply reflecting strong fundamentals.
3. Krugman's criticism echoes the explanation of the collapse of the 1990s' expansion by another Nobel Prize winner, Joseph Stiglitz (2003). It was the perfect markets 'mantra' that drove an increasingly misdirected and ultimately wrong economic policy during the two Clinton administrations. He also concludes that we need to go back to Keynes.
4. John R. Talbott, an investment banker at Goldman and Sachs, anticipated both the Internet bubble and the burst of the real estate bubble as explained in his latest book (Talbott, 2009).
5. '[T]he recession . . . arrived in March 2001' (Stiglitz, 2003, p. 9).
6. Godley's idea is that there was not much investment in the 1990s or, if there was, that it was mainly in R&D. Given this, he would then argue that the government should be running a much more significant deficit.
7. In fact, it might have been one of the main factors sustaining consumption spending, possibly the most important of any wealth effect.
8. See, for example, the announcement of a formidable annual growth rate above 7 per cent in the third quarter of 2003, then revised to 8.2 per cent.
9. Observed inflation in October 2005 was 4.7 per cent, but core inflation was 1.7 per cent, still below the comfortable 2 per cent limit set up by the Federal Reserve, but getting there.
10. For an analysis of the subprime mortgages market see Gramlich (2007).
11. One may wonder whether one would come to the same conclusion by reading economic textbooks, including Samuelson's (1948).
12. This, by the way, might be one of the problems of Japan, a notoriously efficient economy when it comes to introducing automation.
13. The automobile killed off the horse and buggy, petroleum displaced whale oil, electric lights displaced kerosene lanterns, and so on.
14. This seems to have happened in the case of music; the new 'sharing' technologies proved highly destructive, undermining markets, eliminating not only jobs but whole businesses. Newspapers may be next. The distribution of movies is shaky; cell phones are undermining landlines, and the use of the Internet for phoning may further undermine both. It is especially notable that since most of the new products are 'collective' – meaning that consuming them is wholly or in part a joint process – a 'sharing' technology on a network (pirating, sometimes) will make them effectively free. Besides music, this is happening with movies, books, news, some kinds of artwork, and so on. The old forms of marketing no longer apply, and it is often not clear whether new methods will be as profitable.
15. Petit and Soete (2002) have discussed the skill-biased nature of technological change. They pose an emerging duality between those who acquire skills through their jobs, and those who do not. The gap between those who are increasingly left behind in this learning process conceivably affects consumption patterns too.
16. In this light, one can see the success of Google, now contending with Microsoft for a leadership position in the market.
17. The loss of the identity of places in post-modernity is a theme the anthropologist Mark Auge (1992) has popularized.
18. 'Hooked on the Web: help is on the way', *The New York Times*, 1 December 2005.
19. In this respect one should look, for instance, at the work of Jonathan Gershuny. His notion of social innovation (1983) is important for the basic model of the

consumption–growth relationship (Gualerzi, 2001). Some of his more recent work (Gershuny, 2000, 2003) is also relevant for the analysis of the effects of the Internet on time use and the domestic sphere.
20. The price was around 60 dollars a barrel in May 2007, reaching the peak of 147 dollars in August 2008, drifting back to 50 dollars and below from November 2008. They have somewhat come back, due also to the weakness of the dollar, and were in a range of 70–80 dollars in the fall of 2009.
21. To mention an interesting example, Robert William Fogel (2004) argues that the industry of the future is the health industry.
22. An uncertain future – and animal spirits – can certainly be married with the notion of 'a market to be'. When focusing on 'irrational exuberance' and bubbles (Shiller, 2005) we should note that not all bubbles are alike. The technological bubble of the late 1990s was driven by a real transformation. We do not need to subscribe to irrational behaviour to explain what is ultimately driven by the potential for new markets of new technologies.
23. The end of colonialism and the rise of globalization have dramatically changed the world order. The focus on new markets seems useful to examine how such a change intersects with the slowdown of growth and transformation in the main industrial economies.

REFERENCES

Akerlof, G.A. and R.J. Shiller (2009), *Animal Spirits. How Human Psychology Drives the Economy, and Why It Matters for Global Capitalism*, Princeton, NJ: Princeton University Press.

Auge, M. (1992), *Non-lieux: Introduction a Une anthropologie de la Surmodernité*, Paris: Seuil.

Bernanke, B.S. (2005), *Essays on the Great Depression*, Princeton, NJ: Princeton University Press.

David, P.A. (1990), 'The dynamo and the computer: an historical perspective on the productivity paradox', *American Economic Review*, **80** (2), 355–361.

Fogel, R.W. (2004), *The Escape from Hunger and Premature Death 1700–2100*, Cambridge, UK: Cambridge University Press.

Gershuny, J. (1983), *Social Innovation and the Division of Labour*, Oxford: Oxford University Press.

Gershuny, J. (2000), *Changing Times: Work and Leisure in Post-industrial Societies*, New York: Oxford University Press.

Gershuny, J. (2003), 'Web use and net-nerds: a neo-functionalist analysis of the impact of information technology in the home', *Social Forces*, **82** (1), 141–168.

Godley, W. (2000), 'Drowning in debt', The Levy Economics Institute of Bard College Policy Note No. 2000/6, June, available at: http://www.levyinstitute.org/pubs/pn/pn00_6.pdf; accessed 12 September 2010.

Gramlich, E.M. (2007), *Subprime Mortgages: America's Latest Boom and Bust*, Washington, DC: Urban Institute Press.

Greenspan, A. (2004), 'The mortgage market and consumer debt, remarks at America's Community Bankers Annual Convention', Washington DC, 19 October, available at: http:www.federalreserve.gov/boarddocs/speeches/2004/20041019/default.htm; accessed 14 September 2010.

Gualerzi, D. (2001), *Consumption and Growth: Recovery and Structural Change in the U.S. Economy*, Cheltenham, UK and Northampton, MA, USA: Edward Elgar.

Gualerzi, D. (2007), 'Globalization reconsidered: foreign direct investment and global governance', *International Journal of Political Economy*, **36** (1), 3–29.

Gualerzi, D. (2010), *The Coming of Age of Information Technologies and the Path of Transformational Growth*, London: Routledge.

Gualerzi, D. and E. Nell (2010), 'Transformational growth in the 1990s: government, finance and hi-tech', *Review of Political Economy*, **22** (1), 97–117.

Hobijn, B. and Jovanovic, B. (2001), 'The information-technology revolution and the stock market: evidence', *American Economic Review*, **91** (5) 1203–1220.

Krugman, P. (2009), 'How did economists get it so wrong?', *The New York Times Magazine*, 6 September, available at: http://www.nytimes.com/2009/09/06/magazine/06Economic-t.html; accessed 11 September 2010.

Manning, R. (2000), *Credit Card Nation. The Consequences of America's Addiction to Credit*, New York: Basic Books.

Manning, R. (2005), 'Living with debt: a life stage analysis of changing attitudes and behaviors', available at: www.LendingTree.com/livingwithdebt/; accessed 12 September 2010.

Nell, E. (1998), *The General Theory of Transformational Growth*, Cambridge, UK and New York: Cambridge University Press.

Petit, P. and L. Soete (2002), 'Is a biased technological change fuelling dualism?', in M. Setterfield (ed.) *The Economics of Demand-Led Growth. Challenging the Supply Side Vision of the Long-Run*, Cheltenham, UK and Northampton, MA, USA: Edward Elgar, pp. 273–302.

Samuelson, P.A. (1948), *Economics: An Introductory Analysis*, New York: McGraw-Hill; with William D. Nordhams (Since 1985). 18th edition printed 2004.

Samuelson P. (2009), 'Il deficit degli Stati ci salverà', *La Stampa*, 18 July, p. 1 (distributed by Tribune Media Services, Inc.).

Shiller, R.J. (2005), *Irrational Exuberance*, 2nd edition, Princeton, NJ: Princeton University Press.

Steedman, I. (2001), *Consumption Takes Time: Implications for Economic Theory*, London: Routledge.

Stiglitz, J. (2003), *The Roaring Nineties*, New York: W.W. Norton & Company.

Talbott, J.R. (2009), *The 86 Biggest Lies on Wall Street*, New York: Seven Stories Press.

13. Manifestations of the global crisis in a small open economy

Ivars Brīvers

13.1 INTRODUCTION

The extremely high economic growth of the economy of Latvia in 2002–07, which is now ironically called 'the fat years', was followed by a sharp decline in 2008. At the end of 2009 Latvia was close to insolvency and economic catastrophe. At the beginning of 2010 there are some signs of recovery, but the excessively narrow approach to the economy casts doubts that the recovery concerns figures not people.

Could the current economic collapse be the result of those 'fat years'? Latvia can be considered as the most striking example where rapid economic growth has been just the opposite of sustainable development. Normally GDP shows the volume of economic activities on the one hand and the income of population on the other hand. In the case of Latvia there was a significant gap between these two aspects, as its rapid economic growth was followed by a more dramatic increase in foreign debt.

How can we explain the extremely rapid growth of GDP in Latvia? Was it based on technological innovations or a highly increased level of human capital? Could it be the result of a significant increase in the economically active population in Latvia? Not at all. Instead, approximately 10 per cent of the labour force has left Latvia, and even larger numbers of them are trying to leave the country in the near future. However, economic growth took place mainly in speculative sectors of the economy owing to foreign financial means in the form of investment, until there were enough capital assets to be sold, and in the form of foreign credits when most of these assets were already sold. The contribution to the increase in economic potential was negligible.

The Latvian example shows how the model of rapid economic growth works in 'the new democracies' – the initial opening up of the real estate markets causes a significant inflow of foreign capital, which, in turn, causes the increase in demand and the rise in prices. The domestic population cannot compete in this market without looking for loans; domestic banks get large credits from foreign banks and even become their subsidiaries. That causes a further increase in demand and prices, and hence the multiplier effect of growth in such sectors as the building industry, finance and banking, and trading. The growth rate of the GDP is very high, but at the same time this growth does not have a real economic base.

This paper tries to analyse the process, to point out the basic factors of it, and to envisage possible ways of further development. Our methodology is based on the quantitative and qualitative analysis of macroeconomic and financial data, mainly by using statistics from the Central Statistical Bureau of Latvia, the Bank of Latvia and Eurostat.

13.2   A SHORT HISTORICAL INSIGHT OF THE ECONOMY OF LATVIA

13.2.1   The Dynamics of the Process

During the Soviet period the Baltic States were the most prosperous part of the Soviet Union. Nevertheless, Latvians, Estonians and Lithuanians were in the front line in the struggle for independence and accepted with enthusiasm the collapse of the Soviet empire. Latvia's economy during the period of independence has gone through dynamic changes. This period can be divided into five stages:

1.   recession and substantial decrease of GDP during 1990–93;
2.   stabilization of the economy and a slight increase in GDP during 1993–99;
3.   a rapid growth of the economy and a significant increase in GDP during 2000–03 with low inflation;
4.   a rapid growth of the economy and a significant increase in GDP during 2004–07 with high inflation and the first symptoms of recession;
5.   recession and a deep economic crisis in 2008–09.

The significant downturn in the economy after the collapse of Soviet Union and the socialist block is a common feature of economies in all of the former Soviet republics and socialist states in Europe. There is a considerable correlation between the downturn in the economy and the degree to which the economy of a particular state was integrated into the common economic system of the Soviet Union and the socialist block. Latvia was a Soviet republic with one of the highest levels of economic development and perhaps the most integrated one. That's why the downturn in the economy measured by the level of GDP was perhaps the largest

Table 13.1   Indicators of living standards and economic growth

Year	Gross Domestic Product at Constant Prices of 2000 (millions of lats)	Annual Growth of Gross Domestic Product (%)	Gross Domestic Product at Average Prices of 2000 Per capita (lats)
1990*	6771.5	2.9	2542
1991*	5918.3	−12.6	2218
1992*	4018.5	−32.1	1512
1993*	3560.4	−11.4	1366
1994*	3638.7	2.2	1418
1995	3658.2	0.3	1472
1996	3790.4	3.6	1543
1997	4106.5	8.3	1688
1998	4303.4	4.8	1786
1999	4443.4	3.3	1859
2000	4750.8	6.9	2002
2001	5133.1	8.0	2180
2002	5465.4	6.5	2337
2003	5858.4	7.2	2519
2004	6366.7	8.7	2753
2005	7041.7	10.6	3061
2006	7903.1	12.2	3454
2007	8691.7	10.0	3819
2008	8293.4	−4.6	3660

Note: * These dates are not from the CSB, but are the author's calculations.

Source: Data from the Central Statistical Bureau of Latvia (CSB) (until 1995 – from earlier publications) – www.csb.gov.lv.

among the Soviet republics of the European part of the former Soviet Union and socialist countries in Europe. The GDP volume in 1993 was only 52.6 per cent of the one in 1990, so, generally speaking, living standards fell twice. Only from 2004 the standard of living measured by GDP per capita exceeded 1990 levels (Table 13.1). So the assertion that Latvia's economy has been moving forwards faster than most of the other former Soviet republics, Belarus or Uzbekistan for instance, if we only take into consideration the measure of GDP growth, is simply untrue.

The explanation for the changes in the economy and living standards is more complex, and it cannot be measured only with the GDP indicator. First we must point out that the statistics from 1990 only give a conventional notion about the economy, because Latvia was part of the Soviet Union and it was hard to separate the activities that were mainly related to Latvia's economy from those that were more related to the other Soviet republics. The export and import statistics of this period only give a rough idea about the heart of the matter. Among the reasons for the substantial downturn of the economy, there are at least two that explain why the fall in living standards was not as large as the decrease of GDP. One reason is that a substantial part of Latvia's economy during the Soviet period was the military industry. The wages of Soviet Army officers and military people that were situated in Latvia were also included in the GDP of Latvia, as well as the industries that supplied the Soviet Army. After the withdrawal of the Soviet Army, this sector of the economy disappeared. Another reason was that a notable part of the economy moved to a shadow economy. During the period of institutional changes in Latvia's economy and legislation, the legal system was far from perfect and for entrepreneurs and employees it was possible and gainful not to let everyone know what their income was or to use it as a bank transfer payment. So the real downturn in the economy was perhaps not as great as statistics claimed.

To correctly interpret Latvia's statistical data, one must take into consideration the fact that the downturn of the economy was accompanied by high inflation from 1990 to 93. This means that inflation can be explained mostly by supply-side factors. Since Latvia does not have its own energy resources it relies on imports. After the collapse of the Soviet Union, the former Soviet republics, and mainly Russia, exported gas, oil products, coal and so on to Latvia, and sold energy at the market price and this was much higher than the prices of these products in the Soviet Union. The desultory growth in the price of energy resources caused the notable growth in production and transportation costs in almost all enterprises.

At the same time the high level of inflation (Table 13.2) was accompanied by an important change in the price structure. Prices grew faster in the service sector and not so fast in the production sector. As a result the structure of the GDP changed. In 1990 the service sector produced only about one-third of the GDP. Just three years later the share of the service sector was about two-thirds. This unbelievably rapid change of the GDP structure can be explained, partially, by the aforementioned reason – the change in the price structure, partially caused by the fall in output in the production sector, which was bigger than in the service sector. (The fall in the construction sector was over five times greater. It was also sizeable in the fishing and agriculture sectors, but the fall in the service sector was only about 20 per cent.) This must be taken into consideration when one looks at the statistical data of Latvia published in the first half of the 1990s. Even in the middle of the 1990s the base year was not 1990, as in most other countries, but the year 1993, when the change in the price structure took place.

Table 13.2   Indicators of inflation

Year	Annual Inflation Measured by CPI (%)	Annual Inflation Measured by GDP Deflator (%)
1991	172.2	162.6
1992	951.2	979.4
1993	109.2	71.4
1994	35.9	38.3
1995	25.0	14.9
1996	17.6	15.2
1997	8.4	7.1
1998	4.7	4.4
1999	2.4	4.0
2000	2.6	4.2
2001	2.5	1.7
2002	1.9	3.6
2003	2.9	3.6
2004	6.2	7.0
2005	6.7	10.2
2006	6.5	11.1
2007	10.1	13.3
2008	15.3	15.2

Source: Author's calculations, based on data from the Central Statistical Bureau of Latvia – www.csb.gov.lv.

After the period of recession in 1994 a slight increase in GDP took place, which was followed by a decrease in 1995. This was the year when the banking crisis took place. Latvia was one of the first post-socialist countries that underwent this problem. The Baltija Bank, which was the largest bank in Latvia at the beginning of the 1990s went bankrupt. This caused serious direct problems to a large part of the population as well as enterprises and local governmental institutions. Following this it took some time for people's confidence in banks to return.

The end of the 1990s was followed by a slight increase in GDP, and the beginning of the third millennium heralded a significant growth in the economy marked by an increase in GDP. This was a period that generally can be characterized as a recession in the European economy, so the rapid growth of Latvia's economy may be considered as a pleasant surprise. At the same time, the rate of inflation was very low, so the real situation does not seem to be concerned with economic theory.

Since the beginning of the 1990s the foreign trade balance in Latvia has been permanently negative with a tendency to go further into the red until the present economic crisis. The import–export ratio increased from 1.40 in 1995 to 1.94 in 2006, and the foreign trade deficit exceeded 20 per cent of GDP.

Economic growth in Latvia was incredibly high during the first years of the 21st century. The annual GDP increase since year 2000 has been no less than 6 per cent; in the last three years it has been more than 10 per cent. Generally speaking, the economy of Latvia during the recent years has been developing in a most liberal way. From the point of view of economic growth it can be described as successful. A controversial point is the survival of the Latvian nation but in the background of globalization this problem has been considered of little importance.

13.2.2 The Problems of the Economy

It may seem that the extremely rapid economic growth has significantly increased the standard of living and the potential of the economy. But the 'fat years' have brought Latvia to an economic catastrophe and the survival of the state of Latvia and the Latvian nation is under serious threat. Latvia can be considered as an example where there is a rather high discrepancy between the level of economic activity and people's welfare – high growth with low development. Development is a broader process than economic growth, in the same way that welfare cannot be measured only in monetary terms. The analysis of economic processes in Latvia shows that the rapid economic growth in Latvia has caused serious problems from the point of view of sustainable development.

The only strategic goal for an economy of any country, including Latvia, should be sustainable development of the economy, not any other kind. In the case of Latvia the decision-makers have been mixing up the goal with the means – rapid economic growth, low inflation, balanced budgets, and so on. Figures have been considered to be more important than people. This has led to several serious mistakes in economic policy.

One of the most serious mistakes was the opening up of the real estate market. If real estate is used for its main purpose, it is a perfectly non-tradable good with a very low speed of price convergence. When real estate is used for speculative transactions, it is a perfectly tradable good with a very high speed of price convergence.

The opening up of the real estate market in Latvia caused a situation where people, mainly from abroad, with savings, had an opportunity to make more profitable investments than through banks. Real estate became the object of speculative transactions. The demand in this market was increasing very rapidly, along with prices. Latvians, who needed real estate not for speculative transactions, but for dwellings, had to compete in this market by taking out credits leading to a further increase in demand and prices. This caused a situation where not only households failed to recognize the risk of paying back loans but where banks failed to recognize the risks in getting back their money.

Now the real estate market has used up the possibilities of easy profit. At the moment some people with mortgages have been divested of their property and banks are selling it to recoup their loans. It is highly possible that this is only the beginning.

The considerations about rapid economic growth as the main goal have caused another abnormal phenomenon – a long-lasting and significant foreign trade deficit. How is it possible that an economic subject either on a micro- or macro-level spends more money than it earns? In the case of a person there are the following possibilities: he is spending all his savings, or borrowing money, or selling his possessions. In the last decade of the 20th century Latvia was mainly selling its possessions – land, capital assets, and so on, thus acquiring money to cover the foreign trade deficit. A large part of foreign credits were simply stolen, thus persuading public opinion that 'foreign investment' was preferable to foreign credits. Indeed, at least two-thirds of all foreign investment flew into the speculative economy, having no positive impact on the potential of the economy and aggregate supply. In the first years of the 21st century since most valuable things had already been sold, the tune changed from foreign investment to foreign credits. The ratio of the foreign debt to GDP increased from 0.80 in 2003 to 1.35 in 2007, which together with the high foreign trade deficit could not continue like this without having negative effects on the economy and this, given the conditions of the global economic crisis, has turned out to be extremely dangerous.

Economic growth, together with high inflation, has caused a significant increase in social inequality, which is the highest in Europe. The most rapid increase in social inequality in Latvia started in 2004 when there was a sudden flash of inflation. That caused a threat to the social dimension of sustainable development, the deformation of the social environment, the growth of hostility, which intentionally or accidentally was incited by the mass media, which showed examples of senseless splendour among the 'toffs'. Together with the present 'optimization' of the state budget, which means the sacking of police officers and the lowering of wages for those who are left working, it has already caused a rise in the crime rate and social tension. Regional inequality in Latvia is the highest in Europe. The difference in the average standard of living between Riga and Latgale is greater than the difference between Latvia and Denmark.

The attitude of the state towards its citizens has caused a situation where more than 100 000, mainly young, Latvians have left the country. A poll among school graduates shows that more than 50 per cent of them are willing to leave Latvia. Government officials try to explain this away by talking about the difference in wages, not taking into consideration other factors, such as social environment and placing the interests of Latvian people behind the interests of everything else. The ethnical environment is perhaps the only factor that keeps Latvians in their country. The disregard to this environment is, perhaps, the main threat to the survival of the Latvian nation and the future of Latvia. In the case of Latvia the role of agriculture is even more important than in other European countries, as historically Latvians have always lived in rural areas.

13.3 GLOBAL CRISIS AND THE ECONOMY OF LATVIA

13.3.1 What Kind of Crisis Do We Have?

The first decade of the 21st century will remain in our memory as the years of the global crisis. Economists throughout the world have compared the present crisis with the Great Depression of the 20th century, and usually come to the conclusion that the present crisis is not so deep, and that the world will overcome it much easier and much quicker than the Great Depression.

The problem is that the present crisis should be considered differently from the Great Depression. It is not a financial crisis. It is not even an economic crisis. It is global crisis. We cannot get a true feeling for things if we look at it only in one dimension. It is the same with regards to social life, which consists of three dimensions – environmental, economic and social. The main mistake, which is made by politicians and economists, is that they are looking for the way out of the crisis in only one dimension – economic, or even more parochial, financial. This may lead to very harmful consequences – one should remember the consequences of the Great Depression.

The present crisis is an environmental crisis – a large part of the ecosystems throughout the world have been destroyed. There is a serious threat that the changes in the climate have become irreversible. But the environment should be considered in a broader sense than the strictly ecological one – we should also take into account cultural, ethnical and religious factors.

The present crisis is an economic crisis – the notion about the economic goals has turned out to be false. Economic growth in developed countries does not contribute to an increase in real welfare. 'While the rich got richer, middle-class incomes in Western countries were stagnant in real terms long before the recession' (Jackson, 2009, p. 6). Economic growth is unsustainable, as environmental resources at an exponential rate are turned into rubbish, and both of them are close to their limits. Though economic growth is necessary as the increasing productivity and labour substitution by capital allows for the production of the same amount of product with less labour. 'Sir, knowest thou not that out of the luxury of the rich cometh the life of the poor? By your pomp we are nurtured, and your vices give us bread. To toil for a hard master is bitter, but to have no master to toil for is more bitter still' (Oscar Wilde, *The Young King*, 1891). Perhaps, this is the main contradiction of economics in the 21st century and the solution will be the main problem for economics too.

The present crisis should be considered in its social dimension as well – it is a human crisis: moral, educational and institutional. People are confused about the basic values of life – 'added value' has overcome real values. One may well doubt that the level of education in the 21st century is higher than in the 19th century. The concept that higher education should not be elitist has led to the loss of a real higher education. As education has been subjugated to the market, it has lost its moral aspects. The present crisis is an institutional crisis, as the contradiction between individual preferences and social goals cannot be solved without irrational concepts, such as Thorsten Veblen's (1899) institutions. The hope of escape through technological development may turn out to be an illusion as human development significantly lags behind it.

Still a lot of economists pay more attention to the financial markets, considering that the signs of recovery will come from there. This is curious because even during the Great Depression J.M. Keynes considered the labour market not the stock market as the main indicator of recovery. Searching for a way out of the present crisis by putting it down to only a financial crisis may lead to recovery but not welfare.

13.3.2 How to Explain the Present Global Economic Crisis

The words of Schumpeter from his famous book *Capitalism, Socialism and Democracy* (1942) where he mentioned Marx as 'a prophet, a sociologist, an economist and a teacher', also refer to himself. Indeed, Marx and Schumpeter were among those economists, who made long-term forecasts about the development of the world economy. Marx and Schumpeter both came to the same conclusions about the result. Nevertheless, their opinions about the process were different. Not being a Marxist, and never even close to being a socialist himself, Schumpeter considered Marx as the main mastermind of his ideas, arguing that Marx asked the right questions but that he did not give the right answers.

Schumpeter's idea was that economic reality was changing. Moreover, economic theory cannot be considered as complete. The Great Depression caused the birth of modern macroeconomics in a large degree due to the ideas of Keynes and Schumpeter. The present events in the world economy show that economic theory will undoubtedly undergo significant changes.

According to Schumpeter the innovative idea serves as the source of profit and at the same time it is destroying the previous state of things – using Friedrich Nietzsche's term, Schumpeter called it 'creative destruction'. Schumpeter, Keynes and other economists of their time detached the real economy from the 'symbol economy' or speculative economy as it is more often called nowadays. But none of them stressed the possible contradiction between those two sections of economy, which has become perhaps the main problem of the world economy at present – innovative ideas in the speculative economy have destroyed the function of market economy, which equalizes the profitability of different businesses in the long run. The Columbia University professor Jagdish Bhagwati in *The Financial Times*, 16 October 2008, used the term 'destructive creation' as opposed to 'creative destruction' pointing out that with financial innovation the downside can be lethal. Indeed, innovative ideas in the financial markets may be considered as the main perpetrator of the present dramatic situation in the world economy. Since the collapse of the Bretton Woods system, speculative economy has become more and more profitable and innovative ideas there have kept this profitability for more than 30 years, inhibiting investors and entrepreneurs from the real economy. Finally, the profitability of the speculative economy has collapsed with a blast.

The idea of the threat that may cause an excessive growth in speculative economy goes back to the US economist-institutionalist Thorsten Veblen. His far-sightedness lies in the fact that he recognized the separation of production from finance. Making money not goods is the main objective in economics. In this aspect the ideas of Veblen correspond with the Schumpeterian approach. The propensity to introduce technological changes, which come from workers and engineers, is in contradiction to the tendency of the business person to acquire money through 'financial products'. Present events in the global economy show that Veblen's point of view was oracular.

The 20th-century socialist calculation debate has come to the conclusion that markets adjust prices; hence, monetary measures are adequate enough in opposition to planned economies, where the planning organ is incapable of setting adequate prices. 'Destructive creation', using Bhagwati's term, has cast doubts on the adequacy of market set prices.

The Schumpeterian explanation that innovative ideas will function as the 'creative destruction' may seem too pessimistic. In the 21st century there are enough innovative ideas to prove that Schumpeter was not right here. But at the same time one can see that the most profitable ideas arise in the speculative economy, creating money from nothing. Investors are seeking for the most profitable kind of business and almost always it turns out to be in the speculative sectors of economy.

Latvia can serve as a very striking example. The first years of the 21st century were the years of extremely rapid economic growth. The Latvian government boasted about high growth and paid no attention to the structure of it. But now it turns out that this growth was happening, for the greatest part, in the speculative economy. According to the notions of the classical economists (Cantillon, Smith) particular branches of the economy could not maintain high profitability for a long period of time. But innovative ideas in the speculative economy have made this possible in the world for a period of almost 40 years. Ultimately, Cantillon and Smith were right and the profitability of the speculative economy is falling with a resounding crash now.

13.3.3   The Latvian Experience of the Great Depression

The Great Depression affected the economy of Latvia rather softly, compared with the impact of the crisis on other European countries and the USA. Nevertheless, Latvia also suffered from the Great Depression and the standard of living was declining. Latvia did not have world-renowned economists-scientists at the time. The most famous Latvian economist Kārlis Balodis, who furthermore was in opposition to the economic policy of the Latvian government died at the beginning of 1931. Perhaps the most significant contribution in the analysis of the manifestations of the Great Depression in Latvia was made by the editor of the journal *Ekonomists* Alberts Zalts in his book *The Way Out of the Crisis*. It has gathered together general conclusions from different publications of Zalts in the journal *Ekonomists*, among which the most important was the article 'Negotiation of the monetary crisis', published in its first issue in 1932.

Alberts Zalts was a supporter of liberal views on economy. His opinion about the explanation of a crisis is close to the monetary theories of economic fluctuations. Nevertheless, Zalts in his book gives a rather wide range of economic fluctuation theories, including the modern theories of that time, considering the ideas of Fisher, Hayek, Keynes, Ohlin, Cassel, and so forth. Speaking about the measures of economic policy to find the way out of the crisis, Zalts is much less liberal, and some of his suggestions are rather close to the ideas of strong governmental interference in economic processes.

Colliding with his own ideas in the pre-crisis period, Zalts wrote:

> The opponents of governmental interference refer to the classical principle of laissez-faire, laissez-passer in the theories of the physiocrats and the ideas of Adam Smith. At present the impeachment of the necessity of governmental interference means the incapability to understand the real factors of economic development. Such an interference we can see at each step, it becomes stronger each day, and the general conclusion may be, that with the industrial growth, with the development of the international trade and traffic the interference of public institutions in production and consumption processes becomes more and more appreciable. The same fact of interference depends from the level of economic development. . ... And as the industrial growth and international trade is changing the existent capitalist system, the most characteristic feature of the economy in the future will be an organized interference of government or other public institution in the production process and even in the distribution of the goods. (Zalts, 1932, p. 5)

Further, Zalts gives a historical review explaining the reasons why the government should interfere in the economy. First he mentions the social aspects of the economy, then the aspects of international competition. Discussing the situation then, Zalts also mentions the structural aspect and, as he calls it, the 'conjunctural' aspect, meaning, by this, the measures of economic policy in an interpretation that is rather close to the Keynesian one. Alberts Zalts refers to Wladimir Woytinsky's paper, published in 1931, giving a rather long quotation, the main idea of which is that the improvement in any economic situation without interference from public institutions will take a very long time and that there is a lack of advised and sustainable economic policy not only in Germany but in the whole world. Zalts has a further discussion on the ideas of Woytinsky, considering three types of economic policy – US, Russian and German, figuratively calling the first one physical, the second one mathematical and the third one biological.

Discussing the possible tools of economic policy in Latvia, Zalts points out that the economy of small countries significantly differs from that of large ones. Zalts highly favours the fact that economic policy can be put into effect only with deep theoretical knowledge (a rather obvious statement, though things are quite different in today's Latvia). Zalts gives a quotation from *A Treatise on Money* (1936) by J.M. Keynes to the effect that bankers understand the disorder in the monetary field, but they refuse to accept the ideas of economists-scientists. Zalts also cites Walter Bagehot:

one cannot ask for new ideas, how to improve the economy, from bank directors and other people, who are in high positions. Each theoretical investigation
requires large efforts, and those people who are solving practical questions,
have little interest in thinking about the theoretical aspects of their deals. (Zalts,
1932, p. 14)

Alberts Zalts gives a historical review of the events in the economy of
Latvia in 1931 and 1932 when the symptoms of the crisis became cruel.
The problems of the state budget deficit were first solved by cutting back
on governmental expenses, but on 4 December 1931, the Prime Minister
of Latvia, social democrat Marģers Skujenieks, declared the necessity of
increasing income, by founding state monopolies and introducing the
'crisis tax'. Zalts mentions that there was an idea of introducing the 'turn-
over tax', that is, value added tax, but the idea was rejected by the Latvian
Parliament. On 25 February 1932 a 'Price Regulating Commission' was
established, starting the setting of fixed prices on some products, mainly
agricultural ones. In July 1932 there was an increase in import taxes. Zalts
neither glorifies nor criticizes these measures, he only points out that they
were not enough despite being coordinated with each other.

Zalts gives a rather expanded review of the economic stimulation plan
of Kārlis Ulmanis, later the Prime Minister and President of Latvia,
published 1 June 1932. The central idea of this plan is quite Keynesian –
increasing aggregate demand by increasing the inflow of financial means
into the economy. Zalts stresses the common features in Ulmanis's plan
with the ideas of Woytinsky. Being a specialist in agriculture, Ulmanis
considered the deflation of agricultural prices as the most harmful
problem, causing bankruptcies among the farmers. Thus, Ulmanis proposed measures that could increase aggregate demand in the short run
and aggregate supply in the long run in the agricultural sector. The central
proposal of Ulmanis was the setting of fixed prices. As was mentioned
before, the state-established Price Regulating Commission started its work
on 25 February 1932.

In conclusion Zalts wrote: 'These forecasts about the end of the crisis
without exceptions are taken very positively. Nevertheless all these forecasts are fulfilled with some fatalism, as if everything that happens around
us, does not depend on our own actions' (Zalts, 1932, pp. 119–20). This
quote is rather important nowadays when the most popular economists
are those who give their forecasts like this: 'At the end of 2009 the decline
in GDP will be . . . per cent, in the middle of 2010 it will be . . . per cent, but
at the end of 2010 there will be a slight increase of . . . per cent'. The author
is not over-confident in such forecasts, as the process significantly depends
on the economic policy that should take place. Another idea of Zalts that
seems very up-to-date, is that the argument that 'in other countries the

situation is as bad as in Latvia', is not a serious argument, as if the government was not taking measures to make the situation better, but it will not improve itself in a short enough period of time.

Kārlis Ulmanis became the Prime Minister of Latvia and largely put into practice his ideas of how to find the way out of crisis. On 15 May 1934 there was a political coup, after which the Parliament was dissolved, and the authoritarian regime of Ulmanis took political power in Latvia for six years. Not a single person was killed for political reasons during this coup nor after it. From a political point of view this coup cannot be evaluated positively – it turned out that in the long run, democracy was preferable to authoritarianism. But from the point of view of the economy, those six years saw a significant development of the economy of Latvia and a rise in the standard of living. Indeed, the role of state regulation significantly increased; instead of 24 banks only seven remained, two of them with state capital. The fixed price policy in agriculture together with preferential crediting gave a notable impulse for a significant development in agriculture. Latvia became one of the leading exporters of milk products in Europe.

During the Great Depression Latvia suffered from the economic crisis to a lesser extent, on average, than other countries. The government of Latvia took some measures of economic policy that helped the economy to find a successful way out of the crisis. Among those measures were:

- a significant input of financial resources into the real economy, mainly agriculture, by crediting through public banks on beneficial terms;
- using the fixed price policy in the priority sectors of economy;
- the establishment of state enterprises.

The role of the state in the economy of Latvia significantly increased during this period of time and the economy was closer to the 'planned economy' than to the 'free market economy'. Those years are notable, with a high economic development and a significant increase in the standard of living. One may guess that if Ulmanis had restored the democratic state system in 1938, the way forward for Latvia could have been quite different and much better.

13.4 SUSTAINABLE DEVELOPMENT AND THE WAY OUT OF THE CRISIS

Could those measures, which were taken by the Latvian government in the 1930s, help in the current economic situation of Latvia? To a certain extent, perhaps, yes. It is rather obvious that the minds of economists and politicians in the whole world are changing towards a highly necessary increase in the state regulation of the economy. The cutting back of government expenditure and the increase in taxes, in trying to salvage the budget that was passed by the government of Latvia at the end of 2008, has turned out to be a false solution for the crisis. Still very popular is the idea of curing the economy's ills by streaming financial resources into commercial banks. But without radical changes in the financial system where the state could strictly control 'financial products', put high taxes on them or even ban some of them (Schmidt, 2009), this will be no solution, when commercial banks, taking care of their own profits, continue to give credits to the most profitable sectors of the economy, with the highest 'added value', that is, to the speculative sectors of economy. The figures of economic growth will continue to increase but there will be no real benefit from that for society in general. Only if public institutions take the initiative of giving out credits, will financial resources reach the sectors of the real economy. The objective for the crediting institution in this case should not be profit; therefore, credits could be given at a fixed interest rate.

Agriculture was a real priority for the government of Latvia in the 1930s. Today support for this sector of economy is largely fictitious. The main problem for farmers is not the low prices of agricultural products, although it is also of great importance, but uncertainty. The fixed price system, introduced in Latvia in 1932, could be a solution for this problem.

A curious misunderstanding in Latvia is the public opinion created by journalists that problems appear because of the lack of common goals for society. Indeed, the goal should be common for all nations, as is stated by the United Nations – a sustainable development of economy. The present situation leads to the public conclusion about the perplexity of this goal in society – usually it is explained only as nature protection, but sometimes even more erroneous – as rapid economic growth in the long run.

The notion of sustainable development should be understood as a permanent increase in welfare for everyone (not on average), which will not compromise the possibilities of an increase in welfare in the future. The threat for the future arises from the debasement of the environment – not only in its ecological sense, but social, ethnical, cultural and religious as well. The notion of welfare is usually mentioned as something vague and subjective. It concerns such values that most people find necessary for their welfare. To explain this problem, we may consider the Aristotelian approach from his imperishable *Nicomachean Ethics* where Aristotle discusses these eternal problems of human life and human behaviour. For Aristotle happiness (*eudaimonia*) is not a state, but a process:

we must rather class happiness as an activity . . . and if some activities are necessary, and desirable for the sake of something else, while others are so in themselves, evidently happiness must be placed among those desirable in themselves . . . for happiness does not lack anything, but is self-sufficient. (Aristotle, 350 BCE)

Speaking about the factors of the 'quality of life' most people usually mention health and family as they are obviously self-sufficient. Too often people mention money as a factor of welfare, but after a discussion they usually agree that money is not self-sufficient. Using the words of Aristotle: 'wealth is evidently not the good (benefit) we are seeking; for it is merely useful and for the sake of something else' (Aristotle, 350 BCE). The most reliable way to happiness is '*aretē*' – moral virtue or the excellence of character and excellence of intellect. Philosophers are the happiest people. The present approach where education is subjugated to the market is in opposition to the Aristotelian point of view.

The concept of sustainable development cannot be separated from morality and human development. The common understanding of the goal does not guarantee that all the members of society will act in accordance with the goal. Legislating social regulations is not enough to guarantee that all members of society will be acting in accordance with the common goal. Such social institutions as the family, the nation, religion and morality have acted as the guarantee of sustainable development over the years throughout the history of humankind. The present pejorative attitude towards these institutions is the main threat to sustainable development. Thus, a fundamental change in the basic principles of human development is the main goal for sustainable development in the long run. Education should not be considered only as leverage for the labour market; the main goal of the educational process is to develop a virtuous personality who will act with the authority of laws not because she is frightened of being punished but because she cannot act otherwise because of moral principles. To achieve those long-term objectives, Latvia should solve its very complicated short-term problems.

The cutting back of governmental expenditure and the increase in taxes, undertaken by Latvia's government at the end of 2008 in an attempt to save the budget, very soon turned out to be a false solution for the crisis. The effort to increase income by increasing value added tax rate has already turned out to be totally wrong.

As the latest events show, most leaders of the powerful countries understand the necessity of radical reforms in the economy, and the leaders of Latvia sooner or later will recognize that too.

It is more than apparent that the role of state regulations in the economy will substantially increase all over the world. Entrepreneurs could be the main driving force in good times. During wars and crisis the state should take the initiative. This is possible only when people trust the state. These countries that first put into practice this solution will be the first on the way out of the crisis. Sadly, Latvia will be among the laggards in this process, mainly because of its unprofessional and short-sighted state policy.

13.5   CONCLUSIONS

The main reason for the present crisis is the continued profitability of the speculative economy, caused by innovations in the financial and real estate markets. As Professor Jagdish Bhagwati mentions: 'with financial innovation, the downside can be lethal – it is "destructive creation". We have to work hard at defining the downside scenarios' (Bhagwati, 2008).

The most profitable ideas arise in the speculative economy, creating money from nothing. Investors are seeking for the most profitable kind of business and almost always it turns out to be in the speculative sectors of economy.

The first years of the 21st century were years of extremely rapid economic growth. The Latvian government boasted about high growth and paid no attention to the structure of it. Now it turns out that this growth happened, for the greatest part, in the speculative economy. The profitability of the speculative economy is crashing now. Economies like Latvia, Iceland, Hungary and so on, suffer very seriously from it, as the speculative economy has overcome the real economy to too great an extent in these countries. But more or less the problem is the same for the entire world.

The present global crisis has some common causes and similarities with the Great Depression but the main cause of the present crisis is the continued profitability of the speculative economy. For that reason the global economy will not recover with radical reforms and the permanent increase of state intervention in the economy. The understanding of this fact by the government of Latvia is the most necessary condition for the recovery of the economy of Latvia.

BIBLIOGRAPHY

Aristotle (350 BCE), *The Nicomachean Ethics*, as reprinted (1998), Oxford: Oxford University Press.

Bhagwati, J. (2008), 'We need to guard against destructive creation', *The Financial Times*, 16 October.

Brīvers, I. (2008), 'Economic growth vs sustainable development – the case of Latvia', *Journal of Business Management*, **1**, Special Edition, *Sustainable Business Development under Scenarios of Possible Economic Slowdown*, 16–29.

Jackson, T. (2009), *Prosperity Without Growth: Economics for a Finite Planet*, London: Earthscan.

Keynes, J.M. (1936), *Treatise on Money and the General Theory of Employment, Interest and Money*, London: Macmillan.

Krastins, O. (1996), *Latvijas saimniecibas vesturiska pieredze 1918–1940* (The Historical Experience of the Latvian Economy, 1918–1940), Riga: LVAEI.

Schmidt, H. (2009), 'Wie entkommen wir der Depressionsfalle?'(How can we escape from the trap of depression?), *Die Zeit*, 15 January.

Schumpeter, J.A. (1942), *Capitalism, Socialism and Democracy*, as reprinted (1975), New York: Harper.

Veblen, Th. (1899), *The Theory of the Leisure Class*, as reprinted (1965), New York: Augustus M. Kelley.

Woytinsky, W. (1931), 'Internationale Hebung der Preise als Ausweg aus der Krise' (International rising of prices as a way out of a crisis) Berlin: Hans Buske Verlag.

Zalts, A. (1932), *Izeja no krizes* (The Way Out of the Crisis), Riga: Zelta grauds.

14. The aftermath of a long decade of real nil interest rates (Spain 1996–2008)

Óscar Dejuán and Eladio Febrero

14.1 INTRODUCTION[1]

In Westerns, when the sheriff enters a rowdy saloon he shoots the pianist in order to appease the crowd and gain its respect. In sports, when the team is doing badly, it is obvious that the coach should be fired. In a similar fashion, when an economic crisis occurs, politicians, economists and lay people work out who should take the blame. It seems convenient to single out one culprit and punish him firmly in order to restore social confidence and start anew.

Apparently, the culprit of the Great Depression of 1929 was the Chairman of the US Federal Reserve (Fed). According to Milton Friedman (an opinion that has gained followers with the passage of time), the Fed printed out too much money during the 1920s and, suddenly, it cut off the money supply (Friedman and Schwartz, 1963). For many scholars the villain of the Great Recession of 2008 is, once more, the Chairman of the Fed (and the presidents of other central banks who followed suit). They kept the official interest rates too low for too long (from 2002 till the end of 2005, although the policy of low interest rates started in the mid-1990s).

On 7 April 2010, Alan Greenspan (Chairman of the Fed in 1987–2006) was called by Congress to give a public testimony before the Financial Crisis Inquiry Commission.[2] He admitted that the crisis was triggered by the bursting of the bubble in the real estate market and the collapse of derivatives from subprime mortgages. He also admitted that the bubble was caused by historically low real interest rates. What matters for this purpose, he qualified, was not the overnight Fed's rate but the 30-year mortgage rate. The latter became abnormally low (and insensible to the Fed's rate increases after 2005) due to the international savings glut (accruing from China and other developing countries) and to reckless speculative investment from financial institutions unaware of risk. If so, the culprit of the financial turmoil and economic recession was not the Fed, but reckless financial speculators and inept official regulators.

In this chapter, we shall argue that these strands are interwoven, so all agents should take their share of the blame. We want to go beyond the day to day problems in order to appreciate the unsustainability of a new pattern of growth based on artificial credit unaware of the distribution of income and financial risks associated to a debt trap.

The Spanish economy provides a convenient testing ground to analyse the deepest roots of the crisis. (1) It has had the lowest *real* rates in the world for a long decade. Since 1999 Spain enjoyed the European nominal interest rates while its inflation rate kept one or two percentage points above. (2) It has experienced the most pronounced economic boom and bust among advanced economies; this is particularly true with respect to employment. (3) It was not contaminated with the toxic assets derived from US subprime mortgages. The last point is important for our purpose. It makes clearer, that with or without toxic financial assets, with or without an international financial crash, the breakdown of the Spanish economy was obvious at least from late 2006.

Our analysis relies on the Post-Keynesian paradigm based on the principle of effective demand, the endogeneity of money, the hypothesis of financial fragility and so on. If an economist should be singled out, this would be Minsky (1975, 1986). Notwithstanding, we will keep an open dialogue with other schools and will pay attention to the lessons that the current crisis teaches scholars of any stream of thought (except those who believe that they already know everything).

This chapter has been organized in five sections, apart from this 'Introduction'. Section 14.2 offers a graphical illustration of the Spanish boom from 1996 to 2007. Section 14.3 explores the forces behind the financial variables (interest rates, credit and debt), including the active (even 'aggressive') role of banks. Section 14.4 analyses the impact on prices. The moderate inflation in produced goods is contrasted with the speculative bubbles in the real estate and stock exchange markets. Section 14.5 analyses the long-run deflationary effect of debt on output and employment. Our main conclusion (section 14.6) is that, in the long run, over-indebtedness is bound to cause a recession and will hinder economic recovery for years.

14.2 STYLIZED FACTS OF THE SPANISH BOOM (1996–2007)

The story we want to explain can be summarized in seven stylized facts. They will be contrasted with the international situation by means of 12 figures:[3]

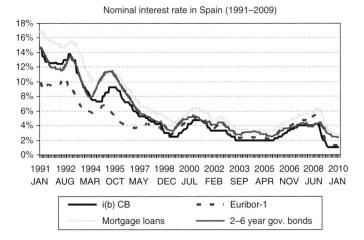

Note: i(b) CB: Base rate fixed by central banks.

Source: Banco de España (BE).

Figure 14.1 A synchronized fall of nominal interest rates in Spain

1. The commitment of the Spanish government to join the European Monetary Union (EMU) and to adopt the euro by 1999, pushed Spanish nominal interest rates to German levels (Figure 14.1). Yet, *real* interest rates were lower in Spain because inflation was one or two percentage points (pp) above the 2 per cent target fixed by the European Central Bank (ECB). From 2002–05 Spanish real interest rates were in fact negative for Euribor-1 (one-year-Euribor), to which Spanish mortgage rates are referenced. On average, for the whole decade 1997–2006, and considering a broader variety of assets, the real interest rate was almost nil. The lowest in the world as we will see in Figure 14.2.

2. Output grew at an average rate of 4 per cent, clearly above other European countries. It was led by the construction industry, which tried to cater for the booming residential investment by households (Figure 14.3). Employment increased even faster because the construction industry had the highest employment multiplier. Half of the new jobs created in the EU between 1996 and 2007 were located in Spain. The unemployment rate shifted from 22 per cent in 1996, to 8 per cent in mid-2008, to go back to 20 per cent at the end of 2010 (Figure 14.4)

3. The trade deficit and the current account deficit (the highest among advanced economies, as seen in Figure 14.5) gave warning signs of trouble ahead for the Spanish economy, which was growing above its

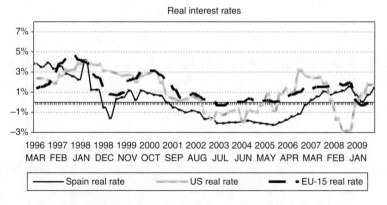

Source: BE and Eurostat.

Figure 14.2   The lowest real interest rate in the world

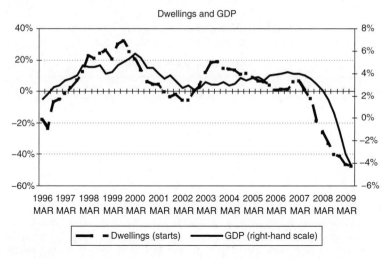

Source: BE.

Figure 14.3   Output boom and bust led by household residential investment

potential and that Spanish society was living above its possibilities. This is the first macroeconomic disequilibrium that, because of the euro umbrella, passed unnoticed for a time. Eventually the balance of payment constraint showed up as a 'debt trap'.

4. Despite the huge increase in employment, nominal wages increased

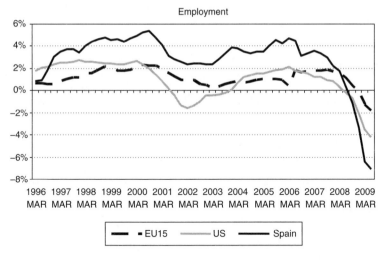

Source: Eurostat.

Figure 14.4   The fastest creation and destruction of employment

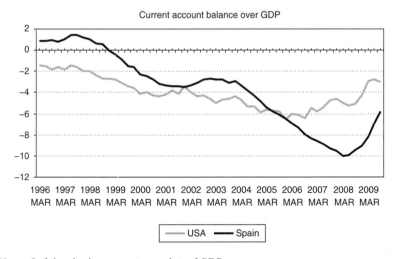

Note: Left-hand axis = percentage points of GDP.

Source: BE.

Figure 14.5   The highest trade and current deficit

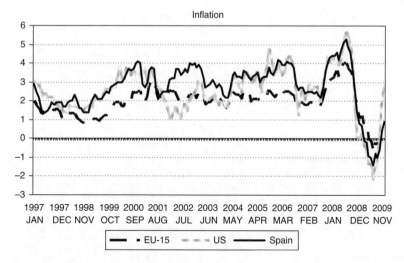

Note: Left-hand axis = percentage points.

Source: BE.

Figure 14.6   Moderate inflation in goods and services

with moderation and the real wage kept constant. The consumer price index (CPI) (which measures the inflation for produced goods and services) increased one or two points faster than in other European countries. Yet, the spread does not look so big if we take into account the Spanish record and compare it with the USA (Figure 14.6).

5.   True inflation occurred in house prices (Figure 14.7). A part of bank credit was deviated to speculative investments in the real estate market and the stock exchange market. The bubbles that originated were among the highest in the world as we can see in Figures 14.8 and 14.9.

6.   The excess of expenditure over the value of the output produced and the incomes distributed, caused most agents to borrow (Figure 14.10). In a few years, the Spanish economy became heavily indebted (Figure 14.11). The debt of households shifted from 40 per cent to 130 per cent of their gross disposable income. The debt of non-financial corporations (NFC) shifted from 150 per cent to 700 per cent of their gross operating surplus (GOS). Foreign debt (that evolved in parallel to the need for borrowing of NFC) shifted from 30 per cent to 120 per cent of the Spanish GDP.

7.   The burden of debt looks particularly risky once we consider the increasing leverage. The ratio 'debt/equity', in NFC, doubled (Figure 14.12).

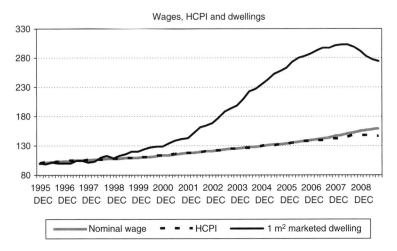

Note: Evolution of costs and prices (1997 = 100). HCPI = Harmonized Consumer Price Index.

Source: BE.

Figure 14.7   True inflation appears in houses

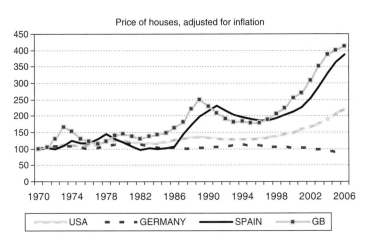

Note: 1970 = 100.

Source: Bank for international settlements (BIS).

Figure 14.8   One of the highest speculative bubbles in real estate

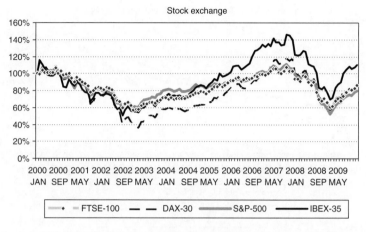

Source: www.uk.finance.yahoo.com and Institute National de Estadistica (INE).

Figure 14.9 The highest speculative bubble in the stock exchange

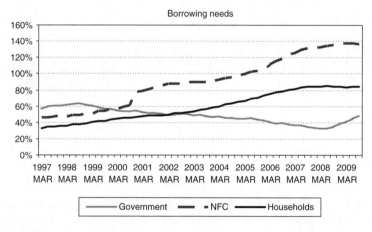

Source: BE.

Figure 14.10 Increasing borrowing needs

14.3 INTEREST RATES, CREDIT AND DEBT – THE 'AGGRESSIVE' ROLE OF BANKS

The empirical evidence presented in Figures 14.1 and 14.2, fits quite well into the Post-Keynesian monetary theory. The interest rate is considered

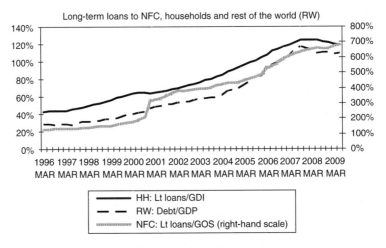

Note: RW includes bank loans, issued debt and other accounts payable.

Source: BE.

Figure 14.11   Increasing burden of debt

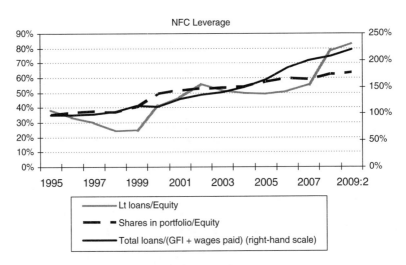

Source: BE and INE. GFI = gross fixed investment.

Figure 14.12   Increasing leverage and financial risk

a monetary variable, in the sense that it can be controlled through the monetary policy implemented by the central banks (CB). In the loans to commercial banks, the CB fixes the 'official' or 'base' rate (i_b). Interbank loans (Euribor, so to speak) are usually pegged to it. Long-term rates (i, that we can link to the mortgage rate) can be derived adding the relevant mark-ups.

$$i = i_b \cdot (1 + \psi + \psi') \tag{14.1}$$

Actually there are two complementary mark-ups. The 'normal one' (y) allows banks to cover unit costs and gain the normal rate of profit on the capital invested (like any capitalist firm). In special circumstances, banks charge a complementary mark-up (y') in order to match the risk of uncontrolled inflation, the risk of default and the risk of illiquidity. After the financial turbulences of 2007–09 and the subsequent recession, the spread between i_b and i rose from one to three percentage points.

The possibility of controlling market rates through the monetary policy has been accepted by the New Macroeconomic Consensus (NMC), which has inspired monetary policy from 1995 on (Woodford, 2003). There is an important difference, however. Following Wicksell (1898), NMC models consider that there is a natural rate of interest depending on forces as stable as productivity and 'thrift' (intertemporal preferences), forces that cannot be violated for too long. Keynes (1936, 1937) argued that the interest rate was not a natural but a conventional phenomenon. People become accustomed to a given rate and use it in their economic decisions. But this convention was 'path dependent' and could be affected by a persistent monetary policy. We should not be afraid of an explosion of prices destabilizing the economy, although some redistribution of income and wealth was unavoidable. The euthanasia of the rentiers could be the cost of such policy.

Let us move forward (and deeper). The exogeneity of the rate of interest is a corollary of the endogeneity of money. 'Money is credit driven and demand determined' (Moore, 1988, p. 19). This is the catchword phrase that summarizes the Post-Keynesian and 'circuitist' theory of endogenous money (Graziani, 2003). The monetary base issued by the CB depends on the requirements of commercial banks, which are committed to satisfying the requirements of economic agents. If the CB issues more/less monetary base than is required, the velocity of the circulation of money will fall/rise in order to ensure the adjustment. Banks deposits (or 'bank money', according to the conventional definition of money) are a consequence of bank credits.

From this perspective, the explosion of legal and bank money that we observe in the period 1996–2007 can be explained as a response by the banking system to the demand for credit by households and NFC, a demand motivated for residential, productive and speculative purposes. Note that this is not a direct and unavoidable consequence of low interest rates because the main determinants of investment lie somewhere else, like economic history shows repeatedly. (1) Most investment booms have occurred in periods of high interest rates (for example, Spain in 1986–92). (2) In recessions, low levels of investment coincide with low interest rates (the dramatic fall of interest rates after September 2008 could not encourage investment). Let us offer a brief review of the main determinants of the different types of investment.

Productive investment by firms is best explained by the principle of acceleration, that is, the expected growth of output times the desired 'capital/output' ratio. A flexible accelerator will admit that investment decisions could speed up (or slow down) if the interest rate falls (rises) over/below the conventional level. Note, however, that the interest rate ceases to exert any effect once the new interest rate becomes the new convention (Baddeley, 2003; Dejuán, 2005).

Residential investment by households depends on three sets of variables: demographic changes, financial conditions and price expectations (Esteban and Altuzarra, 2008; García Montalvo, 2008). For cultural reasons, the rate of house ownership in Spain is quite high (82 per cent). If banks are willing to finance mortgages (as they were from 1996 to 2007), we can expect that the demand for houses will rise whenever there is an increase in the number of adults with a job but without their own house. In the period we are analysing, employment grew by 7 million. Four and a half million of the new employees were immigrants eager to buy a house as soon as they got a job. One million Spaniards, previously unemployed, also had the opportunity to buy their first house. All this represents a kind of endogenous demand for houses in the sense that it is related to the growth of income and employment. The exogenous part derives from the baby boom in the late 1960s and from the demand by ex-pats for villas near the beach after 2002.

Land and financial stocks are a breeding ground for speculative investments. Investors become speculators when they buy an asset, whose value is known to be above its fundamental value, in the hope that it will rise even more (at least for a while). When the expected price increases are in the 10–20 per cent range, a couple of points up or down in the interest rate seem irrelevant. Yet, it's obvious that easy access to credit did encourage speculators between 2003–07.

To end this section we would like to add a couple of observations in order to avoid drawing mistaken conclusions from the theory of money endogeneity. It predicts that an increase in production will call for an increase in credit and money. Yet, not all the new credit is necessarily tied to productive activities. The bubbles in the real estate and in the stock exchange are clear evidence of the presence of speculative forces during the prodigious decade. We can also guess the importance of speculative behaviour looking at the ratio 'loans demanded by firms/productive expenditures of firms (i.e., wages and fixed capital)'. At the beginning of the period (1995–2009) the ratio was around 100 per cent. At the end, it had reached 250 per cent (Figure 14.12).

Second observation. The endogeneity of money does not imply a passive behaviour of banks, despite the suggestion of most Post-Keynesian and circuitist approaches. One of the main lessons of the last boom (1996–2008) is that the financial system can play an active, even aggressive, role.

The fall in interest rates after 1995 and, most of all, 2002, spurred banks to increase the amount of credit lent and to introduce all kinds of financial innovations in order to extract the maximum profitability from each euro entering into the financial system. The securitization of mortgage loans was part of this innovation. Spanish banks did not grant subprime mortgages and did not buy the risky derivatives related to US subprime mortgages. The restrictive regulation after the financial crisis of the early 1990s prohibited these practices in Spain. Yet Spanish banks continually took on excessive risks by lending too large sums for too long a time to workers whose real wages remained constant. To match the increasing price of houses, banks enlarged the average maturity period of mortgage loans (from 19 years in 1996 to 28 years in 2007). So, in the last months of Spanish banks' risky practices, loans were even granted for 40 years. Another risky practice (this one is illegal) was to inflate the market value of the house in order to pay outright 100 per cent of its price (and even expensive pieces of furniture) with the mortgage loan.

This can be considered as an increase in the 'leverage ratio' of households. The important leverage corresponds to NFC and is measured by the ratio 'long-term loans/equity'. It shifted from 30 per cent in 1997 to 80 per cent in 2008. It warns about the increasing financial risks of the Spanish economy by 2006–07 (see again Figure 14.12).

All these events remind us of the 'financial instability' hypothesis of Hyman Minsky (1975, 1986). Note that it is not the unexpected outcome of low interest rates, but the normal by-product of a period of prosperity. In his very last paper he offered a precise summary:

> The first theorem of the financial instability hypothesis is that the economy has financing regimes under which it is stable and financing regimes in which it is unstable. The second theorem of the financial instability hypothesis is that over

periods of prolonged prosperity, the economy transits from financial relations that make for a stable system to financial relations that make for an unstable system. In particular, over a protracted period of good times, capitalist economies tend to move to a financial structure in which there is a large weight to units engaged in speculative and Ponzi finance. (Minsky, 1992, pp. 7–8)

J.M. Keynes also warned about the risks of an economy led by speculative investments, which might happen both with low and high interest rates:

Speculators may do no harm as bubbles on a steady stream of enterprise. But the position is serious when enterprise becomes the bubble on a whirlpool of speculation. When the capital development of a country becomes a by-product of the activities of a casino, the job is likely to be ill-done. The measure of success attained by Wall Street, regarded as an institution of which the proper social purpose is to direct new investment into the most profitable channels in terms of future yield, cannot be claimed as one of the outstanding triumphs of laissez-faire capitalism. . . . (Keynes, 1936, p. 159)

14.4   INFLATION: THE DIFFERENT PERFORMANCE OF THE GOODS MARKET AND THE ASSETS MARKET

Entrepreneurs 'administer' prices by charging a mark-up (β) on unit prime costs in order to obtain a 'normal' profitability on the capital invested. In a macro model, which considers the economy as a huge vertically integrated sector, they are identified with unit labour costs ($w_{n,t}/\pi$ = nominal wage/productivity). Intermediate goods would appear as indirect labour. Only the unit cost of imported raw materials (crude oil, in particular) will appear explicitly (ξ_t). A simple expression of the so-called 'cost push inflation' would look like this:

$$P_t = \left(\frac{w_{n,t}}{\pi} + \xi_t\right) \cdot (1 + \beta) \tag{14.2}$$

The general level of prices will rise over the target rate if nominal wages rise above labour productivity, if the mark-up rises and/or the price of oil rises. See the following expression, where a and a' are parameters that account for the relative weight of each cost):

$$\hat{P} = \hat{w}_n \cdot a - \hat{\pi} \cdot a + \hat{\xi} \cdot a' + \hat{\beta} \tag{14.3}$$

Since wages represent the highest share they deserve particular attention. Most macroeconomic theories postulate that nominal wages rise

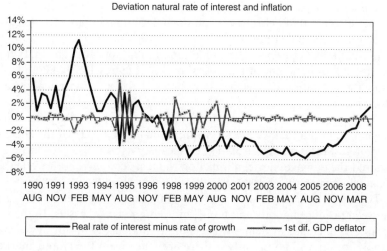

Source: BE.

Figure 14.13   No acceleration of inflation

whenever there are tensions in the labour market, that is, when the unemployment rate decreases. This is, in essence, the Phillips Curve, which relates the rate of inflation to the rate of unemployment.

Economists in the New Macroeconomic Consensus (NMC) have related the natural rate of unemployment to the natural rate of interest, and the NAIRU (Non-Accelerating Inflation Rate of Unemployment) with the NIRI (Non Inflationary Rate of Interest) (Woodford, 2003). This hypothesis has been built on the 'Dynamic Stochastic General Equilibrium model' (DSGE), on which CB's monetary policy relies.

The Spanish experience questions the validity of such a hypothesis. A drop in the unemployment rate from 22 per cent in 1996 to 8.3 per cent in 2007, was bound to exert an inflationary pressure on nominal wages and prices according to the NAIRU doctrine. To explain the paradox they are obliged to assume that the NAIRU evolves with the cycle. This conclusion actually implies that there are no 'natural' rates of unemployment, employment and interest.

Figure 14.13 confirms our suspicions. Inflation did not accelerate in the prodigious decade despite the real interest rate being lower than the potential rate of growth. The one or two points spread with the European average could be considered a kind of 'structural inflation' related to the Balassa-Samuelson effect (Deloach, 2001). It predicts an increase in wages and prices in the country that joins a monetary union of richer countries.

The greater dependence of the Spanish economy on imported oil is a second element that helps to explain the inflation differential (it increased when oil prices rallied up).

In Spain, like elsewhere, true inflation did not appear in the market of goods and services, but in the assets market. Figures 14.7, 14.8 and 14.9 show the formation of speculative bubbles in the real estate market and stock exchange.

By and large, most macroeconomic schools (including the Post-Keynesian brand that we are following so far) have bypassed the effect of low interest rates on the formation of speculative bubbles. They have also ignored the damage they can inflict on the real economy, both while they inflate and when they burst.

To gain a comprehensive vision of inflation, we should distinguish between produced goods and non-produced goods and assets. In the first group, an increase in demand is generally matched with an increase in supply; prices will go up only if there are tensions in the labour market. In the second group, supply cannot adjust (at least at the same pace as demand), so prices will go up. The rise in prices will be proportional to the rise in 'funded' demand. In principle, the supply of new houses was supposed to check this pressure, but supply was always behind demand due to legal or monopolistic restrictions. Time also matters. To obtain a mortgage loan may take a couple of days; to build a house a couple of years.

The price of a standard dwelling (our current concern) is ruled by the maximum amount of money that the purchaser is able to pay. This depends on the amount of money that banks are willing to lend (and the loan-to-value ratio, which we shall assume to be constant and equal to 100 per cent). This, in turn, depends on the current value of the mortgage instalments that banks deem that the borrowing household will be able to set aside for debt service payments. According to Debelle (2004), the price of one house may be computed by the following equation:

$$p_h = \frac{z}{(1 + i)} + \frac{z}{(1 + i)^2} + \frac{z}{(1 + i)^3} + \dots + \frac{z}{(1 + i)^n}$$

$$= z \cdot \left(\frac{(1 + i)^n - 1}{i(1 + i)^n} \right) \tag{14.4}$$

Here z is the amount of each loan instalment, i is the interest rate, and n is the maturity of the mortgage loan. The price of land (a rent) is given by the difference between p_h and the building cost, which we shall assume to be constant.

During the prodigious decade, bank policy consisted in lengthening the redemption period so that all the customers approaching the office would leave it with a mortgage contract. By so doing, banks contributed to the increase in the indebtedness of the household sector and the price of dwellings. Both phenomena are interrelated and created a vicious circle. The expansion of credit pushed the price of dwellings up and obliged purchasers to come back to the office to ask for more credit.

Soon this vicious circle became a speculative one. Under the expectation that the price of houses would always rise (and could never fall), households hurried up to buy a house no matter what the price (provided they got enough credit). Developers hurried up to buy land no matter what the price (provided they got enough credit). Banks competed among themselves to sign the maximum number of mortgages loans. The possible default of some borrowers was not a problem for them since the unpaid house could be re-sold with a profit.

Speculative bubbles cannot last forever. First, because the demand for houses (as for any other durable good) reaches a point of saturation. In early 2007, 15 per cent of all houses were unsold and vacant. Second, because most people realized that the current price of a house was above its fundamental value (the ratio 'rent/price') and that it would be impossible to repay mortgages. Third, because after 2006 banks tightened credit conditions.

The greatest increase in house prices occurred in 2004 (18 per cent). From this year on it started to decelerate. In early 2008 it became lower than the consumer price index (CPI) (5 per cent). In 2009 it fell 10 per cent.

The deceleration in house prices was more a curse than a blessing. 'Ever increasing prices' had been the lure that kept the real estate market buoyant and the construction industry alive. When it was obvious that residential prices could fall, there was no great urgency to buy a house, to build it and to grant mortgage credits.

14.5   OUTPUT AND THE BURDEN OF DEBT

According to the Keynesian principle of effective demand, the equilibrium level of output in year t (Y_t) does not depend on the potential capacity of the economy but on the expected final demand at normal prices. This principle gains full relevance when we introduce the mechanism of the multiplier. The equilibrium output at year t can be expressed as a multiple (m) of the expected autonomous demand for the period (A_t):

$$Y_t = FD_t = C_t + I_t + G_t + X'_t = \mu \cdot A_t \tag{14.5}$$

(*C*: final private consumption; *I*: final private investment; *G*: public expenditures in goods and services; *X*: net exports; *A*: autonomous demand).

By the same logic, the increase of output in a given period will be m times the expected increase in autonomous demand:

$$\Delta Y_t = \mu \cdot \Delta A_t = \mu' \cdot \Delta A'_t \tag{14.6}$$

The multiplier (μ) accounts for induced consumption which represents, by far, the biggest portion of final demand. It can be broadened (μ') to include the acceleration principle, which explains the bulk of productive investment.[4]

In the last Spanish boom (1996–2007), $\Delta A'$ corresponds basically to the new houses built to satisfy the demand by households (residential investment, $\Delta I_{h,t}$). Note that the demand and supply of houses do not always evolve in parallel. In the years 1986–91 the demand for houses rose while supply kept constant. There was no rally of employment led by the construction industry. The full impact of the new mortgage credit to finance residential investment fell on house prices. In the last boom the demand for houses ($\Delta I_{h,t}$) was followed by the supply of houses, which generated a lot of direct and indirect employment. House prices also rose because the supply of houses was always some points below and some months behind the demand for houses.

We can substitute the value of these houses that triggered the multiplier mechanism by the mortgage loans granted by banks to households ($\Delta D_{h,t}$). We should divide by the price deflator of houses ($P'_{h,t}$) to express mortgage loans in real terms (purchasing power).[5] Obviously, what matters is not the amount borrowed but the number of houses that can be purchased (and built) with this credit. The important point to highlight is that to put in motion the same amount of real resources builders and households needed an increasing amount of credit.

The 'multiplicand' ($\Delta A'$) includes a second variable with a negative sign. It is the 'forgone private consumption' ($\nabla C_{o,t}$), which is c times debt service payments ($SD_{h,t} = i' \cdot D_{h,(t-1)}$). In this expression $D_{h,(t-1)}$ stands for the mortgage debt accumulated until the previous year. After multiplying by i' we obtain the service of debt (interest plus redemption). Then we multiply by the propensity to consume (c) in order to represent the burden of debt in terms of forgone consumption.[6]

The preceding analysis allows us to write:

$$\Delta Y_t = \mu \cdot (\Delta I_{h,t} - \nabla C_{o,t}) = \mu' \cdot \left(\frac{\Delta D_{h,t}}{P'_h} - c \cdot SD_{h,t} \right) \tag{14.7}$$

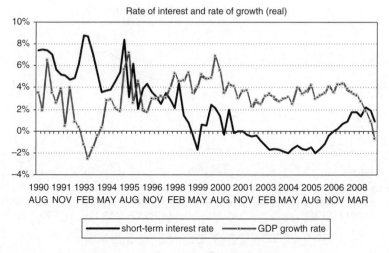

Source: BE.

Figure 14.14   First short-circuit: real interest rate > rate of growth

With a simple inspection of (14.7), we conclude that there will be a recession if $c \cdot SD_{h,t} > (\Delta D_{h,t}/p'_h)$. Output and employment are bound to shrink if the issue of new loans that allows building and buying new houses turns out to be lower than the service of debt. 'Debt service payments' account for the part of the income generated in period t going to the financial sink. There is no guarantee that it will return to the economic circuit as new investment. This is the basic tenet of the so-called 'stock-flow consistent models' (Godley and Lavoie, 2007; see also Wray, 2009).

The fragility of over-indebted economies becomes evident either when the interest rate rises or when the rate of growth falls.[7] Figure 14.14 shows that both variables crossed in 2007 causing a dangerous 'short-circuit'. The increase in the rate of interest accelerated the service of debt. The deceleration of the growth reduced, at a greater scale, the issue of new credit.

The interest rate rose as a result of a tighter monetary policy and more 'prudent' bank practices. To prevent the consolidation of inflationary expectations when the price of oil was rallying up, the ECB decided to increase the base rate step by step, from the 2 per cent rate ruling in December 2005 to 4.25 per cent in mid-2008. In turn, commercial banks charged a higher mark-up in order to match for the increasing risk of default. As a consequence, payments associated to debt rose. Until 2006, and despite price increases, banks managed to keep the debt service

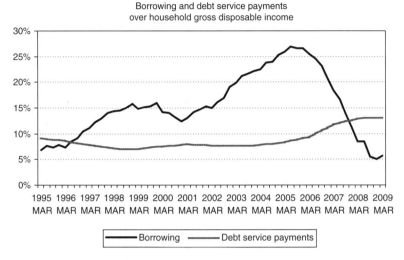

Source: BE, INE and authors' calculations.

Figure 14.15   Second short-circuit: debt service > borrowing

constant (at 25 per cent of household gross disposable income) by length-ening the redemption period. After 2007 this procedure was not enough. In two years, the burden of debt service rose from 25 per cent of household disposable income to 40 per cent.

The fall in the rate of growth of the economy since 2007 was a consequence of the exhaustion of its only engine: residential investment. The saturation of the demand for dwellings and the puncture of the speculative demand for land and houses led to the deceleration of the building industry.

Figure 14.15 shows the second short-circuit of the Spanish economy, closely related to the former. By 2007 the service of debt (a proxy for 'forgone consumption') outstrips new borrowing (a proxy for the demand for and supply of new houses). (Both variables are measured in terms of gross disposable income.)

The Spanish story we have just commented upon, reminds us that debt has a deflationary effect on aggregate demand. It may take time to show up. But the negative impact will be felt for a long time after debt stops piling up.

Note that this effect depends on the type of debt. In this respect, domestic public debt is the least harmful, while foreign debt (private or public) is the worst. The interest paid by the government to their citizens increases household disposable income, which is the source of private consumption. On the contrary, the service of foreign debt implies a direct subtraction of domestic income and domestic demand. It could be reversed through the import of Spanish goods by foreign countries, but such a reversion is not warranted at all. We remind the reader (Figure 14.5, above) that, during the last boom, Spain experienced the highest trade deficit and current account deficit among advanced countries (10 per cent of GDP). Spain's membership of the EMU allowed Spanish banks and NFC to finance this deficit easily. The balance-of-payments constraint did not show up in the usual ways: credit restrictions or currency depreciation (McCombie and Thirwall, 1994). Spanish banks managed to finance, in international markets, the increasing need of borrowing of NFC. They pumped a foreign debt ball that in a few years proved to be a heavy and dangerous burden. The burden of foreign debt is the new expression of the balance-of-payments constraint.

The deflationary impact of household debt is also important; more than economists tend to admit. An increasing share of household income (up to 120 per cent), went to the financial sink under the label of 'services of mortgage debt'. There was a chance that this money would return to the economic circuit as 'residential investment'. But this did not happen after 2007 (as we saw in Figure 14.15). Note that the stock of debt is expressed in nominal terms, so speculative bubbles increase the burden of debt. If the price of a house doubles from year 1 to year 2, the service of the new debt doubles. And it will continue at this level for the whole redemption period (20 or 30 years) even if in year 3 the market price of the house falls to the original level.

14.6 CONCLUSIONS

The aftermath of a long decade of very low real interest rates has seen one of the largest booms in Spanish history, followed by the deepest recession since 1929. The Spanish economy experienced a credit boom, which is synonymous for debt and was bound to exert a deflationary pressure on aggregate demand for many years. This credit propelled parallel booms in residential investment, output and employment. They brought about an enormous current account deficit. It constitutes the first serious disequilibrium, which was somehow hidden because of the euro, but was bound to exert deflationary pressure on aggregate demand. Credit also spurred speculative investments, which inflated bubbles in the real estate and the stock exchange.

From the Post-Keynesian approach developed in this paper, there is no

direct and strict causality between low interest rates and the rally of residential and productive investment. Economic booms have occurred both
with high and low interest rates. A fall in interest rates may be insufficient
to release the economy from a recession, as we see nowadays.

Yet, the historical fall in interest rates after 1995 (and even more so
after 2002) pushed banks towards a more active (even aggressive) role that
paved the way for a brand new pattern of finance. This is the distinctive
element of the last upswing. In order to keep profitability high, financial
institutions did their best to multiply the amount of mortgage loans to
households and to introduce financial innovations (most of them related
to the securitization of these loans). Banks were also eager to finance
entrepreneurs and speculators who took advantage of low interest rates
to lever their profits. When the credit-funded demand was massively
addressed towards non-reproducible assets, the formation of bubbles was
unavoidable.

Should we blame central banks as the ultimate culprits of these speculative bubbles, financial turmoil and economic recession? In the introduction we referred to the defensive position of the former Chairman
of the Fed, Alan Greenspan.[8] Now we support him against the oppor-
tunistic opinion of John Taylor (2007). He cannot criticize the Fed for
failing to abort the house price bubble, because asset inflation is absent
from his much celebrated 'Taylor's monetary rule'. Yet, the current
crisis teaches two important lessons to Greenspan and incumbent presidents of central banks. They should start concerning themselves about
speculation and asset inflation, which have proved to be more sensitive
to interest rates and more dangerous to real activity than the usual inflation of goods and services. They should also improve the regulation of
banks to avoid the ongoing fragility of the financial system. It is not just
an issue of 'toxic assets'. The enlargement of the redemption period of
mortgages was a key element of the debt bomb, which passed unnoticed
to regulators.

In our opinion the roots of the 2008 financial and economic crash go
beyond low interest rates and toxic assets. The crisis represents the terminal state of a pattern of growth propelled by a single engine (residential
investment) and artificially fed by artificial credits. 'Artificial' because of
the lack of awareness of the distribution of income and financial risks.

The normal pattern of growth in capitalist economies is led by entrepreneurs that reinvest a part of the profits obtained in the process of
producing and selling goods and services. The Spanish pattern of growth
from 1996 to 2007 was led by households investing in homes whose price
was rallying up. Since the real wage stayed constant, households had to
borrow increasing amounts of money that banks distributed à la carte to

households for as many years as they needed. After a decade of reckless borrowing ('reckless lending', would be a fairer statement), households fell into a major debt trap. The same happened to NFC and to the Spanish economy as a whole.

Under these circumstances, an increase in interest rates and/or a deceleration in the rate of growth was bound to cause massive default and a fall in the value of real and financial assets directly or indirectly related to the house business. This happened in September 2008, after the Lehman crash, although the first symptoms had already showed up a couple of years before. In early 2007, the service of debt by households was already outstripping new credits granted to build new houses.

An unpleasant corollary, to end with. The recovery of Spanish economy will take longer than in other European countries because Spanish households and firms are more indebted.

NOTES

1. John McCombie (University of Cambridge) discussed this paper in the 'International Workshop on the Recession of 2008', jointly organized by the UCLM (University of Castilla-La Mancha) and ESHET (European Society of the History of Economic Thought) in Albacete (Spain). His comments have been very helpful.
2. See Chapter 11 in this book and Greenspan (2010).
3. For a more detailed description see Banco de España (BE) (2009a, 2009b), ECB (2010), Eurostat (2010) and IMF (2009). The main source of data for the graphs is BE (2009b). Specific data about the building industry appears in Fundatión BBVA (2009).
4. The standard expression of the 'super-multiplier' (or multiplier-accelerator) is: $m^* = 1/[1 - c(1-t) + m - kg]$. Where c: propensity to consume; t: tax rate; m: import propensity; k: desired 'capital/output' ratio; g: expected growth of autonomous demand to which aggregate demand and output adjust.
5. Actually, $p'_{h,t}$ stands for the difference between the increase in house prices and the CPI. In the years 2004–07 the CPI was 3.5 per cent while the house deflator was 15 per cent. This yields a $p'_{h,t}$ equal to 11.5 per cent.
6. Consider the simplest consumption function: $C = cY_d$. Disposable income will be: $Y_d = Y - T - SD = Y - t \cdot Y - i \cdot D_{(t-1)} = Y(1 - t) - i \cdot D_{t-1}$. ($T$ stands for direct taxes and t for the tax rate). Therefore: $C = c \cdot Y(1 - t) - c \cdot i \cdot D_{t-1}$. The last part of this expression is 'autonomous' and should appear in the 'multiplicand', the same as investment expenditures.
7. The price deflator of houses does also play an important role that we analysed in the previous section.
8. See Chapter 11 in this book and Greenspan (2010).

REFERENCES

Baddeley, M.C. (2003), *Investment. Theories and Analysis*, New York: Palgrave, Macmillan.

BE – Banco de España (2009a), *Informe Anual 2008*, Madrid: Banco de España.

BE – Banco de España (2009b), *Cuentas Financieras de la Economía Española*, Madrid: Banco de España (yearly editions).

Debelle, G. (2004), 'Macroeconomic implications of rising household debt', BIS Working paper No. 153.

Dejuán, O. (2005), 'Paths of accumulation and growth: towards a Keynesian long-period theory of output', *Review of Political Economy*, **17** (2), 231–252.

Dejuán, O. (2007), 'The conventional *versus* the natural rate of interest: implications for central bank autonomy', *Journal of Post Keynesian Economics*, **29** (4), 645–666.

Deloach, S.B. (2001), 'More evidence in favor of the Balassa-Samuelson hypothesis', *Review of International Economics*, **9** (2), 336–342.

ECB – European Central Bank (2010), 'Statistics', available at http://www.ecb.europa.eu/stats; accessed 13 September 2010.

Esteban, M. and A. Altuzarra (2008), 'A model of the Spanish housing market', *Journal of Post Keynesian Economics*, **30** (3), 353–374.

Eurostat (2010), 'Statistics', available at http://epp.eurostat.ec.europa.eu; accessed 13 September 2010.

Friedman, M. (1977), 'Nobel Lecture: inflation and unemployment', *Journal of Political Economy*, **85** (3), 451–472.

Friedman, M. and A.J. Schwartz (1963), *A Monetary History of the United States: 1867–1960*, Princeton, NJ: Princeton University Press.

Fundatión BBVA (Banco Bilbao Vizcaya Argentaria) (2009), 'El *stock* de capital en viviendas, 1990–2008', *Cuadernos Capital y crecimiento*, 10.

García Montalvo, J. (2008), 'El sector inmobiliario Español a principios del siglo XXI: entre la demografía y las expectativas', *Revista Económica de Castilla-La Mancha*, **11**, 57–79.

Godley, W. and M. Lavoie (2007), *Monetary Economics. An Integrated Approach to Credit, Money, Income, Production and Wealth*, New York: Palgrave, Macmillan.

Graziani, A. (2003), *The Monetary Theory of Production*, Cambridge: Cambridge University Press.

Greenspan, A. (2010), 'The Crisis', BPEA papers, Spring, Brookings Institution, Washington, DC, 15 April 2010, available at: http://www.brookings.edu/~/media/Files/Programs/ES/BPEA/2010_spring_bpea_papers/spring2010_greenspan.pdf; accessed 13 September 2010.

IMF (2009), *World Economic Outlook. Crisis and Recovery*, Washington, DC: International Monetary Fund.

Keynes, J.M. (1936), *The General Theory of Employment, Interest and Money*, London: Macmillan.

Keynes, J.M. (1937), 'The *ex ante* theory of the rate of interest', *Economic Journal*, **47** (188), 663–668.

McCombie, J.S.L. and A.P. Thirlwall (1994), *Economic Growth and the Balance-of-Payments Constraint*, New York: St. Martin's Press.

Minsky, H.P. (1975), *John Maynard Keynes*, New York: Columbia University Press.

Minsky, H.P. (1986), *Stabilizing an Unstable Economy*, New Haven: Yale University Press.

Minsky, H.P. (1992), 'The financial instability hypothesis', The Jerome Levy Economics Institute Working Paper No. 74, New York.

Moore, B.J. (1988), *Horizontalists and Verticalists: The Macroeconomics of Credit Money*, Cambridge: Cambridge University Press.

Taylor, J.B. (2007), 'Housing and monetary policy', in Federal Reserve Bank of Kansas City, *Economic Symposium. Proceedings*, August, pp. 463–476.

Wicksell, K. (1898), *Geldzins und Guterpreise*, English translation (1936), *Interest and Prices*, New York: Macmillan.

Woodford, M. (2003), *Interest and Prices*, New Jersey: Princeton University Press.

Wray, L.R. (2009), 'Money managing capitalism and the global financial crisis', in E. Hein, T. Niechoj and E. Stockhammer (eds), *Macroeconomic Policies on Shaky Foundations*, Marburg: Metropolis-Verlag, pp. 283–307.

Index